AF845334

A Practical Guide to Digital Marketing Analytics

a practical guide to

DIGITAL MARKETING ANALYTICS

Track KPIs, Build Dashboards, and Make Data-Driven Decisions in the Age of AI

Syndicate Business Publishing

A Practical Guide to Digital Marketing Analytics

Copyright © 2026 by Nick Kastner. All rights reserved.

No part of this book may be reproduced, stored in a retrieval system, or transmitted in any form or by any means, electronic, mechanical, photocopying, recording, or otherwise, without the prior written permission of the publisher, except in the case of brief quotations embodied in critical articles or reviews.

This book is primarily educational and instructional in nature. It features screenshots, data, and references from various third-party platforms, including Google Analytics, Google Search Console, Data Studio, and YouTube (Google LLC), Microsoft Clarity (Microsoft), Instagram and Facebook (Meta Platforms), Semrush, SE Ranking, and Sprout Social to provide analytical examples, commentary, and step-by-step guidance.

All product names, logos, brands, and screenshots are trademarks™ or registered® trademarks of their respective holders. The inclusion of these visual and textual elements is for educational, illustrative, and critical purposes under the fair use doctrine (Section 107 of the U.S. Copyright Act).

This book is independently authored and published. It has not been authorized, sponsored, endorsed, or otherwise approved by Google LLC, Meta Platforms, Inc., Microsoft, or any other third-party platform or company mentioned herein.

Publisher's Note

The information in this book is provided on an "as is" basis. The author and publisher have made every effort to ensure the accuracy of the information herein, but provide no warranties and assume no responsibility for errors, omissions, or damages resulting from the use of the information contained in this book. Digital platforms frequently change their interfaces and algorithms; readers should expect variations over time.

Published by Syndicate Business Publishing
Murrayville, GA, USA

Hardcover ISBN: 979-8-9971332-0-7
Ebook ISBN: 979-8-9971332-1-4

First Edition: August 2026

This book is dedicated to my wife, my children, my work family at Forum Communications, and the thousands of students I've been blessed to teach over the years.

A Practical Guide to Digital Marketing Analytics

Preface

In December of 2008, I received a call from then-Dean Katie Simmons at what was Gainesville State College. She needed someone to teach marketing part-time after the previous faculty member left just two weeks before the semester began. I met the requirements to teach — five years of marketing experience and an MBA — and, at least from my perspective, she was desperate enough to be calling me (ha!). At the time, I served as a director at an agency, and while I had always been interested in education — even started college as a music major considering education as a career — I wasn't so sure I would be a great fit. She disagreed, and so after some very brief deliberation (time was of the essence), I agreed. If you had told me then that I would eventually write a book on analytics, I would have called you a liar. Analytics was my least favorite part of the job! But, that unexpected opportunity to teach would eventually shape the direction of my career in ways I never anticipated. Fast-forward eighteen years later and here we are — a complete book on one of the topics I've had the privilege of teaching along the way.

So, how did we get here? After a string of difficult clients and a need for something new, I found myself full-time at the University of North Georgia (UNG), not as a faculty member teaching marketing, but as the marketing manager for the Mike Cottrell College of Business. The College's namesake sought to build a brand for it, and the College's development director (and someone who had become my mentor) Mike Banks, thought I would be a good fit. I was fortunate that they allowed me to continue teaching when I took on the full-time role as marketing manager in 2013, teaching fundamental courses in marketing and management. As digital marketing continued to grow as a field, I asked Dr. Donna Mayo, then dean of the College, to allow me to test market a new class in digital marketing that I hoped one day would become a program. From that first summer class with eight students, the program steadily grew, leading to a concentration in digital marketing that includes courses in digital marketing, social media and content, and the subject at the heart of this book — digital marketing analytics.

Now, why write a book on this topic of all things? Honestly, there is a significant need for a practical book about digital marketing analytics. I've read a number of the books available and consistently have been disappointed that I didn't learn anything new or that the content was so dated it wasn't applicable. Only one book on the topic, *Lean Analytics* by Alistair Croll and Benjamin Yoskovitz, has been worth the effort. I've even used it as a tool in the classroom because of the lack of quality textbooks on the topic. For the few that do exist, they are just cumbersome to read and are too busy explaining theory to actually show how the work is done in practice.

By now you're probably thinking — oh, so you wrote a book for your class because you didn't think any other book was good enough so it's textbook for a course. That's kind of true, but not entirely. There is a whole new generation of marketers and analysts, whether in a classroom or behind a desk, trying to figure out this thing called digital analytics. There are classes to teach you software and there are articles you can read, but few stop to say, "Hey, wait a minute. Here's what this stuff actually means." In addition, while I did dedicate a few years of my career to education marketing, education has always been my side hustle, if you will. Really, I've always wanted to write a book and why not write it on a topic that I've studied and taught for a long time.

This is a preface so a few thank yous: I've been blessed that people like Dr. Donna Mayo, Dr. Mohan Menon, Dr. Caroline Muñoz, Dr. Laura Pricer, and Dr. Wendy Walker — all from the University of North Georgia — have allowed me to pour into students all these years. And even when I left the University to return to the agency world at Forum Communications, they've allowed me to continue teaching.

I came to this project with specific goals in mind. I wanted to write a book on digital marketing analytics that isn't full of vague language and examples that don't reflect how marketing actually works today. Now, it is analytics so some of that's here. It's sort of a requirement. But, that's certainly not the entirety of the book. Many analytics books focus heavily on theory. In practice, marketers often need to make decisions quickly with imperfect data. The goal of this book is to help you understand what the metrics are and which metrics actually matter when making real marketing decisions.

Again, this book is the culmination of years of refinement of a course called "Digital Analytics" and my own nearly twenty-five years of marketing for organizations large and small.

Much like the digital analytics course I've taught over the years, this book follows a deliberate structure. To understand where we're going, we have to know where we've been, so this book starts with a brief history of marketing analytics and the web. From there, we'll take a brief but meaningful detour into financial metrics that matter most to marketers. Why? Because you need to understand how digital marketing analytics affect the bottom line, not just your follower count. Then we jump headfirst into the important stuff — digital marketing analytics — reviewing each of the primary marketing channels, what we measure, why we measure it, and best practices for each. We'll wrap up with some of the latest on data governance, privacy, and — did I mention that Lean Analytics is one of my favorite analytics texts? We'll briefly review some of the key concepts from that text and how they apply to digital marketing.

There's a lot of ground to cover, but I'll do my best to make it worth reading. And while I know any book on analytics — even this one — can be dense at times, I hope you find it practical, useful, and worth the purchase.

God bless and thank you for trusting me with your time.

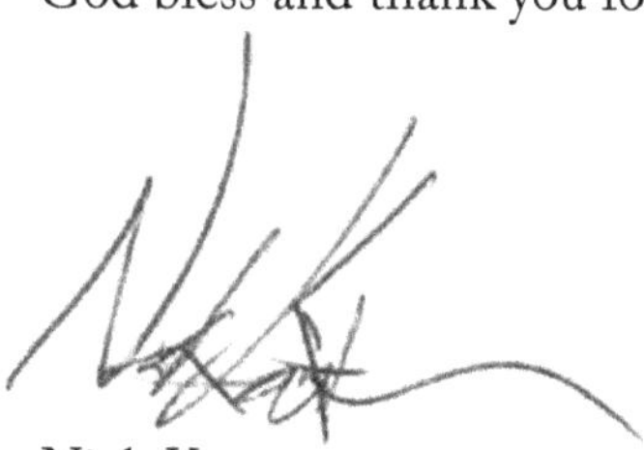

Nick Kastner

Chapter 1
A Brief History of Marketing Analytics & the Web

Why start with history, of all things? In teaching young marketers for the past eighteen years, I constantly have reminded myself that those of us who are 'a certain age' remember so much from the beginning of the web. And, understanding where things begin can tell us so much about not only the past, but the future.

For years, marketers have been challenged to connect the art of communication to the bottom-line results most businesses seek. Frankly — that's hard. It requires analytical and statistical skills that don't always come naturally to people drawn to marketing's creative side. At least from my experience, marketers tend to enjoy storytelling, copywriting, generating creative ideas, and developing Instagram Reels. At the heart of marketing lies a balance between creativity and the ability to measure results. That's why Alexander Chernev defines today's marketing management as part art and part science.

If you consider how long business and trade have been around, marketing analytics is relatively new. Buying, selling, and trading of goods and services have been happening for centuries. Some trace the earliest known logos to roughly 1500 BC while widespread marketing as a commercial activity didn't truly take shape until the invention of the printing press around 1450 AD. It took almost 500 years before marketing (not just advertising and communication) became important to businesses.

Around 1950, Harvard advertising professor Neil Borden began speaking of the 'marketing mix' — the blend of activities that define marketing. A decade later, E. Jerome McCarthy distilled it into the four Ps we still use today: Product, Price, Place, and Promotion. This strategic framework for marketing has been used for years and only recently has begun to expand. In the 1970s, statisticians from the University of Chicago built the first statistical models to help quantify the connection between marketing and sales. These tools were great... for big business. Small and medium-sized businesses at the time simply didn't have the manpower nor the skill set to pull off these highly detailed and heavy math-oriented measures.

In the 1980s, marketing mix modeling (or MMM) — a statistical approach using regression analysis to connect marketing activities to business results — began to take hold. However, again, these activities were limited to large businesses due to the human resources and computing power required at the time. Again, another resource issue. Are you sensing a theme here?

Insight: Traditional Marketing Measurement

A company sends 10,000 postcards promoting a sale. Two weeks later, sales increase by $5,000. Did the postcards cause the increase?

Before digital analytics, marketers often struggled to answer questions like this.

Most businesses simply didn't have the staff, time, or financial resources to truly develop marketing analytics as a function of their marketing effort. It's also why a lot of business owners still struggle with marketing and its value today. Most businesses, up until the advent of the web, tracked revenue in comparison to marketing spend over time. If you mailed 10,000 postcards, how much in sales did you generate over the two weeks after those postcards reached mailboxes? Or, if you ran an ad in the newspaper, how much in sales did you generate?

This has always been a challenge in marketing. How can you prove that your marketing efforts generated a conversion, a sale, or any measurable outcome? Here I have to reiterate: from the 1980s through the early 2000s, with traditional marketing activities, many large businesses used models and statisticians to measure marketing. Small and medium-sized businesses struggled to determine whether marketing generated value at all. Even in the early days of my own career, proving the direct value of your efforts was very difficult especially in the services industry.

Then, the internet. Many point to 1990–1991 as the web's official birth, and at that time, it was truly the Wild, Wild West. It began with text and links, soon to advance to coding with images, Adobe Flash animations, and more. And today, it's advanced so far to be a critical part of our daily lives.

The web was initially developed simply to deliver and receive information. Website owners either did not track website traffic or simply tracked file hits or opens directly from the web server to determine success. Simply measuring the number of times files were accessed was similar to the reactive approach most small and medium-sized businesses had relied on before, but at this time, still reserved for larger businesses with tech teams that could afford to do so.

Then, in 1995, the first true web traffic analysis tools arrived. A free log-file analysis program called Analog was released that year, followed three years later by Urchin, launched in 1998 by Urchin Software Corporation. Remember that name — it comes back twice in this book. All of these tools measured hits. **Hits** were simply a count of how many times a file on a website was loaded into a web browser — like counting the number of people who walk through a retail store (and, every item they carry in with them). Hits were also used to track online advertising views and their subsequent clicks. Analog arrived the same year the first two major e-commerce marketplaces (Amazon and eBay) launched.

Tip: Why "Hits" Were a Bad Metric

Early analytics tools counted every file loaded on a webpage — including images and scripts. This made "hits" a misleading measure of website popularity. Modern analytics focuses instead on users, sessions, and events.

Because marketers, information technology professionals, and data technicians all wanted more detailed information, they began developing ways to make tracking more precise. So, hits very quickly became more detailed — introducing the idea of page views. **Page views** are simply the total number of web pages viewed over a given period. The time between 1990 and the early 2000s on the web is referred to as Web 1.0.

Web 1.0

Web 1.0 is a critical time in the history of the web. This period is before cellular phones were web dominant and before social media. Data speeds were very slow and most users like me used the internet for emails, MapQuest and early online shopping primarily using eBay as an online thrift store and Amazon for books. We connected with friends on our large desktop computers using tools like ICQ and AOL Instant Messenger. Websites were built from static HTML code and were uploaded "server side" and there was no content management system. In 1997, both Amazon and eBay completed over 1 million transactions. Google and Yahoo! became marketing tools through practices like search engine optimization, and in 2000, Google monetized search by debuting Google AdWords, allowing businesses to advertise when users searched a given key phrase. Email marketing also matured during this period with the launch of tools like Eloqua, Mailchimp, and ExactTarget, alongside CRM platforms like Salesforce. Metrics like **open rate** (the ratio of email opens to emails sent), **bounce rate** (in email, the ratio of messages that never reached an inbox to messages sent and not to be confused with website bounce rate), and **email click-through rate** (the rate of clicks on links to emails sent) for email were introduced. However, this rapid period of growth on the web also led to speculative investment in internet companies. From 1995 to March of 2000, the NASDAQ rose by 400% driven by these fast growing web companies. By October 2002, the dot-com bubble had burst, falling 78% from its peak and giving up all of its gains. During this time, companies born of that speculative frenzy — Pets.com, Boo.com, and several communications companies among them — failed.

Web 2.0

Web 2.0 was defined by two major changes: an emphasis on user-generated content and the idea that the web could be a platform for software. **User-generated content** (UGC) is exactly what it sounds like:

content created by the people using the platform — in this case, the web. While many of us used the web to communicate via chat or forums prior to 2003, the first social media platform to reach true mass adoption — MySpace — launched in 2003. The second shift (the web as a software platform) is what made UGC possible at scale: consumers now had the tools to publish and share on their own.

This period, typically spanning the early 2000s through 2010, was defined primarily by the emergence of platforms like MySpace, Facebook, Reddit, and Wikipedia. This period also saw the first mass creation of personal websites, blogs, and content aggregation. This ability for consumers to create and share their own content online helped pave the way for the next major shift — the smartphone, beginning with the first iPhone in 2007. Web technologies also advanced. **Cascading Style Sheets** (CSS), introduced in the late 1990s, became more widely and creatively adopted during this period to manage the visual design of websites — and remain standard practice today. During this period, we also saw wide adoption of website animations in Adobe Flash and several other web-related technologies including XHTML, DOM, and more.

Just as the web changed, so did analytics. Over time, marketers and software engineers developed ways to turn hits into groupings. The web saw wide adoption of server side hit tracking and Urchin was becoming a widely adopted solution for many organizations.

In 2005, Google purchased Urchin, and later that same year launched the very first iteration of Google Analytics. This new tool presented us with a clear way to review information from the web. Also, this new tool became attainable to all because it was free. In my opinion, the launch of what we now call Google Classic Analytics is the very moment that the expectations of marketers changed forever. Now, everyone, not just marketers and analysts, could use a snippet of JavaScript at no cost to track web behavior.

These tools tracked users using these snippets of code (which we call cookies and define later). If the user came from an individual **Internet Protocol (IP) address** — the unique network address assigned to an individual device — marketers assumed that if someone used the same device from the same location frequently, it represented one person or user. A **user**, thus, was a single IP address appearing from a single location. That single user could visit a website multiple times. Therefore, a **visit** was a group of website **page views** that occurred from an IP address within a certain amount of time. These concepts were used in the development of the next iteration of web analytics tracking.

In addition to website analytics, social media platforms also began providing metrics including likes, page reach, and visits.

While the tools available to us were better than ever, web futurists in the early 2010s saw more. They saw a future that would eventually pull together all societies and information. Tools that would break walls between countries. And even further, a web that could change society as we know it. That leads us to Web 3.0.

Web 3.0

Coined in 2014 by English computer scientist Gavin Wood, Web 3.0 provided a future of decentralization and democracy of the web. Tim Berners-Lee, the inventor of the World Wide Web, had earlier described a related vision he called the semantic web.

The conceptual ideas of Web 3.0 were driven by blockchain technologies, digital and cryptocurrencies, edge computing, non-fungible tokens, and the metaverse. That's a lot of buzzwords. Web 3.0 simply asked the question – could we make the web become its own entity? Like a shared digital reality with its own money, own environment, and more. While I'm not sure that's actually what has happened, the web certainly has taken on new life and has become an integral part of modern society. Let's define some of these ideas:

A **block** is a record stored within a database ledger.

A **blockchain** is the distributed database that stores and links these records together. Each block contains a cryptographic reference to the previous block, creating a secure and traceable chain of information.

Non-fungible tokens (NFTs) are built using blockchain technologies and are simply records of ownership of anything digital that has an NFT attached and can be bought, sold, traded and ownership transferred. NFT trading alone increased from $82 million in 2020 to $26.3 billion in 2022.

Digital currencies and **cryptocurrencies** represent currencies that are decentralized, unlike standard government-backed currencies, but represent a value that is established by the web community. At the time of this writing, online games like Axie Infinity and others actually have high value cryptocurrencies that are bought and traded in-game and on secondary markets. Also, and for a variety of reasons, 2023 saw NFT trading volume drop to $13.7 billion, but the cryptocurrency market, which is built on the framework of blockchains, hit an all-time high at the time with a market capitalization of $3.71 trillion on December 9, 2024.

Edge computing is defined as moving the actual data storage and processing to the edge of a given network. Ideally, this reduces the latency or lag from data access. Many of you have already experienced cloud computing or use of the cloud for data access. If you've ever pulled a photo off iCloud or Google Drive, you've already used the ecosystem that edge computing is trying to extend.

And, finally, the **metaverse** — a shared digital reality that allows users to connect with each other in real time. Some of you may have experienced the metaverse through various platforms like Roblox or other online interactions in games like Fortnite or through virtual reality (VR) headsets.

When these concepts were discussed in 2014 / 2015 they were simply dreams as to where the web could go. However, these ideas are now driving decisions for brands and are becoming more and more a part of our everyday lives.

Analytically, another pivot point arrived in this era: Universal Analytics (or UA for short), which Google announced in 2012 and fully released in 2014. This new tool allowed for tracking and the separation of data between device type (desktop, tablet, mobile), integration of metrics, and the possibility of using Google's Application Programming Interface (API) to interface into other systems touched by customers. This represented a massive shift in the marketplace — one still echoing today as Google and others continue merging data platforms.

At the time of this writing, the dreams and ideas behind Web 3.0 have not been fully implemented because the market has changed. Many Web 3.0 enthusiasts were aiming to change the world. The world certainly changed — just not entirely in the way they predicted — and new technologies may be leading us somewhere different still: machine learning, artificial intelligence, and quantum computing.

I would be remiss not to acknowledge that today's technologies are built on the foundation of Web 3.0, but futurists will argue today that what we are seeing is just Web 3.1 — not Web 4.0. Who's to say, and I frankly am not sure that it matters, but the web is certainly changing.

Web 3.1 or Web 4.0?

For marketers, the greatest benefit to digital marketing since its inception is a marketer's ability to track users across their web presence. As tracking technology grew sophisticated enough to tie behavior to an individual, privacy activists quickly saw the problem: a skilled marketer could follow a user across the web right down to their personally identifiable information.

In May 2018, **General Data Protection Regulation (GDPR)** took effect in the European Union. It remains the most demanding privacy law any government has actually put on the books, and it applies to you whether or not you have a single customer in Europe. This law imposes rules on all organizations with a web presence – not just those within the European Union – requiring that users be able to manage how they're tracked on the websites they visit.

Compliant website owners now give users the option of selecting which behaviors can be tracked. GDPR has also heavily influenced laws here in the United States, including the California Consumer Privacy Act (CCPA). Each of these new laws directly affect all organizations that use analytics tools to track users on the web.

Beyond privacy, one of the big shifts that could lead to the next generation of the web is the widespread adoption of **artificial intelligence** and **machine learning**. In late 2022, OpenAI's ChatGPT arrived, and the internet reorganized itself around it in about ninety days when the platform was released to the public for beta testing. Soon after, companies from Meta to Google rushed to release their own AI models. In just a few years, AI has rebuilt the web's toolset — images, video, copywriting, social media management, data analysis. It has changed the face of search marketing and both simplified and complicated the marketing environment at the same time. Even academic institutions are scrambling to adjust now that students can generate essay and exam responses on demand.

Insight: Analytics Will Continue to Evolve

The evolution of the web has always shaped marketing analytics.

Web 1.0 → Basic traffic measurement
Web 2.0 → User behavior and engagement metrics
Web 3.0 → Data integration, NFTs, Edge Computing
Web 4.0? → AI, privacy regulation, and machine learning

As technology evolves, the tools marketers use to measure success evolve as well. AI is already beginning to assist marketers with forecasting trends, analyzing data, and generating insights. However, marketers must still understand the underlying metrics to interpret AI-generated insights correctly.

Machine learning is a subset of artificial intelligence that focuses on identifying patterns, making decisions based on those patterns, and essentially teaching itself through experience. These tools use algorithms trained on massive datasets to imitate how we as humans learn. Organizations are using these technologies to develop software that assists marketers — or in some cases, makes decisions on their behalf entirely.

Artificial intelligence and its use across the web are bringing about rapid and massive change. Consider this: a marketing agency is paid to develop content for a new website and over 100 blog posts in a given year. This content can now be generated via artificial intelligence in a matter of moments. The question now is where the ethical line sits — and who gets to draw it. While some of this is yet to be determined, AI-generated images, video, and copy are improving at a startling pace — and the gap between machine-made and human-made content narrows by the month. We actively see clients at our agency send us sample creative design or content developed by AI. While some claim that artificial intelligence and machine learning are part of Web 3.0, it could also be argued that these elements, along with discussions around user rights and privacy, are bringing about a new iteration of the web.

Also, as noted with each new iteration of the web, it seems analytics tracking also changes. In 2023, Google fully rolled out its latest iteration of Analytics — Google Analytics 4. Announced in late 2020, this iteration would now allow for the integration and measurement of apps (remember Web 2.0's mention that the web could be a platform for software?) AND websites. Google Analytics 4, or GA4, has built-in tools that account for new privacy laws and uses AI and machine learning to help do so. As of 2026, Google measurement tools were used on a combined 55% of websites that use analytics globally.

Whether Web 3.0, 3.1, or 4.0, today's marketers seek to track every element of a user's journey on the web while balancing this activity with meeting privacy requirements. The end goal of these tracking efforts is to:

1. Create value for the person or organization doing the tracking — the owner of the website, app, account, or page;

2. Create the best user experience possible for the end user / consumer delivering real value to them;

3. And, to make decisions that allow for both of these activities to occur.

The tools we use to measure marketing today weren't designed in a vacuum. Every update — from simple hit counts to GA4's machine learning models — was a response to a real limitation the previous tool couldn't solve. That pattern hasn't changed and won't. Whatever comes after GA4, it will exist because the market demanded something the current platform couldn't deliver. Understanding that cycle is, I'd argue, as important as understanding the platforms themselves.

Before we get into the analytics themselves, though, there's a detour worth taking — one that a lot of analytics books skip entirely. To make sense of why any of these metrics matter, you need to understand how marketing connects to the financial health of a business. That's where we're going next.

References

A brief history of website analytics. (2020, June 5). Leady. https://leady.com/blog/a-brief-history-of-website-analytics/

Artificial Intelligence (AI) vs. Machine Learning. (n.d.). Columbia Engineering. https://ai.engineering.columbia.edu/ai-vs-machine-learning/

Ash, A. (2023, November 29). *What is Web 4.0? Worth Explaining Now*. Lizard Global. https://www.lizard.global/blog/what-is-web4-explained

Aulakh, N. (2024, March 27). *The History of Market Mix Modeling*. Arima Data. https://arimadata.com/company/blogs/the-history-of-market-mix-modeling/

Blockchain: Six considerations for securing your software supply chain. (n.d.). Synopsys. https://www.synopsys.com/glossary/what-is-blockchain.html

Chernev, A. (2018). *Strategic Marketing Management* (9th ed.). Cerebellum Press.

Dot-com bubble. (n.d.). Wikipedia. https://en.wikipedia.org/wiki/Dot-com_bubble

e-Bay: from the auction of a piece of toast to the ideal marketplace. (n.d.). expando. https://www.expan.do/post/ebay-marketplace

Edge Computing. (n.d.). Accenture. https://www.accenture.com/us-en/insights/cloud/edge-computing-index

History of E-Commerce: Facts, Stats, & Tips on What's Next. (n.d.). George Washington University. https://healthcaremba.gwu.edu/history-of-ecommerce

History of the Internet. (n.d.). Wikipedia. https://en.wikipedia.org/wiki/History_of_the_Internet

Hunter, N. (2024, August 2). *Every iPhone Generation: A Full History of Release Dates*. IGN. https://www.ign.com/articles/all-iphone-release-dates-in-order

Katte, S. (2025, March 7). *NFT trading volume has tumbled 63% since December*. CoinTelegraph. https://cointelegraph.com/news/nft-trading-volume-down-63-since-december

Kubinec, J. (2024, January 18). *NFT volume fell $14.5B in 2023: CoinGecko*. Blockworks. https://blockworks.co/news/nft-trading-volumes-fall-from-2022

Lapenta, N. (n.d.). *Google Analytics Generations*. Data Consultant. https://www.nicolalapenta.com/google-analytics-generations/

Lee, R. (2026, January 21). *Google Analytics Statistics 2026: What's New and What's Next*. SQ Magazine. https://sqmagazine.co.uk/google-analytics-statistics/

Mohammad, W. (2012, August 11). *Amazon 1997-2003: An Insight into the Rise of the E-Commerce Giant*. menabytes. https://www.menabytes.com/amazon-1997-2003/

Non-fungible token. (n.d.). Wikipedia. https://en.wikipedia.org/wiki/Non-fungible_token

Oseni, M. (2023, April 20). *Google Analytics Statistics in 2023 (GA4 Included)*. Narrative BI. https://www.narrative.bi/analytics/google-analytics-statistics-in-2023-ga4-included

Taylor, J. (2024, February 21). *The History of Email Marketing*. Knak. https://knak.com/blog/history-of-email-marketing/

The History of Marketing in Under 5 Minutes. (2023, January 9). Ocreative. https://ocreative.com/the-history-of-marketing-in-under-5-minutes/
Timbó, R. (2023, March 14). *What is Web 3.0?*. Revelo. https://www.revelo.com/blog/what-is-web-3-0

Urchin – the first Google Analytics. (n.d.). Tracking Garden. https://tracking-garden.com/knowledge/web-analytics/systems/urchin/

Vailshery, Lionel S. (2023, November 27). *Web analytics software market share worldwide 2023*. Statista https://www.statista.com/statistics/1258557/web-analytics-market-share-technology-worldwide/

Web 3.0 Explained, Plus the History of Web 1.0 and 2.0. (2024, August 8). Investopedia. https://www.investopedia.com/web-20-web-30-5208698

What is GDPR, the EU's new data protection law?. (n.d.). GDPR.EU. https://gdpr.eu/what-is-gdpr/

Chapter 2
Marketing and Finance

Marketing and finance are often perceived as separate disciplines that operate in silos. In one corner is marketing, which focuses on communicating value to consumers and gathering insights about their behavior — all activities that come with associated costs. In the other corner, finance focuses on operational efficiency and delivering value at the lowest possible cost to maximize profit. I've seen this firsthand working in one role where the CFO would openly state marketing had little value because its value wasn't apparent in the income statement.

Both functions exist to deliver value to the customer. They just don't always trust each other's methods. Some finance professionals view marketing as a function that increases costs while struggling to prove its value. As a result, marketing can sometimes appear to overpromise and underdeliver. Unchecked or poorly guided marketing can produce a negative return on investment. On the other hand, a finance function too focused on cost-cutting can ultimately underdeliver on customer value and erode what the organization means to its customers. That, too, can become unsustainable — and produce the same outcome.

The key is alignment between the two disciplines. For businesses to thrive, marketing professionals must understand the financial metrics that underpin their strategies. A 2021 Deloitte study found that among companies generating positive revenue growth, more than 70% reported strong C-suite alignment on which marketing metrics mattered most. Connecting digital data points to financial outcomes is essential to ensuring that marketing efforts contribute to the organization's bottom line.

For marketing to build trust with finance and organizational leadership, marketers need a working understanding of how finance thinks — the goals they're trying to hit and the metrics they reach for first. This chapter walks through the data points marketers need to know if they want a seat at the table.

Converging Marketing and Finance

Here's the way I've always thought about it: marketing creates the demand, and finance keeps score. When those two functions are working well together, they're reading from the same playbook. When they're not, marketing teams spend budget on campaigns finance didn't buy into, and finance teams cut programs that were actually working because no one translated the results into language they recognized. The bridge between the two is data — and understanding the financial documents and metrics that finance runs on is how you start speaking that language.

To understand how marketing contributes to financial performance, marketers must first understand the financial documents used by organizations to measure success. Those in finance usually start with the income statement. I'm starting with the cash flow statement, because cash flow is where a marketer's spend actually shows up first — and it's the document most likely to explain why your budget increased or got cut.

The Financial Statement

Financial statements typically consist of three primary documents: the cash flow statement, the income statement, and the balance sheet. Each of these documents provides valuable information for marketers on the success (or failure) of their efforts. They also help us as marketers answer a variety of questions:

- Can we analyze current financial strengths and weaknesses?
- Can we do comparative analysis over time periods for financial metrics we care about? And if so, do we know why these ups and downs occur?
- Can we evaluate alternative strategies to create momentum? Introducing new products? Revising budgets up or down? Can we learn from the data — for example, reviewing landing pages to determine which pages / products / services drive higher sales volumes?
- Can we forecast or effectively budget for success?

These documents provide a great deal of information as well as allow us to calculate data that is helpful. This includes calculating information directly from financial statements as well as looking at more detailed information from ancillary documents used daily by the finance team. Some of the things that matter to marketing are:

- Customer Acquisition Cost
- Return on Investment / Return on Marketing Investment
- Customer Lifetime Value
- Gross Margin
- Revenue Growth
- Sustainable Growth Rate
- Contribution Margin (for Marketing)
- Payback Period
- Conversion Rate
- Retention

The Cash Flow Statement

Cash flow statements speak directly to sales volume, expenses, inventory, and labor costs. The cash flow statement can also show purchases of new assets — like buildings and equipment — as well as repayments on long-term debt. In the end, this document shows us how much cash came in, how much was spent, and our ending cash balance over a period of time. It also shows us net cash flow, so we can see whether cash flow was positive or negative for the period.

On the following page is a sample of a cash flow statement for a coffee shop. Take the time to read through the various points of the cash flow statement and see if you can find any data points that might be important from a marketer's perspective. Marketers utilize the cash flow statement in a few ways. Ultimately, the cash flow statement helps answer four key questions:

Sample Statement of Cash Flows

Bean & Bar Coffee Company

For the year ended December 31,	2023	2024	2025
Cash at Beginning of Period	$ -	$24,450	$167,215
Cash Receipts from Operating Activities			
Cash from Sales	336,100	582,275	805,318
Cash Payments from Operating Activities			
Cash paid from Inventory	(75,304)	(142,066)	(175,254)
Cash paid from Direct Labor	(137,653)	(143,215)	(156,032)
Cash paid for Advertising	(6,109)	(6,356)	(6,531)
Cash paid for Accounting	(945)	(1,543)	(1,562)
Cash paid for Point of Sale Services	(2,456)	(2,419)	(2,579)
Cash paid for Transaction Fees	(25,194)	(37,981)	(56,437)
Cash paid for Insurance	(2,945)	(3,483)	(3,749)
Cash paid for Rent	(36,174)	(37,429)	(38,241)
Cash paid for Supplies	(5,600)	(5,945)	(6,050)
Cash paid for Miscellaneous	(900)	(1,350)	(1,462)
Cash paid for Utilities	(4,800)	(4,850)	(5,100)
Cash paid for Dues and Subscriptions	(1,100)	(1,325)	(1,325)
Cash paid for Repairs & Maintenance	(1,043)	(1,350)	(1,540)
Cash paid for Salaries	(51,200)	(53,200)	(115,300)
Cash paid for Loan Interest Expense	(5,743)	(5,820)	(5,125)
Cash paid for Income Tax	-	(6,325)	(26,450)
Cash from Operating Activities	**($21,066)**	**$127,618**	**$202,581**
Cash from Financing & Investing			
Cash from New Loans	135,000		
Cash paid on Loan Principal	(9,234)	(12,853)	(13,520)
Cash paid (from sale) for Fixed Assets	(80,250)	28,000	-
Net Cash from Financing & Investing	**$45,516**	**$15,147**	**($13,520)**
Cash at End of Period	**$24,450**	**$167,215**	**$356,276**

- Where is cash coming from?
- Where is cash being spent?
- Why do the ins and outs of cash occur?
- And, can we attribute any marketing activity to the ins and outs of cash during the period of time measured?

As you saw on the prior page, in 2023 the coffee shop represented here had no cash at the beginning of the year. Our assumption is this is the first year the shop was in business. During the year it generated just over $336,000 in sales but spent all of those funds and more on operational costs. Operationally, the shop actually lost money in year one — about $21,000 more went out than came in. What saved them was financing: a $135,000 loan covered the shortfall, the equipment purchases, and left $24,450 in the bank. This is exactly why the cash flow statement matters — the sales number alone would never tell you this business started underwater. And what did they sell in 2024 for $28,000? An espresso machine? A delivery van? The statement won't tell you — which is a good reminder that financial documents raise questions as often as they answer them. As marketers, we would also note that they spent very little in advertising and continued that trend in 2024 and 2025. As you look through this cash flow statement, what other insights can you identify?

All three of those columns are actuals. But look at the trajectory and project it forward: this business is planning on serious growth while spending almost nothing on advertising. How? Is the owner an influencer? Do they have a cult following, or are they assuming one? Are they in a prime location? Somebody needs to answer that question before they sign a lease on a second location. All of these things would need to be taken into account regarding extreme growth with little paid promotional effort.

The Income Statement

The **income statement** is focused on incoming sales volume and the cost to operate the business. It answers a simple question: how much money did we make? On the following page is an Income Statement from a company called Outdoor Gear, Inc.

Sample Income Statement

Outdoor Gear, Inc.

Income Statement

For the Year Ended December 31, 2025

Item	Amount ($)
Revenue	
Product Sales	1,250,000
Service Revenue	150,000
Net Sales	**1,400,000**
Cost of Goods Sold	
Materials	420,000
Direct Labor	210,000
Manufacturing Overhead	120,000
Total Cost of Goods Sold	**750,000**
Gross Profit	**650,000**
Operating Expenses	
Salaries and Wages	220,000
Marketing and Advertising	85,000
Rent and Utilities	72,000
Insurance	18,000
Office Expenses	15,000
Depreciation	30,000
Total Operating Expenses	**440,000**
Operating Income	**210,000**
Other Income and Expenses	
Interest Expense	(20,000)
Interest Income	4,000
Total Other Income (Expense)	**(16,000)**
Income Before Taxes	**194,000**
Income Tax Expense (25%)	48,500
Net Income	**145,500**

While marketers often focus on sales, every organization must also consider the costs required to operate. Driving high sales volumes without the appropriate operating structure can lead to business failure just as quickly as poor sales can. The income statement itself is about efficiency — not effectiveness. The goal for most organizations is to maximize revenue and minimize expenditures, thus increases in revenue and decreases in costs (including marketing) can drive higher margin. So, both successful and unsuccessful marketing campaigns will eventually appear in the income statement; if higher revenues coincide with higher marketing expenditures, marketing may be proving its value. Inflationary pressures, declining prices, and margins on sales also appear when reading an income statement.

Net sales, the total dollar value of sales recorded during the period under review, appears at the top of most income statements. This number can indicate great work by your sales or marketing team – or lack thereof. It also can indicate economic pressures dependent on industry and timing.

Cost of sales (or cost of goods sold) explains the cost of production of goods and services. Increasing costs from suppliers or even inflation can negatively impact even successful sales and marketing efforts. Subtracting cost of sales from net sales (you'll sometimes see this labeled Total Revenue) provides you with the gross profit of your products and services. Using gross margin as a measure, marketers can consider product pricing from a financial standpoint. Product marketers can also look at ways to cut production costs to improve gross margins for higher profits later assuming they are not cutting the quality or value perceived by the consumer (we'll define gross margin properly in a few pages).

Operating expenses represent the overhead for your efforts. This typically includes general and administrative expenses and can also include marketing and sales expenses. Some organizations include research and development in operating expenses, while others fold it into cost of sales, depending on their organizational structure.

Operating income subtracts the cost of sales and operating expenses from net sales. This number indicates how much money was actually made prior to adding other income or expenses as well as any provisions set aside for taxes or provisional product losses. Once these additional measures are added or subtracted, you reach net income. **Net income** simply starts with net sales and subtracts all costs as well as adds any additional ancillary income present on the income statement.

Insight: Marketing is an Investment

Marketing should not be viewed simply as a cost. When executed effectively, marketing becomes an investment that generates measurable returns in revenue, customer loyalty, and brand equity.

Each of these metrics can be applied later to determine other measures including corporate return on investment (ROI), sustainable growth rate (SGR), contribution analysis, and more.

The Balance Sheet

The **balance sheet** lays out the assets, liabilities, and equity owned by a business. It's called a balance sheet because total assets should equal total liabilities plus equity. For marketers, there are a number of things that can matter in a balance sheet. Things like accounts payable (how much we owe), accounts receivable (money owed to the organization by its customers — revenue earned but not yet collected), cash on hand, current assets (things we own), debt, and equity all can matter. Brand equity itself won't show up as a line item unless it was acquired — but you'll see its fingerprints in intangible assets and goodwill when brands change hands.

For instance, major increases in inventory on a balance sheet could be because of a poorly performing campaign OR a ramp up to prepare for a campaign. Increases in intangible assets may be due to brand growth or strength. Accounts payable being larger than accounts receivable can be detrimental unless cash and equivalents are high. Marketers can even get a better gauge of the availability of cash and accounts receivable to determine how much room they actually have for an upcoming campaign.

Acme Candy Company
Balance Sheet

Assets	2023	2024	2025
Current Assets:			
Cash	$167,971	$181,210	$183,715
Accounts Receivable	$5,100	$5,904	$6,567
Prepaid expenses	$4,806	$5,513	$5,170
Inventory	$7,805	$9,601	$9,825
Total current assets	$185,682	$202,228	$205,277
Property & Equipment	$45,500	$42,350	$40,145
Goodwill	$3,580	$3,460	$3,910
Total Assets	**$234,762**	**$248,038**	**$249,332**
Liabilities			
Current Liabilities:			
Accounts Payable	$3,902	$4,800	$4,912
Accrued expenses	$1,320	$1,541	$1,662
Unearned revenue	$1,540	$1,560	$1,853
Total current liabilities	**$6,762**	**$7,901**	**$8,427**
Long-term debt	$50,000	$50,000	$30,000
Other long-term liabilities	$5,526	$5,872	$5,565
Total Liabilities	$62,288	$63,773	$43,992
Shareholder's Equity			
Equity Capital	$170,000	$170,000	$170,000
Retained Earnings	$2,474	$14,265	$35,340
Shareholder's Equity	**$172,474**	**$184,265**	**$205,340**
Total Liabilities & Shareholder's Equity	**$234,762**	**$248,038**	**$249,332**

Key Financial Metrics for Marketers

Marketers can learn a great deal from the financial statement alone. However, with some additional manipulation, marketers can learn even more about their own efforts and their success or lack thereof. There are a few simple metrics that all marketers should be keenly familiar with. While not exhaustive, I've included some of the most frequently used of these metrics as well as their definitions and formulas for your use.

Consider this a quick guide to some of the many tools you can use to build better relationships with your financial counterparts.

Customer Acquisition Cost (CAC)

Customer Acquisition Cost, or CAC for short, represents the total expense incurred to acquire a new customer. This includes costs related to advertising, sales, and any associated tools or platforms. Marketers should regularly calculate CAC to assess the efficiency of their campaigns.

To calculate the CAC, simply take the total cost of sales and marketing divided by the number of customers acquired.

$$\text{Customer Acquisition Cost} = \frac{\text{Total cost of sales and marketing}}{\text{\# of customers acquired}}$$

Remember to include all marketing costs related to acquiring new customers including:

- Wages of sales and marketing teams
- Taxes
- Benefits
- Travel
- Agency Fees
- Advertising costs
- Marketing software and tools
- Production costs

A local retailer spent $85,000 on marketing and advertising last year and acquired 1,700 new customers. Their CAC is $50.

Low CAC can indicate that a company is acquiring customers cost-effectively. High CAC can signal significant inefficiencies or expensive acquisition channels. By optimizing campaigns and focusing on higher-performing channels, marketers can lower CAC and improve the return on investment (ROI).

Return on Investment (ROI) / Return on Marketing Investment (ROMI)

When most people think about marketing analytics in general, return on investment is usually the first metric discussed. That's because ROI is one of the calculations that "proves" marketing's efforts generate direct financial value. **ROI** and **ROMI** are the primary calculations for marketing efficiency. In simple terms, ROI is the return received for the investment made. In marketing terms, ROMI measures the profitability of marketing campaigns by comparing the revenue generated to the cost of the actual campaign. The two calculations are frequently mentioned together in marketing as they are very similar. Simply remove all of the marketing references in the calculation below to determine the calculation for ROI (ROI = (incremental revenue - costs) / costs).

ROMI is calculated as such:

$$\text{Return on Marketing Investment} = \frac{\text{Incremental revenue generated by marketing} - \text{Marketing costs}}{\text{Marketing costs}}$$

As an example, if a company spends $10,000 on a marketing campaign and generates $100,000 in new sales, their ROMI is 900%. So, for every dollar spent, the company got its dollar back plus $9 in return.

Calculating ROMI can be difficult because of the complexities in determining attribution and the time between the marketing effort and its results. Nonetheless, ROMI helps marketers measure success, justify expenditures and identify high-performing marketing campaigns. It also provides clarity on which efforts are driving tangible financial results.

Customer Lifetime Value

Customer Lifetime Value (CLV, also referred to as LTV) is a highly valuable and variable measure that estimates the total revenue a business can expect from a single customer over their lifetime.

The simple CLV / LTV has three components: the period of time we're measuring, average revenue per customer and average customer lifespan. Both the average revenue and average lifespan must be measured in the same type of period of time.

CLV = Average Revenue per Customer x Average Customer Lifespan

For a coffee shop, let's say that we are measuring in months. Their average revenue per customer per month is $14 over the average life span of, we'll say, 24 months. The average CLV would be $336.

The other way to look at this same calculation is this:

CLV = Average Order Value x Purchase Frequency (per year) x Average Customer Lifespan (in years)

If the same coffee shop was calculated in this way, we would say the average order value is $7, consumers tend to buy twice a month so the purchase frequency is 24 per year, and the average customer lifespan is 2 years. So, $7 x 24 x 2 is $336.

The problem with calculating CLV typically lies in a lack of exact data. If an organization doesn't track average spend per customer — how much and how often individual customers buy — this metric is nearly impossible to produce. The same is true if the organization doesn't actively maintain data on customer lifespan. Both of these are easy to calculate IF you track the data and establish methodology in how your organization wants to keep up with this information. For instance, an organization that wants to measure average annual customer spend needs to ensure that they are using some type of customer relationship management (CRM) system that tracks user purchases. Also, the organization may be able to use their point of sale (POS) system as well for this tracking. To track average customer lifespan, an organization must establish metrics on the average time between purchases and at what point a consumer is considered "dead" or no longer purchases from your organization so that the lifespan can end. For newer or smaller organizations, this process can be challenging and may not seem worth the effort. However, the long term value of this calculation is enormous as it can dictate what types of customers you want more of and even how you budget for your marketing efforts.

Tip: Focus on the CLV to CAC Ratio

One of the most important metrics for marketers is the relationship between Customer Lifetime Value and Customer Acquisition Cost.

A healthy benchmark is typically 3:1, meaning a customer generates three times the revenue it costs to acquire them.

When the data is available, many times marketers will refine this calculation further to use profit rather than revenue as it provides a more accurate portrayal of the consumer's value back to the organization. If I'm calculating CLV for a customer, this is the method that I prefer.

CLV (profit-based) = Average Revenue per Customer x Gross Margin (as a percentage) x Average Customer Lifespan

So, back to our coffee shop: our average revenue over a month is $14 and our average customer lifespan remains 24 months. Now, based on our gross margin (I'll show you how to calculate this on the next page) is 65%. If I multiply $14 times 65% (0.65) times 24 months, our CLV is $218.40.

That means that the average customer is worth $218.40 in profit over their lifetime as a customer.

Comparing CLV to CAC allows marketers to determine the value of acquiring and retaining customers. CLV can also be segmented into different groupings of customers to determine which types of customers provide the highest value. A high CLV relative to CAC indicates healthy customer relationships and effective marketing strategies.

Gross Margin

Gross margin represents the percentage of revenue remaining after deducting the cost of goods sold. While not directly controlled by marketing, gross margin impacts decisions on pricing and promotional strategies.

$$\text{Gross Margin} = \frac{\text{Net Sales - Cost of Goods Sold}}{\text{Net Sales}}$$

Back to our coffee shop example: calculated as $1,300,000 ÷ $2,000,000, or 65%. That tells me a great deal about how much room they have to spend on acquiring a customer. The average gross margin for a coffee shop is between 60% - 70% making their current marketing efforts on point for the industry.

Tip: Percentages and Calculations

Throughout the remainder of this book you'll see a number of "rates" that should be displayed as percentages. Rather than reiterate every time in a calculation to get to a percentage you have to multiply the number by 100, that is just assumed. If you see a rate and it states it should be a percentage, and then you calculate the rate, remember to multiply by 100. An example: let's say, the result is 0.52 — that's not the final number. The actual number is 52%.

Marketers need to understand gross margin to design campaigns that align with profitability goals while also understanding product costs for research and development. For example, third-party e-commerce platforms may increase sales volume but may erode margins due to additional costs.

Many times, I've asked clients what their gross and net margins are to better determine the value of their existing sales and marketing efforts. If margins are relatively low, that tells me how much room they realistically have to spend on marketing to drive volume.

Revenue Growth Rate

Revenue growth rate measures the percentage increase in revenue over a specific period. Marketing efforts often drive this growth, making it a critical metric for campaign evaluation.

The formula for this calculation is relatively simple:

$$\text{Revenue Growth Rate} = \frac{\text{Current Period's Revenue} - \text{Previous Period's Revenue}}{\text{Previous Period's Revenue}}$$

For example, if the revenue for a company in the first quarter of 2025 was \$120,000 and \$100,000 in the first quarter of 2024, then the revenue growth rate would be 0.20, or 20%.

By tracking revenue growth, marketers can align their strategies with broader business objectives and demonstrate their contribution to the organization's success. While marketers and business leaders may want to track marketing success to net income growth, marketing has little control over the additional costs of the business beyond marketing expenditures.

Sustainable Growth Rate

Sustainable growth rate is a very important metric in understanding an organization's ability to grow. Imagine your agency is approached by a

CEO focused on growth. In your analysis, the organization's staff is struggling to maintain pace at their current rate and the organization itself is hitting a leadership ceiling. To grow, new hires should likely be brought on in addition to your agency to support marketing.

Think: Marketing and Growth

What financial information would you want to attempt to collect to assist with not only the marketing budget, but to provide additional business advice to help the organization continue growing?

Sustainable growth rate is the counterpart to revenue growth rate. Where revenue growth rate shares how fast an organization is currently growing, sustainable growth rate determines the rate at which an organization can grow without the need to borrow or to seek additional investment. Basically, do you have enough capital to grow at a pace that is sustainable? For small businesses, this may dictate how much money ownership can draw from the bottom line or whether the owners may need to invest further to continue growth.

For marketing, sustainable growth rate can serve as a benchmark — a case for improving performance, for asking leadership to increase budgets, or occasionally for pumping the brakes before growth breaks the business.

The calculation is multi-faceted as you need access to specific data. To accurately calculate sustainable growth rate you'll need to calculate the organization's asset utilization rate, profitability rate, equity multiplier, return on equity, dividend rate and business retention rate.

Asset Utilization Rate

This simple calculation is the first step in calculating return on equity, which is required to calculate sustainable growth rate. **Asset utilization rate** shows how well an organization is leveraging its existing assets to drive sales.

$$\text{Asset Utilization Rate} = \frac{\text{Total Sales for the Year}}{\text{Total Assets at Year End}}$$

To keep the example simple, let's say that total sales for the year were $20,000 and total assets at year end were $100,000. This would mean that our asset utilization rate is 0.2, or 20%.

Profitability Rate

Profitability rate is the second calculation necessary to determine return on equity. Another simple calculation, profitability rate shows how much value your sales actually drive after the organization's other expenses.

$$\text{Profitability Rate} = \frac{\text{Net Income}}{\text{Total Sales for the Year}}$$

In this simple scenario, let's assume that net income was $5,000 for the year and, if you'll recall from the previous calculation, total sales for the year were $20,000. This would mean the profitability rate was 0.25, or 25%, over the term.

Equity Multiplier

The last of the calculations for return on equity is the **equity multiplier** (you may also hear finance professionals call this "financial leverage"). On its own, the equity multiplier shows how much of an organization's assets are financed by its owners versus its lenders. The higher the number, the more leveraged the organization is.

$$\text{Equity Multiplier} = \frac{\text{Total Assets}}{\text{Total Equity}}$$

Again using our example thus far, remember that total assets at year end were $100,000. Total equity is calculated by subtracting total liabilities from total assets. If our liabilities over the term are $50,000, then our total equity is $50,000. $100,000 divided by $50,000 is 2 — or 2.0x. In plain terms, every dollar of owner equity is supporting two dollars of assets.

Return on Equity

Return on equity (ROE) is the amount of money an organization generates for its owners relative to what they've invested — money that can be kept and used to fuel future growth.

To calculate ROE, we simply multiply our asset utilization rate, profitability rate, and equity multiplier together.

Return on Equity = Asset Utilization Rate x Profitability Rate x Equity Multiplier

Going back to our example: if our asset utilization rate is 20%, profitability rate is 25%, and equity multiplier is 2.0x, then multiplying these together, our return on equity is 0.10, or 10%.

Want to check the math? There's a shortcut. ROE is ultimately just net income divided by total equity — $5,000 divided by $50,000 is 10%. So why bother with three separate ratios? Because the three-part version tells you where the return comes from: how hard the assets are working, how much profit each sale keeps, and how much leverage is amplifying it all. Finance professionals call this three-part breakdown DuPont analysis, and dropping that term in a meeting is a very inexpensive way to earn credibility with your CFO. We'll hold this value for our calculation of our sustainable growth rate.

Dividend Rate

The dividend rate is the percentage of your organization's earnings that you give back to your shareholders (or to yourself if you are a small business owner).

$$\text{Dividend Rate} = \frac{\text{Dividend}}{\text{Net Income}}$$

For our example, we'll assume a dividend of $500. Using our net income of $5,000, our dividend rate is a simple 0.1, or 10%.

Business Retention Rate

Our last calculation before determining our sustainable growth rate is the business retention rate. This calculation is the percentage of net income that an organization keeps for itself after dividends are paid.

$$\text{Business Retention Rate} = 100\% - \text{Dividend Rate}$$

This element is critical, as it allows our sustainable growth rate to account for any dividends the organization pays to shareholders or owners in the future, assuming that dividends are paid at the same rate.

With this complete, we're now ready to calculate our sustainable growth rate.

Sustainable Growth Rate = Return on Equity X Business Retention Rate

If we utilize the calculations we've already made, our return on equity is 10% and our business retention rate is 90%. Multiplying these two together, our sustainable growth rate is 0.09, or 9%. If we go back to our revenue growth rate from earlier in this chapter of 20%, we're growing more than twice as fast as we can sustain. As a recap:

Revenue Growth Rate = 20%

Asset Utilization Rate = 20%

Profitability Rate = 25%

Equity Multiplier = 2.0x

Return on Equity (ROE) = 10%

Dividend Rate = 10%

Business Retention Rate = 90%

Sustainable Growth Rate = 9%

If an organization's revenue growth rate is higher than the sustainable growth rate, it's likely that the organization will or is beginning to struggle to maintain pace. You may not have enough cash on hand to meet business needs or the right staff in place to continue growth. This can also show as staff burnout due to overwork, frequent loss of staff, issues with business collaborators, vendors, or even the pace you are able to get parts to manufacture products.

If an organization's revenue growth rate is lower than the sustainable growth rate, the organization may continue to grow at a faster rate with little financial risk. It also may be evidence that your organization is poorly performing and changes are necessary to improve performance.

Tip: Growth Must Be Sustainable

Rapid growth can be exciting, but if an organization grows faster than its financial resources allow, it can create operational strain. Sustainable growth rate helps leaders understand how quickly the organization can grow without taking on additional debt.

Contribution Margin (for Marketing)

This metric evaluates the total revenue generated through variable costs inclusive of marketing expenses.

$$\text{Contribution Margin} = \text{Total Sales Revenue} - \text{Variable Costs}$$

This metric can highlight the direct contribution of marketing on the organization's bottom line. This makes sense if the organization's marketing campaigns tend to drive direct and measurable return. It also helps prioritize strategies that drive the most significant revenue. For organizations where marketing heavily influences top of funnel strategies, that is efforts focused on brand awareness or those that don't directly drive a conversion, then this particular metric can work against marketers.

Payback Period

The payback period measures how long it takes to recoup the customer acquisition cost (CAC) from a customer's revenue contributions.
A shorter payback period reduces financial risk and indicates efficient customer acquisition strategies.

$$\text{Payback Period (in months)} = \frac{\text{Customer Acquisition Cost}}{(\text{Average Monthly Revenue per Customer X Gross Margin \%})}$$

If it costs $50 to acquire a customer, that customer spends $40 a month, and your gross margin is 50%, you're earning $20 a month against a $50 cost. Given the data, your payback period is 2.5 months.

Conversion Rate

As we start to wrap up the various metrics that frequently cross over between finance and marketing, there are two additional metrics that help provide additional trust between marketing and leadership. The first of these metrics is conversion rate.

Conversion rate reflects the percentage of users who complete a desired action, such as making a purchase, completing a form, or signing up for a newsletter. This is typically measured across websites, ad platforms, and other marketing efforts. For instance, if you send 1,000 direct mail pieces to consumers, and 10 of those individuals take action, that results in a 0.01, or 1% conversion rate.

$$\text{Conversion Rate} = \frac{\text{Number of Conversions}}{\text{Number of Opportunities}}$$

Conversion rate directly relates to a number of the financial metrics discussed. For instance, using the direct mail campaign example above, if we know that we typically generate a 1% conversion rate, we can then consider our budget versus the actual value of those conversions. We also can share conversion rate data as a metric to be transparent in our efforts with finance and leadership and to determine ways to improve our overall efforts. Now, in digital marketing, not every conversion leads to a direct sale. As mentioned previously, sometimes conversions are form completions, white paper downloads, and newsletter signups. While these all provide value, they are more closely related to marketing effectiveness, not the financial efficiencies anticipated by the finance team.

To take the example further, we can also use conversions and conversion rates to apply other financially driven metrics and show value. If the direct mail campaign cost $750 for 1,000 direct mail pieces and it generates a 1% conversion rate, what is the actual value of the direct mail in terms of return on marketing investment (ROMI)?

If every conversion is on average worth $100 and we multiply this by the 10 conversions that occurred, that means this campaign generated $1,000 for a cost of $750. If you run the calculation for return on marketing investment, then this particular campaign generated an ROMI of roughly 33%. The campaign was profitable, so an argument can be made that it generated value. Astute financial professionals may try to consider actual profit margins and not just the marginal return on marketing investment.

They may push to margin-adjust the return. Be careful which margin. Gross margin is fair game as it's the same adjustment we made for CLV and payback period. Net margin is not: it already has your marketing budget baked into it, so running ROMI against net margin charges your own spend twice.

So, all of these thoughts, and how an organization operates play a role in determining how many of these metrics are applied. Understanding conversion rates is critical to digital analytics as it allows marketers to identify bottlenecks in the customer journey and optimize campaigns for better performance. Higher conversion rates typically correlate with lower CAC and higher ROMI.

In addition to conversion rate, let's briefly discuss another metric that can build trust between finance and marketing — retention rate.

Retention Rate

Retention rate measures the percentage of customers who continue doing business with an organization over a given period.

$$\text{Retention Rate} = \frac{(\text{Customers at End of Period - New Customers Acquired During Period})}{\text{Customers at Start of Period}}$$

If you begin a month with 500 customers, gain 50 customers over the course of the month, and finish with 480 customers, the calculation would work like this: (480 - 50) / 500. This means you retained 86% of your original customer base during the month. Marketing strategies that focus on retention are often more cost-effective than acquisition. A high retention rate contributes to a higher CLV and consistent revenue streams.

Bridging the Marketing / Finance Gap

Understanding financial metrics empowers marketers to design strategies that drive sustainable growth and create value within the organization. To foster collaboration between marketing and finance, organizations should:

1. **Align strategic goals:** Defining shared objectives between marketing and finance including revenue growth or improved profitability creates cohesive strategies that influence collaboration and trust. This trust is critical to the partnership between both departments.

2. **Leverage data:** Today's marketing strategies are built on data. Using analytical tools to track and report financial and marketing metrics in real-time makes it easier for marketing teams to adjust campaigns and show financial awareness. Plus, it helps to continue to build the vital trust needed between both departments.

3. **Communicate results:** Regularly sharing marketing outcomes in financial terms builds trust and demonstrates value.

4. **Invest in training:** Equipping marketing teams with financial literacy training improves understanding of the broader business context.

By bridging the gap between creativity and fiscal accountability, marketers can contribute to long-term profitability and demonstrate their direct value to the organization.

As you've read, marketing and finance are closely connected functions within any organization. While marketing focuses on generating demand and creating value for customers, finance ensures that these activities contribute to profitability and long-term growth.

By understanding financial statements and key metrics such as CAC, CLV, ROMI, and revenue growth, marketers can better demonstrate the value of their efforts and strengthen their relationship with organizational leadership. It builds trust and ensures that everyone is fighting for the same thing and playing on the same team. Remember that CFO who said marketing had little value? Our job is to make the value visible in the statements he already trusts.

References

Allred, S., & Murphy, T. (2021, October 14). *Marketing and finance - a partnership for growth*. Deloitte. https://www2.deloitte.com/us/en/insights/topics/strategy/impact-of-marketing-finance-working-together.html

Customer Acquisition Cost (CAC). (n.d.). Product Plan. https://www.productplan.com/glossary/customer-acquisition-cost/

Formula to calculate & reduce customer acquisition cost. (n.d.). Paddle. https://www.paddle.com/resources/customer-acquisition-cost

How to Calculate Customer Lifetime Value (LTV): Formula and Examples. (2026, March 15). KISSmetrics. https://kissmetrics.io/blog/how-to-calculate-lifetime-value-of-a-customer

Korczynska, E. (n.d.). *Revenue Growth Rate: Definition, Formula & How to Improve It*. UserPilot. https://userpilot.com/blog/revenue-growth-rate/

Lewis, Michael R. (2024, September 28). *How to Calculate the Sustainable Growth Rate*. WikiHow. https://www.wikihow.life/Calculate-the-Sustainable-Growth-Rate

Lincoln, J. (2023, October 26). *Crunching the Numbers: ROMI Formula and its Impact on Strategy*. Ignite Visibility. https://ignitevisibility.com/romi-vs-roas-marketing-metric/

ROMI: The Key Metric for Unlocking Your Marketing Success. (n.d.). Polymer. https://www.polymersearch.com/glossary/return-on-marketing-investment-romi

The Relationship between marketing and finance. (2019, September 24). IMM Graduate School. https://imm.ac.za/the-relationship-between-marketing-and-finance/

Russo, K. (2025, February 17). *What Is a Good Retail Profit Margin?*. Oracle NetSuite. https://www.netsuite.com/portal/resource/articles/accounting/retail-profit-margins.shtml

Stobierski, T. (2020, May 28). *How to Read & Understand an Income Statement*. Harvard Business School. https://online.hbs.edu/blog/post/income-statement-analysis

Trivedi, H. (2024, September 17). *Customer Acquisition Cost (CAC): Formula, Benchmarks & More*. Factors.AI. https://www.factors.ai/blog/customer-acquisition-cost

What is Revenue Growth? How to Calculate and Improve it. (2025, April 4). RevVana. https://revvana.com/resources/blog/what-is-revenue-growth-how-to-calculate-and-improve-it/

Chapter 3
Building an Analysis Strategy

When analyzing an organization's digital marketing efforts, it helps to start by remembering what we're actually trying to accomplish. Marketing is often seen as a primary driver of growth within organizations. However, marketing should be about creating value and value can mean a lot of different things to different people. There's the obvious meaning in driving actual profit for the company, but we can also create value in other ways. We can build brand equity through greater awareness. We can grow social media followings that support loyalty and advocacy. We can even create value by increasing traffic to our website or mobile app.

Marketing is more than simply creating value for the organization. When marketing is effective, it also creates value for the organization's customers and its collaborators. For customers, the focus is providing a value to match the cost of the good or service sold. For instance, what should a $3 candy bar taste like versus a $10 candy bar? It may seem obvious but in order for the consumer to believe they received significant value for what they paid, there should be a definitive difference. We can also create value for the consumer in terms of the perceived value of owning the product or using the service like a pair of collectible sneakers or trading cards – or even intrinsic value in how the product or service makes the customer feel. For collaborators, we want good relationships with the other organizations that we work with so value is also present. Whether that is in our relationship with the collaborator or even in our vendor / client relationship in buying goods or services to make our own products and services, those also matter.

Now that we've clarified marketing as a function, what does marketing analysis provide? A marketing analyst reviews data and information to further improve the value relationship that is occurring between a company, its customers and its collaborators. Typically, marketing analysis looks at the past to better understand the present and eventually predict the future. To do so, marketers analyze a lot of different variables. Chapter 2 worked to explain some of the financial metrics that are used for marketers — all in an effort to start understanding how marketers use these metrics — and other variables — to make decisions to increase value.

Traditionally, marketers relied solely on comparing expenses to returns, and on calculating brand awareness through telephone and mail surveys. Later, marketers used regression analysis to attempt to determine the future based on past behaviors through marketing mix modeling; however even this data can easily be skewed without significant data samples.

As we've discussed, the web and digitization have changed everything providing new capabilities in tracking that allow us to even further measure marketing results. Today, we utilize digital marketing metrics as one of the primary tools to measure the value that marketers are providing to the company, its customers and its collaborators. Digital marketing is done across a wide variety of channels and platforms so there is no "one size fits all" approach. In fact, the basis on which some metrics are even tracked can change frequently, requiring constant education and explanations to upper management as to why and how these analytical changes affect ongoing tracking.

Using these various platforms, marketers can now review activity across channels and over time to make quick and informed decisions to move the organization forward to provide more value than ever to all parties involved. All of these tools help us determine what works, what doesn't, and what patterns we can follow to continue to drive this value. One of the primary benefits of digital marketing channels compared to more traditional marketing efforts is first the simplicity in how the data is collected and second the amount of data that can be tracked.

And with all of this information, it seems that analysis should be easy. Simply look at the data provided to you and make a decision. However, marketers have so much data available to them, it can be difficult to ascertain exactly which marketing platforms to pull data from to determine how to measure anything! This is called **marketing data fragmentation** — where we have multiple platforms to pull from, but no single source to review.

There are so many different platforms that digital marketing analytical data are pulled from. Web analytics platforms. Social media platforms. Paid media platforms. Demand side platforms (DSPs). Retail media. Video. Customer relationship management (CRM) platforms. Email service providers. I could go on. Many times, these disparate platforms have to be forced together to speak to one another and in some cases — they don't. According to data platform Adverity, data fragmentation may be the single largest challenge for marketing agencies today.

As was just mentioned, all of the metrics that we collect today look at the past. How successful was your most recent pay-per-click campaign? How many purchases occurred via your website last month? How many new followers did we gain on a social media platform last quarter? However, the goal of analyzing these insights is to determine the next best step in your marketing efforts — and sometimes predict future actions that will drive value.

Insight: Artificial Intelligence and Analysis

Now, as you work through the remainder of this book, keep in mind that there are tools now, and that are being developed, that will allow you to use artificial intelligence to complete some of the most difficult calculations. However, note that the direction, prompts, and information you provide these systems will determine the results you receive from these platforms. Accurate data, clear requests, and an understanding of digital marketing analytics are crucial to ensure that the information you receive from AI platforms is reliable.

Creating a Digital Marketing Analysis Strategy

Determining your analysis strategy starts with a simple question: What do you want to accomplish?

For example, your organization may want to track website traffic, online campaigns, social media advertising, and other digital marketing channels.

In this review, you want to evaluate how effectively you are reaching your target audiences. With all of these varying resources, where do you even start? And, why are you tracking these metrics?

Developing an analysis strategy requires marketing to evaluate several key factors:

1. What are our goals?

2. What do we need to measure to determine if we are meeting those goals?

3. What other factors may influence reaching those goals? What secondary or tertiary measurements are needed to ensure those goals are met?

4. Why do the ups and downs occur?

5. How do we alter our strategies to move these measurements in the right direction?

While there's no secret formula for establishing a digital marketing analysis strategy, we must first ensure that our data is reliable before measuring performance against goals. Given the amount of data we now have access to, ensuring data accuracy is mission critical to any successful analysis effort. You cannot compromise data quality and be successful.

Adverity defines **quality data** as consistent, accurate, up-to-date, and complete, with no missing or incoherent data. **Consistent data** is data that is tracked uniformly across platforms. **Accurate data** is collected from the

Insight: Data Quality Determines Insight Quality

Even the most advanced analytics tools cannot produce meaningful insights if the underlying data is inaccurate or incomplete.

original source and has not been altered through unnecessary processing. **Up-to-date data** is in real-time when possible and allows for quick decisions. **Complete data** contains no missing or incorrect value. And, most importantly, the data is logical and correct.

For instance, let's say that you work for a marketing agency and a client provides you access to their data platforms. In the client's web analytics, you find that year over year they have seen a 300% increase in overall website traffic but no increase in sales or lead volume. An experienced analyst would immediately question the quality of the data and investigate what may be wrong. Is it spam traffic? Is something broken in terms of lead tracking? Was there data that wasn't tracked from the prior year? Has the team created thought leadership content that isn't converting? Just because the data is reported from a reputable source – your analytics platform – does not mean it is accurate nor does it mean it was installed correctly. These are the sort of fine details that impact any digital marketing analytics strategy. If quality data is a goal in digital marketing analytics, another would be finding some semblance of organization in the chaos of disparate systems (and thus this book) and data fragmentation as mentioned earlier. Platforms like Zapier and application programming interfaces (APIs) allow for integration, but they don't always pull the data together in a way that is consumable by leadership. Thus, the invention of the marketing dashboard.

Side Quest: Understanding Target Audiences

How do you know who your target audience is? Or, really, what is a target audience? While I'm aware this book isn't about targeting or target markets, understanding target audiences is a very important aspect of managing or implementing digital marketing analytics for an organization. So before we jump head-first into dashboards, let's talk target audiences.

A **target audience** is defined as the group of consumers or prospective customers for whom a product or service is designed. Every product or service created by an organization exists to solve a problem, meet a need, or create value for a specific group of people. That group represents the organization's target audience. *In simple terms, a target audience answers the question: who are we creating value for with our product or service?*

Without this information, marketing efforts can become unfocused, messaging may reach the wrong people, and analytics data can become very difficult to interpret.

In practice, organizations use several different terms to refer to this same general concept. The language used may vary across industries as well, but it largely means the same.

Some of the common terms used include:

Target Market: A target market refers to the broader group of consumers an organization intends to reach. This term is often used in academia, traditional marketing strategy, or in market segmentation discussions.

Target Audience: Target audience is commonly used in marketing communications and digital marketing. While similar to target market, the language emphasizes the users receiving the communication.

Ideal Customer Profile (ICP): An Ideal Customer Profile represents the type of customer that receives the most value from the organization's offerings and, in turn, provides the most value to the organization. This language is used frequently in B2B industries where organizations want to clearly define the buyer that will most likely convert to a long-term customer.

Personas (or Buyer Personas): Personas are fictional, data-driven representations of a typical customer within the target audience. Personas humanize the audience giving these representations real names, goals, challenges, motivations, and media preferences.

While all of these terms are used differently across organizations and industries, they all answer the same question. These profiles also often include similar information that may include:

Demographic Characteristics

- Age
- Gender
- Income Level
- Education
- Geographic Location

Psychographic Characteristics

- Attitudes
- Interests
- Values
- Lifestyle Preferences

Behavioral Characteristics

- Media Consumption Habits
- Social Media Activity
- Purchase Patterns
- Website Usage Behavior

Together, these characteristics help marketers understand why a customer would find value in a product or service.

For example, imagine an organization that sells air fryers. Their target audience may include those who value convenience, healthy cooking, or time-saving kitchen tools. When creating a persona for this target, marketers may define groups such as:

- Busy parents looking for quick meal solutions
- Young professionals living in apartments with limited kitchen space
- Health-conscious consumers seeking an alternative to deep frying

Each persona helps the marketing team better understand *how and why a consumer might purchase the product.*

Building a meaningful audience profile starts with data you actually trust. I've worked with clients who spent six figures on research and still couldn't tell you why their best customers chose them — and I've worked with small businesses that cracked their target audience wide open by doing 20 fifteen-minute customer interviews over a week. Both examples point to the same truth: there is no substitute for actually talking to and listening to the people who buy from you, and there is no substitute for checking whatever you think you know against real behavioral data. Marketing teams rarely rely on assumptions alone (unless there is no other option). Instead, they gather insights from multiple sources to understand who their customers are and how they behave.

Common sources used to build personas or ICPs include:

First-party research like customer surveys, interviews with existing customers, data from your customer relationship management (CRM) system, or sales team insights;

Third-party research including industry research reports, data providers like Nielsen or Statista, or marketing research firms;

And, **digital marketing analytics**. Digital analytics platforms can play a critical role in understanding the target audience. Data collected from websites, search engines, social media platforms, and advertising tools can reveal valuable insights including:

• The demographics of website visitors

• What devices customers use

• Which marketing channels drive engagement

• How users interact with digital content

By combining traditional research with digital analytics data, marketers can create audience profiles that are both descriptive and measurable.

Understanding the target audience is essential for interpreting digital analytics data because it provides context. Without context about who the organization is trying to reach, it becomes difficult to determine whether marketing performance is actually successful.

For instance, if your target audience consists of primarily younger consumers, a marketing analyst may expect to see higher mobile device engagement, strong performance on social media, and lower engagement from desktop traffic. However, if you don't see these expected behaviors, did your marketing team miss the target?

In other words, audience insights help analysts set expectations for user behavior and help confirm whether those expectations are accurate.

Digital Marketing Dashboards and Dashboard Design

What is a digital marketing dashboard?

With such high volumes of data available, organizing it into a usable format has become absolutely critical. Trained analysts can look at the data and understand it, but when it needs to be reported and maintained, a digital marketing dashboard is a simple way to do just that.

Digital marketing dashboards are simply a visual representation of digital marketing data in an easy-to-understand format. For instance, not every element of data is important to every marketing team. Understanding how people engage with your website may be important to the analyst, but understanding conversion volume is important to the majority of the team. The goal of a marketing dashboard is to report the most important data that helps the marketing team make real business decisions.

Tip: Start with the Question

Effective analytics begins with a clear question. Before reviewing dashboards or reports, marketers should define what decision they are trying to make.

How to Design a Dashboard

Digital marketing dashboards should always be designed with the use case in mind. The goal is to simplify the data into an easy-to-understand format so that the end user can easily see the data that is most important to them. The key for analysts is to make sure they understand what is actually important to the end user.

For instance, in an e-commerce business, most teams will want to know:

- Sales over a time period compared to a similar prior time period
- Most popular products in views
- Most popular products in sales
- The source (search, paid search, social media, email, etc.) from which sales are coming
- The geographic location of sales and users
- The site's conversion rate compared over time
- The site's conversion rate compared to the industry average
- The user journey and locations where the users may not complete the purchase
- Or, ROI for advertising campaigns.

Tip: Dashboards Should Simplify Decisions

A good dashboard does not simply display data — it highlights the metrics that matter most for decision-making.

Each of the data points above points to some element of success or failure in your process. It also reports trends over time and against the industry as well as the most valuable marketing efforts by the team. The measures that are found in a marketing dashboard don't typically all come from the same data sources. For instance, website data may come from Google Analytics 4, social media analytics may come directly from Facebook Insights or Instagram Insights, and email analytics data may come from Constant Contact, Mailchimp or directly from your customer relationship management (CRM) system. The power of the marketing dashboard is the ability to pull these various data sources into one location so you and your marketing team can look at what really is important for your organization.

There are a variety of marketing dashboard tools that can pull these data sources together, including Google Data Studio (formerly Looker Studio, and free to use) as well as other paid platforms like Tableau. Most require additional tools that would allow you to pull data from these multiple data sources.

I'll expound upon what data may be needed from each of these various sources as we introduce the different kinds of metrics we can track by marketing channel.

A Simple Framework

Beyond the analysis strategy, marketers can also frame their entire marketing organization around collecting and using data effectively. One way to frame marketing with analytics might look something like this:

#1: Business Objectives

First, we would start with what the organization is trying to achieve. Every organization is different and will have different goals. As an example, some organizations may be focused on increasing revenue or generating more leads. Others may be focused on improving customer retention or building brand awareness. Each of these goals is different and requires different metrics to establish a baseline and determine whether your marketing activities are moving the key performance indicators related to these goals in the right direction. No matter the goal, analytics exists to support business outcomes. Therefore, we must define our objectives first.

Think: What to Track?

If an organization's goal is to increase online sales by 20%, which of the five framework elements would determine **what data should be measured to track progress toward that goal?**

#2: Marketing Strategy

Now that we have objectives, how is marketing supporting those objectives? Are we working to optimize conversion rates on the website? Are we using organic and paid search marketing efforts to support the objective? Are we focused on brand advocates on social media? Is it related to an email campaign or maybe paid advertising? Metrics and strategy are two different elements of marketing, but they are interrelated because analytics tracks the success or failure of the strategy. Defining what we are doing to meet the objective provides critical information for determining how analytics should be used to measure performance and guide marketing decisions.

#3: Key Metrics

So we have objectives and we know the marketing strategy. What do we measure to determine our next move? We will explore this topic in more detail in the next chapter, but ideally analytical measures should align with objectives, strategies, and the sales process. For instance, if we're measuring awareness, we may look specifically at the number of times an ad is seen (impressions) or how many people in our target audience that have seen our advertisement (reach). If our strategy is engagement-driven, we may look at how many times an ad is clicked (click-through rate) or the amount of time a video is viewed (video watch time). If conversion is our target, we may focus on leads generated, marketing-qualified leads, sales-qualified leads, purchases, or signups. The key is defining what should be measured to determine whether we are meeting our objectives and implementing our strategy effectively.

#4: Data Sources
Once we know what we want to track, we must define where the data comes from. With the fragmentation of data found in marketing, it could be from a myriad of sources: Google Analytics, Google Search Console, CRM systems, advertising platforms, email platforms, or social media. The key is knowing which metrics to track and where to find them.

#5: Insights and Decisions
Finally, we arrive at the purpose of analytics: what should we do differently based on this data that we've collected? This could involve improving landing page user experience or shifting budgets between marketing channels. We may need to refine our messaging or re-consider certain aspects of the campaign. We may also find that we missed our target by over- or under-segmenting our audience.

In the end, analytics is meant to support decisions, not simply report statistics. While the framework above outlines how analytics supports marketing decisions, effective analysis begins with understanding the people those marketing efforts are meant to reach.

Target Audience Research (Personas and ICPs)

You've already been introduced to the concept of target audiences, but how they are discussed in actual business speak is a bit different. Your target audience comprises the group(s) of individuals most likely to purchase your goods and services (or to donate to your organization or to volunteer for your organization, etc.). In industry, you may hear this referred to as personas or ideal customer profiles (ICPs). I'll never forget the first time I heard someone in a meeting refer to ICPs. As a long-time marketer and educator, I had always heard the term personas or target markets / audiences. So, when it was mentioned, I immediately thought "why are we making references to the Insane Clown Posse in a business meeting?"

Regardless, for any successful marketing effort — or analysis strategy — we need to understand who these individuals are and how they behave. This effort provides guidance in understanding how they may behave across various marketing channels.

As an analyst, you'll likely need to understand the target audience(s):

- Demographic profile including age, gender, income, etc.
- Psychographic profile including attitudes, interests and other criteria.
- User behavior including social media participation, media consumption, website behavior and usage, etc.

Understanding your target audience can drive expectations for further analysis. For instance, if you know your target audience skews younger and, while they use search, they rarely click on links in the results, then you can fully anticipate that your organic search traffic may be lower than that of competitors whose target audience may be older. Or, if your audience is older then they may choose certain social media platforms over others. All of these elements can factor into your understanding of your analytical data.

Competitive Information

Three chapters in and our focus thus far (and even throughout the text) is internally focused on the organization. But, as a marketing professional, understanding your competition's position is critical to understanding your own position. When reviewing competitive information from a digital perspective, we must rely on sources that can be collected. For instance, a competitor's website data is not directly accessible. However, we can do competitive research to find:

- Paid search advertising placements and budgets
- Organic search performance

- Organic social media followership and engagement
- Digital public relations efforts
- And more.

This competitive information provides us some idea of where we stand in the competitive landscape. It also provides us with some basic idea of how to benchmark our efforts against others. I'll dive more into this topic in later chapters. Even while the data regarding our competition is helpful (and, more helpful in some marketing channels than others), the real competition is ourselves in where we have been and where we are going.

Company Performance

The entire purpose of establishing a strategy for digital marketing analytics is to determine marketing performance. In Chapter 2, financial metrics related to marketing were discussed and are also a critical element in determining whether marketing activities are successful or not. But, financial metrics provide more of what happens at the end of the marketing effort. Think of financial metrics as the score at the end of a game. To be successful, you have to know the score throughout, your position, and what next steps have to be taken to get the score you want at the end of that game.

From a business standpoint, marketing's tracking efforts support upper management's efforts to determine the company's performance as well as the performance of marketing efforts. Many organizations choose to include financially relevant marketing metrics alongside traditional and digital marketing metrics in their digital marketing dashboards. Combining this data in one place allows marketers and organizational leaders to better understand the overall performance of marketing efforts and how various data points contribute to success or failure. Organizations may also use this type of information, particularly weekly or monthly revenue data, as part of their marketing mix modeling efforts to determine what marketing channels produce direct return on investment.

Next Steps

Analytical strategy is the first step in any analytical effort. Marketers frequently pull data from various digital marketing platforms but may not have an overarching strategy for how to leverage that data. With groundwork set on understanding analytical strategy, the next step is to understand the various metrics for each digital marketing channel. Over the next nine chapters, we will examine digital marketing channels, their related metrics, and the data that matters most to your organization.

References

What is data quality? An In-Depth Guide for Marketers to Achieving High Standards. (2021, October 14). Adverity. https://www.adverity.com/data-quality-a-complete-guide

Chapter 4
Website Analytics

For as long as digital analytics has existed, the focus of digital metrics has been the website. The website has historically been the destination to which all other digital marketing channels point — and where success or failure is measured. Whether a call to action on social media, a digital ad, search engine results, paid search advertisements, and other channels, it has all led to the website. Of the more than 1.1 billion registered websites in the world, just under 18% — about 193.9 million — are active.

We track the results of a website's success or failure through **website analytics** — the process of gathering, measuring, tracking, and reporting the activities that occur on a website. This includes how many people visit the website, which marketing channels were used to reach the website, and the behaviors of users during their visit. Website data in review can serve as a powerful marketing research tool for the organization and provide data that allows the organization to make a variety of improvements to its website and other marketing efforts.

For example, let's say a non-profit organization is seeking to increase the number of online donations generated. They recently added a new video to the page to assist with this effort, but it doesn't seem to be providing any additional value in terms of donations. In reviewing their website analytics, they note that website visitors frequently visit the donation page and remain on it for a considerable amount of time, but often leave without donating. What is wrong?

Given that users are visiting the page at a high rate and remaining on the page for a considerable amount of time, this could indicate a few different issues. The first may be that consumers are confused on arrival as the ads or other marketing efforts driving users to the page may not align with the consumer's expectations of the page. The second option may be that users are visiting and watching the video based on how long they are remaining on the page, but an issue with the donation form may be present. The third option may drive us back to reviewing our video data. We may need to review video completion rates to see if users are staying to watch the video and not converting (meaning the video is poorly performing), the video is preventing the page from loading, or otherwise. It could also be that the video is driving interest and greater time on site but does not lead to conversion. The data from website analytics, in any case, has led us to consider all of these alternatives because we now know how users behaved on the page.

Insight: Website Analytics Tell a Story

Website data is most valuable when it helps explain user behavior. The goal is not to collect metrics, but to understand what those metrics reveal about how users interact with the website.

This is just one example of how website data can help us make decisions to improve our marketing efforts. Generally speaking, many of the basic website metrics that we track are the same for all websites. For that reason, marketers sometimes rely heavily on these more global metrics because they are measurable across sites and industries. These types of metrics can easily become vanity metrics because they are easy to measure and, because we're human, we can use them to benchmark and compare a website against others in its industry. However, doing so is short-sighted.

Take, for instance, the number of website visitors a website receives. Some organizations are quick to utilize this measure as the primary measure of success for a website. The problem with this is its reliance on the input. Any marketer can increase traffic to a website given any reasonable budget. However, the challenge is influencing the user visiting to complete the goal at hand. No matter the organization, every website has a goal or set of goals that the organization wants the consumer to complete. Every organization is different and the activities organizations want a consumer to complete on a website can be different.

And while they are different in structure and specifics, the primary goal of a website comes down to just a few primary activities:

1. Making a purchase (e-commerce or donation)

2. Completing a form (contact us, appointment request, gated content download, etc.)

3. Consuming content (blog, user-generated content, etc.)

4. Or, making a phone call.

Tracking of these activities is how most website owners know that their website and even digital marketing efforts are successful. However, a dysfunctional website can also make other marketing channels look like they are providing poor performance.

We start here with a simple question. What defines success? We know we want users to complete an activity, but which activity and how often do these activities need to occur to be successful? What path do they take to get there? Compared to ourselves and others, how do you know that your efforts are fruitful and meet the goal of the site? These are the questions that website analytical tracking can answer.

As mentioned previously, there are roughly 193.9 million websites on the web. Of those that use analytics, roughly 55% utilize Google Analytics as their primary analytics tracking software. It's frequently used because of the platform's price (free). For those that do not use Google Analytics, there are a number of websites that utilize no analytical tools or use analytical tools built into their own website through its content management system (CMS). Others use high-powered analytical platforms that come with a significant cost like Adobe Analytics, FullStory, Glassbox, Kissmetrics Analyze, Quantum Metric, and others. These platforms may add a number of additional benefits including simple integration, custom dashboarding, artificial intelligence tools, and more. Even Google Analytics offers an additional product called Google Analytics 360 that offers additional scalability, customization, and enterprise-level support. These robust platforms are great for organizations where their web traffic is paramount to their business success.

While there are a number of on-site platforms, many use similar language in terms of metric descriptions. For the purpose of this book and given the platform's price, the most practical platform to learn from is Google Analytics 4 which will be our focus. In addition to using Google Analytics 4 as the on-site platform for discussion, it's worth saying that there are off-site analytical platforms that track users on other platforms ranging from social media to email, and these are much of what we'll discuss throughout the remaining chapters of this book. Even with that said, one's website analytics platform is the primary host of data for any digital marketing effort. One of the platforms that crosses both on-site and off-site behavior is Google Search Console.

Google Search Console tracks what happens on Google's side of the transaction, before the user ever reaches you. It shows the keyword searches (and now the AI Overviews) in which your site appears, along with clicks, impressions, and any errors Google hit while crawling your pages. This tool offers direct integration into Google Analytics 4 and will also be discussed within this chapter.

Let's first begin by understanding how on-site website analytics tracking works.

How Website Analytics Track Users

Tracking users on any given website (or mobile application) starts with some sort of tracking mechanism. Given that we're working to stay practical, we'll start with the most common of these methods: a snippet of code known as a web tracking tag. Some may refer to this as a website tag or tag. This snippet of code is embedded on individual pages of your website or mobile app and collects data and sends the information to servers for tabulation.

These snippets of code typically install a cookie — a small text file stored in your web browser when you visit a site that uses them. These cookies track your behavior either only on the website you are visiting or across the internet, based on the type of cookie used on the website or mobile application. For instance, a **session cookie** would track your behavior during the given session, or period of time you are on the website for that session. With session cookies, the website or mobile application can save important information such as shipping information in e-commerce or whether you want a video to auto-start. **Persistent cookies** stay with the user over a longer term and can save things like usernames, passwords, time zones, and other information. Both types of cookies can improve the user experience and/or allow for tracking for website improvement.

When it comes to cookies, we also have to consider "who" is installing the cookie on the user's browser. Is it the website owner? Or, is it a third-party that is trying to track the user's behavior? If you've heard the terms first-party and third-party cookies, this is where that conversation actually starts.

First-party cookies are cookies/tags that are triggered by the website owner. With first-party cookies, the data is usually only used to improve the website you're visiting or for its use. For instance, a first-party cookie may be triggered and saved in your browser related to preferences on the site including use of cookies, preferred language, etc. While some website owners do sell access to their data to marketers and other third parties, that is not typical. The popular Google Analytics 4 (GA4) utilizes first-party cookies to collect data.

Third-party cookies are different in that the tracking is not done by the website owner, but by another party. News sites, select e-commerce sites, and others frequently utilize third-party cookies to optimize your experience across the web. For example, your favorite news site may allow third-party advertisers to track your behavior to better optimize or tailor their ads for your experience. Think about the times you've added something to a cart or browsed a product on an e-commerce site, only to have that exact product follow you around the web for the next week. That's because those sites allowed the e-commerce provider to install a third-party cookie for this tracking (typically not directly but through an advertising platform).

A third and less common option is the **fourth-party cookie** — typically deployed by advertising networks that allow partner cookies to feed behavioral data back to their platform to tailor ads to your preferences.

An additional method is using beacons or pixels. Similar to the idea of cookies, pixels are frequently a single pixel transparent image that is installed for tracking. These pixels work similarly to cookies in that they can monitor your behavior on the page where the pixel is installed, across pages, and are typically used for advertising. Meta, LinkedIn and other advertisers frequently use pixels to track user behavior in relation to the advertiser's own advertising efforts.

An increasingly common technique is **browser fingerprinting**. This technology allows websites to identify individual users based on their web browser. Data including operating system, time zone, preferred language, history on the website, existing browser plugins, device and model, screen resolution, and more are passed to the website.

The use of these website tracking utilities is widely debated due to user privacy. While first-party tracking is easily understood, these third-party and fourth-party cookies have come under intense scrutiny due to privacy concerns. For instance, once a user is logged in to an account online and is personally identifiable, can that data be sent to third-party cookie providers? This personally identifiable information (also called PII) creates complications. If this PII data is sent to a third-party, then the consumer becomes personally identifiable across the web anywhere this third-party cookie exists and therefore the third-party cookie owner could know not only the user's behavior online, but who the user is by name! This has led to worldwide debate and new privacy laws implemented at varying levels of government that affect not only the use of third-party cookies, but web behavior. We'll explore this topic in detail later in Chapter 15.

Setting Up Analytics

Setting up analytics tools on a website or app is fairly straightforward with some HTML know-how, or through a content management system that supports plugin installation. The "cookie" or code snippet required for tracking must be uploaded to the site, typically in the site's <head> section of HTML. Different website analytical platforms have different requirements for setup, but this is the most common.

In your initial setup, you'll be provided with this snippet of code that should be uploaded to every page of the website and verified. If you plan on using more than one snippet of code or more than one analytics or tracking tool (Google Analytics, Meta, LinkedIn, and other platform tools), creating a Google Tag Manager (GTM) account should be considered. Google Tag Manager is a free tool provided by Google that allows you to install GTM code once and then upload any further code snippets to GTM. Tag Manager also allows you to provide customizations to Google Analytics and other platforms, which can simplify capabilities moving forward. The process is simple and just like that of most analytics or cookie snippets, adding GTM to your website is fairly simple.

A code snippet like that listed below is added to the <head> section of your site's HTML and can be done either by hard-coding this snippet to every page OR by uploading via your website's content management system or via a plug-in on your website. The bolded X's below represent your GTM container ID.

```
<!-- Google Tag Manager -->
<script>(function(w,d,s,l,i){w[l]=w[l]||[];w[l].push({'gtm.start':
   new Date().getTime(),event:'gtm.js'});var f=d.getElementsByTagName(s)[0],
   j=d.createElement(s),dl=l!='dataLayer'?'&l='+l:'';j.async=true;j.src=
   'https://www.googletagmanager.com/gtm.js?id='+i+dl;f.parentNode.
insertBefore(j,f);
   })(window,document,'script','dataLayer','GTM-XXXXXXX');</script>
   <!-- End Google Tag Manager -->
```

This code snippet triggers Google Tag Manager to activate the code snippets present in your GTM account. An additional code snippet provided below also is to be placed immediately following the <body> tag of your website's pages. This is a failsafe so if the browser does not have

JavaScript enabled, some tracking is still possible. Your GTM container ID would be placed where the X's are present in the code snippet below as well.

```
<!-- Google Tag Manager (noscript) -->
<noscript><iframe src="https://www.googletagmanager.com/ns.html
?id=GTM-XXXXXXX"
height="0" width="0" style="display:none;visibility:hidden"></iframe></
noscript>
<!-- End Google Tag Manager (noscript) -->
```

Note that all tags, whether GTM, Google Analytics, or otherwise, look similar and have similar functions. Using Google Tag Manager simplifies this process so all tags can be managed in one location. It also is helpful for testing, as GTM offers a test mode so you can test code before pushing it live to your website to ensure that all additional tags trigger correctly and in the right order.

Session-Based Analytics

When website tracking first became popular, website owners primarily tracked hits, a simple server-side measure of the number of times files were loaded within the web browser. Think about how many times you might open a single document on your computer. Each of those file opens would have been counted as a 'hit.' Websites that loaded multiple image files or HTML files within browsers would receive multiple hits every time a webpage was loaded. While this metric may have allowed website owners to understand website popularity, it did little else, as a measure of files opened on a website points to nothing other than the popularity of those particular files.

Today, measurement capabilities are much more sophisticated. Marketers took what they learned from these early server-side measures of tracking and advances in web technologies to begin tracking not just hits, but the way users consumed information on the web. Marketers began to consider a user's experience on a website more like that of visiting an organization's office or their physical brick and mortar location. So, in essence a person (or user) could "visit" the site and have a grouping of behaviors during that visit. Think of someone visiting a retail store, looking through the various shelves of the business and leaving. Then, that same user could come back to the store, look through the shelves, place a few items into a cart, and then check out at the register. This would be a single user with two sessions and similar but differing behaviors during each session. This concept was used to develop session-based analytics.

Session-based website analytics tools have been available for some time and focus on tracking a user's **session** — the collection of page visits and activities that occur during a specific timeframe. This was the structure of Google's prior website analytics platform and the structure of a number of other platforms that still exist today.

Let's break down how these types of platforms work.

In a session-based website analytics platform, all of a user's behaviors pivot on the session. The assumption with session-based website analytics is that marketers care about the volume of website sessions and the number of users that choose to visit the site over a period of time. Remember that the first iteration of website tracking elements was based on hits and page counts, not conversions. Session-based analytics starts its measurement with which channel the user came from (thus where the session starts) and how it ends. From there, the system measures how long the session lasts, how many pages are visited during the session, what conversions occurred during the session, and so on. To understand the other interactions that occur on the website or mobile application, you then must set up another activity that is referred to as an event. In the case of a session-based analytics platform, events would have additional descriptors that describe the event and how it is triggered. Consider things like video views or form completions. These would be events.

Prior to GA4, the most widely used platform was Google's Universal Analytics (UA). In UA, event descriptors consisted of four parts: category (the type of event, such as video or file), action (what took place, such as 'click' or 'view'), label (whatever name you assigned to the action), and value. Additional custom descriptors could also be created. Use of these events and related descriptors was the only way to track phone call clicks or specific button clicks across the site.

The power of the session-based analytics platform lies in its simplicity of reporting. At first glance, session-based analytical tracking is very simple. Wise digital marketers and sharp laypersons could easily implement analytical tracking on their website and track the metrics they believed they needed. Even digital marketers didn't need to fully understand how the platform worked because it, well, worked. This is why session-based platforms still exist.

However, session-based analytics were also limited by the concept of time. Because sessions begin and end based on time, a user who remained on a site but left their browser open for a certain amount of time would be reset when they re-engaged, which would count as another session. Also, real-time data was difficult because the user's sessions technically needed to end for the data to be complete due to the limitation of time. While this may not be a pressing issue for a small business, it was detrimental to large businesses who wanted to make decisions and improvements in real-time. Doing so was near impossible.

As the largest provider of analytical tools on the internet, Google continued to modify Universal Analytics in an attempt to address some of these issues. As new needs became apparent, Google worked to provide some semblance of real-time analytics and better event tracking, and as mobile platforms grew in use, it worked to allow better tracking for mobile applications as users adopted mobile devices as their primary means of web use. However, change did not stop there. New privacy regulations required tools that would allow for user privacy and advances in machine learning and artificial intelligence were changing the industry quickly. In response, Google began development of its new event-based analytics platform Google Analytics 4 in 2019, launching formally as GA4 in 2020.

Event-Based Analytics

Event-based analytics use a different measurement model focused on events and parameters. In session-based analytics, page views, clicks, and more are all classified as hit types that occur during the session. With event-based analytics, they are all counted as events with separate parameters. You may also recall that session-based analytics are in measures of sessions with the constraints of when the session begins and ends. Event-based analytics are not limited by time, thus analytics tracking can occur in real time and provide detailed reports on user behavior. In addition, rather than needing to create separate activities as events, the system is built on events with views and all other elements all tracked as events. Event-based analytics are more complex to configure, but they offer the real-time flexibility and customization that today's marketing decisions require.

In Google Analytics 4 (GA4), the system captures four categories of events. The first are those that are automatically collected and somewhat similar in name to that of its predecessor Universal Analytics. Next are enhanced measurement events that allow analysts to collect more data without any additional configuration. Third, because GA4 utilizes machine learning, the platform also creates recommended events that would be best suited for your website or application. Last, custom events are available which allow the marketing analyst to set up any measure that they would want to track that may not already exist in the other three categories. This new model allows for many of the same details to be tracked, just in a much different way.

Event-based tracking is genuinely more powerful than session-based tracking, but I want to be honest with you: it's also significantly harder to set up correctly and easier to misread if you haven't spent time in the platform. Let me show you what I mean.

Since the system measures events and not sessions, it is possible to track actions across devices or platforms. Also, because it is possible to track across devices, analysts garner a better understanding of the customer, their behavior, and the additional ability to create custom lists based on actions. While these changes are immensely helpful, the challenge with event-based analytics is how difficult it can be to establish the right reporting.

Insight: Events are the Foundation of GA4

GA4 is built around events. Understanding how events work is essential to understanding conversions, reporting, and user behavior in the platform.

Because the platform is built to be customized, if the analyst or digital marketer doesn't understand how the platform works, then establishing reporting can be very difficult. GA4 takes far more time to customize, review, and report. Standard, simple reports that were present in Universal Analytics no longer exist. These reports were great for small businesses and digital marketers who did not have time to expand beyond basic reporting. In addition, users could easily filter out bot traffic or internal traffic within Universal Analytics. In GA4, customization creates complication. Reports are all customizable and for good reason — different organizations have different needs. This flexibility creates the ability for modern marketers to create more accurate reports for their organization and to track what matters most. However, for the new digital marketer or analyst, it requires a significant learning curve. While Google has established certain pre-established events and reports in GA4, these reports are very surface-level when you're looking to track something specific. Also, because new events can be added, historical reporting is a bit tricky. New events that are added within GA4 are only available from the date in which they are created. This creates challenges in terms of standard reporting and accuracy. All of these capabilities are great for users who understand the event-based analytics model and understand analytics, but for those that do not, GA4 can be quite difficult.

To create accurate reporting in GA4, users must either have a complete understanding of GA4, use Google Data Studio to develop custom marketing dashboards (more on this topic later) or utilize other external marketing dashboard tools to create custom reports. From my personal experience, using GA4 directly for reporting is challenging. In addition, other marketing dashboarding platforms like Google Data Studio and Tableau do a better job of filtering traffic due to the limitations of GA4 to filter traffic without additional costs. If the organization wants consistent and accurate data, then the analyst needs to ensure that proper filtering is present and that reports are consistently pulled from the same source. In my current work, we do this by pulling data consistently from Google Data Studio where we have already manipulated the information to remove any bot or internal traffic as well as considered any new events that may have been added for tracking purposes.

Today's digital marketers typically start their web tracking efforts with GA4. For that reason, and now with an understanding of how these platforms work, let's jump into the language and tracking capabilities of event-based tracking.

The Language and Metrics of Website Analytics & GA4

Website analytics (or website tracking) is focused on the behavior of the user on the website (and in some cases behavior on mobile applications). Many who are not in the industry will use language like "website analytics," "web analytics," and "digital marketing analytics" interchangeably — but they are not the same. 'Digital marketing analytics' is the broadest category, encompassing all digital channels. 'Web analytics' refers to any analysis conducted on the web, and can overlap with digital marketing analytics. 'Website analytics' is the most specific: it refers to user behavior on a particular website or app.

So what do we actually measure using GA4? Properties. Google defines a **property** as a website, app, or other digital property that can be tracked in GA4. When an account is first created in Google Analytics 4, the user creates an **account** and within that account, the user can add up to 2,000 properties. So, for those organizations that may have multiple properties inclusive of websites and other applications, this allows users to track these different properties in separate groupings while using a single account.

When starting the account, the user would then define where the data for a property will be coming from—whether the web, an Apple-based mobile application using the iOS operating system, or a Google-based mobile application using Android. These are called **data streams**. While there is logic in creating individual properties for each of these, there can also be incredible value by combining all of your various data streams into a single property. I personally always think about the scene from the original Ghostbusters movie when they're told not to cross the streams but when they do, it creates an immense amount of power. In GA4, pulling multiple data streams into a single property allows the analyst to track user behavior across different platforms all within the same group of data. This unified analysis can provide a comprehensive view of your efforts across platforms. In addition, if you have multiple websites under a property, you can configure your efforts for cross-domain tracking so you can track users as they navigate between different websites.

Beyond data streams, users of GA4 also have the ability to **import data** into GA4, allowing them to import data ranging from costs to offline events that can further enhance their analytical capabilities. The strategies to implement data streams and data imports will be different for every organization. For that reason, I won't belabor this topic further, but know that it is certainly possible and the larger the organization, the more valuable these features become. Further information on the best strategies for implementation of different data streams and data importing can be found in the references section for this chapter. Now, as discussed thus far in this chapter, GA4 is an events-based tracking system, thus the first term that we have to define is an event.

Events and Conversions

The goal of most websites is to drive some type of conversion. This can be as simple as a page view and as complex as the e-commerce checkout process. Tracking of conversions is also the primary key performance indicator for most websites. In Google Analytics 4, this starts with utilizing the platform's events-based tracking. As defined by Google, an **event** allows you to measure anything that happens on your website or app. For example, events measure when pages on a site load, when a user clicks a link, or completes a purchase, or even measures site or system behavior, such as when an app crashes or an impression is served.

An event is basically any user interaction or system event on your website or app. If you go back in time and consider where website analytics began with hits, an event is somewhat like a hit in that it is tracked in real-time and it is an action that takes place. However, what makes events different than hits is that they are defined and those definitions can be customized.

In GA4, there are a number of **automatically collected events**. These are events like page views, session starts, and when a user first visits the site. These types of events would need to be tracked on practically all websites and applications. Furthermore, GA4 offers enhanced measurement events that are also tracked automatically, but only when enhanced measurement is enabled on your GA4 property. These **enhanced measurement events** are part of the real power of GA4 and one of the key enhancements made from its predecessor. Examples of these automatically collected events (inclusive of enhanced measurement events) include:

- when a user's session starts (automatically created);

- the first time a user visits a website (automatically created);

- when a user actively engages with the site by action (automatically created);

- when a user clicks a link leading to a downloadable file (enhanced);

- each time a user clicks a link that leads away from the primary domain (enhanced);

- the first time a user reaches the bottom of each page (enhanced);

- when a video starts playing (enhanced), and more.

Google also provides a list of **recommended events** that are tailored based on your industry or organization's category. These recommended events must be set up using Google Tag Manager. There are four groups of recommended events: events for all business verticals, for online sales, for lead generation, and for games.

The recommended events built for all business verticals may not be needed for every vertical. For instance, if your site isn't e-commerce, then there are recommended events that aren't relevant for your business. The same is true for a variety of these events. However, Google recommends any of the following events to be setup if they apply to your organization:

- an ad_impression event that would trigger when a user sees an advertisement (for apps only);

- an earn_virtual_currency or spend_virtual_currency that triggers when a user would earn or spend virtual currency;

- sales-related events like purchase and refund;

- lead generation events related to when leads are generated;

- and, other events related to when a user may login, join a group or sign up to your site, search your site, select certain content elements, share content, or begin or complete a tutorial.

Events for online sales provide a ton of valuable feedback for marketers related to behaviors in how users interact with the category and products, the shopping cart, and throughout the checkout process. These include viewing items, item selection, wishlist interactions, adding and removing products from the cart, and every step of the checkout process. These tasks can also be helpful beyond retail and e-commerce, including for travel and real estate. Data from these recommended events populate the standard e-commerce and purchases report as well.

There are times that you as an analyst may want to measure something that is not included as an automatically collected or recommended event. These are referred to as **custom events**. Custom events are events that you can define so you can collect information that is relevant to your organization. These can be custom events for everything from measuring a specific page view to data importation. In tandem with other custom measurements and reporting, this makes Google Analytics 4 incredibly powerful and provides the ability to truly turn GA4 into a platform that is specifically customized for your organization.

From the many events available to you, you can designate specific ones as key events — what GA4 also calls conversions. A **conversion** is simply an action that we want a user to take as we define it. This can be a form completion, an e-commerce transaction, and really anything that your organization would mark as a conversion. Because GA4 is event-based, GA4 refers to these conversions as **key events**. I know that can be confusing as key events and conversions can be practically interchangeable in the way they are discussed and even used in GA4. In terms of GA4 and Google Ads, the term conversions is saved for key events that are also the target activity we want users to take from Google Ads. Specifically, from Google's Analytics Help section: conversions data is eligible for bidding and reporting in Google Ads and a Google Analytics conversion can also allow you to measure actions from organic channels like search, email, and social for cross-channel campaign measurement. Rather than complicate this, throughout this book the term conversions and key events may refer to the same thing — an action we want users to take that can be measured — except when in discussion about Google Ads and paid search.

Of the hundreds of events that you can set up on a website or app that are worth tracking, not all of them will or should classify as a key event / conversion. There are events that you may want to track like refunds or when a user starts to play a video, but those activities may not be worthy of a key event or conversion. In GA4, you can create an unlimited number of events, but only up to 30 key events as conversions within a single GA4 property.

With conversions, one of the other determinants that has to be considered is who gets credit for the key event / conversion. This matters in Google Ads as it can dictate with certain ad setups how budgets are allocated and frankly, may also matter as to how you allocate budgets for your other marketing efforts. For instance, if all of your conversions come from a single source — say "email" — then why would you not put more effort in email to drive additional conversions? GA4 uses a data-driven attribution model that assigns credit to channels based on the number of touchpoints (visits) from that source and how it believes it influences conversions. In other words, it estimates the impact of the interaction based on how each interaction changed the probability of the key event occurring. Users can change this attribution model and shift to a model known as "last click." The last click attribution model simply provides all of the credit to the last click the user made before the conversion. For instance, a user may visit the website multiple times from organic search, direct traffic, or even an ad, however with last click attribution the last click before the conversion would get the credit. One of the issues with GA4's paid and organic last click attribution model is that it purposefully ignores direct traffic; thus, direct traffic will not receive credit for a conversion even if it was the last click. For this reason, Google's data-driven attribution model is likely better than the last-click model, but note that if your website doesn't receive significant traffic or the data for a given conversion is insufficient, Google may fall back to the last-click attribution model.

Dimensions

Marketing researchers frequently discuss two types of data: qualitative and quantitative. In these terms, **dimensions** are the qualitative attributes within Google Analytics 4. Dimensions provide the characteristics of a website's user and their interactions. They describe the data using text rather than numbers. These dimensions include:

- **Country**: the geographical location of the user inclusive of country, region, and city

- **Browser:** the browser used to access the website or app

- **Source / Medium:** where the website or app traffic comes from and how the user arrived (i.e. instagram / social)

- **Language:** the language of the user's web browser or device

- **Page Location:** the URL visited by the website user

- And more.

While most dimensions are easily explained, Channels & Sources / Mediums can be confusing to those not accustomed to the language of digital marketing. Website traffic is driven by a variety of sources and those most consistent are direct traffic (traffic from users typing your website's URL directly into their browser's search bar), organic search traffic (traffic from users who completed a search in a search engine and clicked a non-paid link to visit your website), paid search traffic (traffic from users who completed a search in a search engine and clicked a paid link to visit your website), referral (traffic from users who clicked on a link from another website that was not a search engine), social traffic (traffic from users who clicked a link to visit your website from social media), etc. These groupings are referred to as '**channels**.' Within each channel, sub-categories called '**sources**' describe the specific platform (YouTube, Bing, Yahoo) and the method of arrival (CPC, referral, organic, email, social).

Custom dimensions are also available that can be created by the analyst. These may include new sources like large language models (LLMs) for tracking AI-driven traffic, e-commerce related dimensions like color, size, and category, or even loyalty or user role based on prior user history. When inside GA4, the columns on the left side of all standard reports are dimensions. The columns on the right side represent the *metrics* related to these dimensions. All primary dimensions are used to sort the report. For instance, the "Traffic acquisition: Session primary channel group (Default Channel Group" report shown below (found within the Acquisition > Traffic acquisition report listing) shows the default channels where traffic comes from to the website. The primary dimension in this case is the Session Primary Channel Group. A sample of this report is shown below.

	Session primary...Channel Group)	Total users	Sessions	Engaged sessions	Engagement rate	Average engagement time per session	Events per session	Event count All events	Key events All events
	Total	224,554 100% of total	353,639 100% of total	200,568 100% of total	56.72% Avg 0%	49s Avg 0%	5.64 Avg 0%	1,992,919 100% of total	4,560.00 100% of total
1	Organic Search	144,455 (64.33%)	240,721 (68.07%)	148,668 (74.12%)	61.76%	57s	5.86	1,410,690 (70.78%)	2,702.00 (59.25%)
2	Direct	58,725 (26.15%)	73,496 (20.78%)	34,981 (17.44%)	47.6%	28s	5.11	375,626 (18.84%)	650.00 (14.25%)
3	Paid Search	15,433 (6.87%)	19,949 (5.64%)	11,884 (5.93%)	59.57%	57s	5.98	119,283 (5.99%)	1,020.00 (22.37%)
4	Display	5,193 (2.31%)	5,349 (1.51%)	321 (0.16%)	6%	4s	3.17	16,935 (0.85%)	0.00 (0%)
5	Unassigned	3,368 (1.5%)	3,580 (1.01%)	1,614 (0.8%)	45.08%	1m 23s	6.93	24,820 (1.25%)	46.00 (1.01%)
6	Organic Social	2,564 (1.14%)	2,774 (0.78%)	1,234 (0.62%)	44.48%	18s	4.61	12,776 (0.64%)	13.00 (0.29%)
7	Referral	2,408 (1.07%)	3,139 (0.89%)	2,141 (1.07%)	68.21%	1m 23s	7.22	22,676 (1.14%)	119.00 (2.61%)
8	Paid Social	1,654 (0.74%)	1,711 (0.48%)	252 (0.13%)	14.73%	7s	3.43	5,877 (0.29%)	2.00 (0.04%)
9	Paid Other	641 (0.29%)	712 (0.2%)	131 (0.07%)	18.4%	9s	3.30	2,348 (0.12%)	0.00 (0%)
10	Cross-network	113 (0.05%)	114 (0.03%)	104 (0.05%)	91.23%	1m 35s	9.43	1,075 (0.05%)	8.00 (0.18%)

Source: Google Analytics 4, 2026

One of the powerful capabilities of Google Analytics 4 is the ability to cross-tabulate dimensions. A "+" is located directly beside the channel grouping seen here to do so. Once selected, a drop-down appears with the dimensions available for this function.

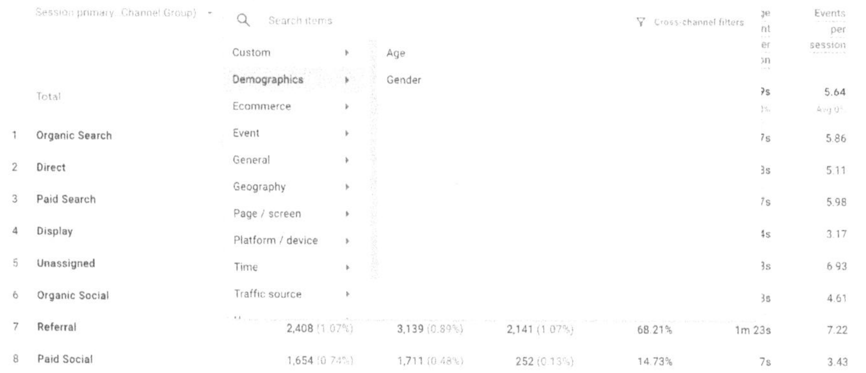

Source: Google Analytics 4, 2026

Adding an additional dimension like "region" which in the United States represents States allows for the same traffic acquisition report we reviewed on the prior page to be extended to include Regional data. Note that the primary dimension is present first with the Region also present in the second column. This now provides further detail and breaks up the first dimension in addition to the Region data. In the prior report, 144,455 total users visited the site during the time period from Organic Search. The new report now divides that number to show that roughly half of that amount of users came from the state of Georgia.

	Session primary Channel Group	Region	Total users	Sessions	Engaged sessions	Engagement rate	Average engagement time per session	Events per session	Ev...
	Total		224,554	353,639	200,568	56.72%	49s	5.64	
1	Organic Search	Georgia	76,366	135,962	86,699	63.77%	1m 07s	6.25	850,3
2	Direct	Georgia	21,037	31,064	16,270	52.38%	41s	5.61	174,
3	Direct	(not set)	10,816	10,536	5,741	54.49%	1s	3.81	40,
4	Paid Search	Georgia	10,247	12,509	7,821	62.52%	1m 01s	6.10	76,
5	Organic Search	Florida	10,156	12,540	7,756	61.85%	43s	5.15	64,
6	Organic Search	Virginia	7,489	8,902	5,513	61.93%	38s	4.83	42,
7	Organic Search	New York	7,262	8,543	5,370	62.86%	35s	4.78	40,
8	Organic Search	North Carolina	6,498	7,705	4,937	64.08%	47s	5.21	40,
9	Organic Search	Ohio	5,708	6,559	4,094	62.42%	36s	4.65	30,
10	Direct	Virginia	5,481	5,636	1,727	30.64%	16s	4.33	24,

Source: Google Analytics 4, 2026

Given users can also add data via import and create custom dimensions, if mapped appropriately the power of GA4 to connect with offline data or other collected data is immense.

Metrics

Metrics represent how users behave while they are on the website or app in relation to dimensions. These metrics allow you to understand how users interact and to make determinations on what works and what doesn't. When analysts talk about website analytics, they're really referring to collecting and reviewing metrics.

Metrics are broken down into two types: *default* and *custom* metrics. Default metrics are those most commonly used and are all measured within a specified date range including:

- **Total Users:** the total number of users interacting on the website or app

- **Active Users:** users who had at least one engaged session during the period

- **New Users**: the number of users who have visited your website or app for the first time
- **Returning Users**: the number of users who have visited your website or app before within the date range
- **Sessions**: the group of user interactions that occurred within your website or app
- **Engagement Rate**: the percentage of engaged sessions
- **Engaged Sessions**: sessions where users have spent at least 10 seconds on the site, had at least one conversion or key event, or had at least two page views
- **Average Engagement Time**: the amount of time on average a user spends engaged with the website or app
- **Page Views**: the total number of pages viewed on the website or app
- **Event Count**: the total number of events that occurred on the site
- **Conversions**: the total number of conversions (that is events marked as conversions) that occurred on the website or app
- **Conversion Rate**: the percentage of users who completed a conversion
- And various others.

As you work through each available metric, it's important to understand how these metrics relate to each other.

All metrics are based on time. So when reviewing data within GA4, you need to first understand the time period that you are reviewing. You can only review data after GA4 is installed on the site so there will be no metric data available prior to that installation. This is important because many times we as analysts want to review data in comparison to prior time periods. Comparing data week to week, month to month, quarter to quarter, and year to year can all be helpful to see how marketing efforts are impacting site or app behavior. However, you cannot compare data that you don't have—so if historical data is not present, it cannot be compared.

It's important when reviewing data in comparison to prior time periods that you consider what happened beyond just the data. For instance, you may run a large campaign in November and December of each year. Comparing month over month data from October to November may look as if November was incredible in comparison. However, considering that additional marketing efforts and expenditures happened that month, October isn't necessarily a poorly performing month, it's just different. That's also true if you compare the 4th quarter (October, November, December) to the 3rd quarter (July, August, September). The 3rd quarter may not have underperformed; it is simply being compared to a very active period for your organization. In my own experience, I've found that the most useful data is year over year data (if available) as it does tend to compare to similar user behaviors and is a better measure of success or opportunity. But, there are times where even week to week data can be meaningful based on the industry and situation. It's important to always go back to what we're measuring and why to determine the time period that matters the most.

Many of the metrics within GA4 are also interrelated. For instance, there is a significant relationship between users, sessions, and page views. A single user can have multiple sessions across a given time period.

Sessions include multiple page views. Thus, there will generally be more page views than sessions and more sessions than users. Each of these measures also has other metrics tied to it, including engagement rate, which calculates the rate of engaged sessions, and bounce rate, which is the percentage of sessions that were not engaged. (Note: GA4 de-emphasizes bounce rate in favor of engagement rate, discussed on the following page.)

Metrics are grouped into a variety of sub-categories to make it simple to understand how they are related to different aspects of a user's experience.

Think: Metrics in Context

A website shows increasing sessions but declining key events.

What questions should an analyst ask before recommending a change in budget or strategy?

There are **User Metrics** like users, new users, sessions and returning users that serve as measures of site usage and volume. **Engagement Metrics** inclusive of engagement rate, engaged sessions per user, average session duration, event count, conversions, and other metrics which measure how engaged users are on the site. **Revenue Metrics** track revenue and orders for sites with e-commerce and/or donation elements. And, **Other Metrics** that don't fit neatly into one of these other categories. Custom metrics may fit into any of these categories which could include "video views" or a variety of other options dependent on your needs. Some of these metrics are available for review in the same report we reviewed in our discussion about dimensions seen again on the following page.

Tip: Traffic is Not the Same as Success

A website can generate more users, more sessions, and more page views without actually improving business performance. Traffic should always be reviewed alongside engagement and conversions.

All metrics are seen in measurement against a dimension. In this particular report, we're looking at the session's primary channel which represents how users arrived on this particular site over a given time period. What we quickly learn is that most users and sessions arrive at the site from organic search, but the most engaged users are from the channel cross-network which tends to be representative of advertising. Last, the majority of key events that occurred on the site are also from organic search and paid search. Each of these points to user behavior and can be reviewed further to determine which pages these users arrived on, exactly which key events users completed along their path, and which pages in sequence were viewed to drive such a high number of key events. All of this information can be reviewed to help make further improvements on other pages of the site and within advertising via other channels.

	Session primary Channel Group	Total users	Sessions	Engaged sessions	Engagement rate	Average engagement time per session	Events per session	Event count All events	Key events All events
	Total	224,554	353,639	200,568	56.72%	49s	5.64	1,992,919	4,560.00
1	Organic Search	144,455	240,721	148,668	61.76%	57s	5.86	1,410,690	2,702.00
2	Direct	58,725	73,496	34,981	47.6%	28s	5.11	375,526	650.00
3	Paid Search	15,433	19,949	11,884	59.57%	57s	5.98	119,283	1,020.00
4	Display	5,193	5,349	321	6%	4s	3.17	16,935	0.00
5	Unassigned	3,368	3,580	1,614	45.08%	1m 23s	6.93	24,820	46.00
6	Organic Social	2,564	2,774	1,234	44.48%	18s	4.61	12,776	13.00
7	Referral	2,408	3,139	2,141	68.21%	1m 23s	7.22	22,676	119.00
8	Paid Social	1,654	1,711	252	14.73%	7s	3.43	5,877	2.00
9	Paid Other	641	712	131	18.4%	9s	3.30	2,348	0.00
10	Cross-network	113	114	104	91.23%	1m 35s	9.43	1,075	8.00

Source: Google Analytics 4, 2026

According to an article by Databox, the 11 most frequently used metrics are users, bounce rate, sessions, average session duration, percentage of new sessions, sessions by channel, pages per session, event count, page views, conversions, and engagement rate. From my experience, this is accurate; however, much of that is because these have represented the easiest metrics to understand. As the web continues to change, some of these measures aren't as meaningful in tracking as they once were.

Insight: Dimensions and Metrics Work Together

Dimensions describe the data. Metrics quantify the data. Strong analysis depends on understanding how the two work together in reports.

AI is actively changing how people use the web. There will always be a place for each of these metrics in terms of understanding how users use websites and apps, but what dictates success is changing and will continue to change. Historically, we as marketers utilized the number of users and the number of sessions per channel (that is did the user come from paid advertising, directly to the site, organic Google searches, referred from another website, etc.) as whether marketing activities were first driving traffic to the site. Then we would look at user behavior in terms of engagement or conversions. With the adoption of AI across most of the web, users are now finding information before they arrive on the website or app reducing traffic from organic search (Google, Bing, etc.) thus causing a reduction in overall users and sessions, particularly from organic search channels. This should be noted in considering "which metrics" to use in measuring success as well as changing user behavior that is actively impacting which KPIs to choose to measure.

Before we jump into actual measurement, let's first gain a quick understanding of the enhanced measurement capabilities of GA4.

Enhanced Measurement

When you set up your data stream in GA4, you have the option to enable Enhanced Measurement. As has already been discussed, GA4 is highly customizable to meet your organization's particular needs. But such high levels of customization require additional knowledge of how to set up these features. If you're not quite sure what to measure, how to measure it, or how to set up your account correctly, this is where Enhanced Measurement provides a great deal of value.

Enhanced Measurement allows you to collect additional events that can be noted as key events or conversions without needing to create custom tracking or customization within Google Tag Manager. In Universal Analytics, setting up some of these measures (not all) required quite a bit of know how. With GA4, Enhanced Measurement allows for these same analytics to be tracked without additional coding or programming requirements. With that said, these events are not perfect. To ensure accuracy in most of these enhanced measurements, some customization may be needed.

If Enhanced Measurement is enabled, it will automatically track the following:

- Page views
- Outbound link clicks
- Site search usage
- And, Form interactions.
- Scrolling behavior
- File downloads
- Video engagement

Each of these can be enabled / disabled within the Enhanced Measurements section of GA4 and can also be set up or controlled within Google Tag Manager to ensure accuracy. These enhanced measurements have specific parameters that are followed as well that can be modified via customization.

Measuring the Ups and Downs

Now that we have a base knowledge of how website analytics, and more specifically GA4, works, how do we actually measure user behavior? Much of the answer to this question lies with our organization's goals.

Beyond conversions, every website or app has different key performance indicators (KPIs). Generally speaking, all website or app owners want more traffic and more users visiting their websites or apps. However, any marketer can drive more traffic by spending more money in advertising. Then driving more traffic and users from specific sources and mediums may be a KPI. But, if those users don't engage with the website or app then why are we encouraging them to visit the site or app? The next metric we would consider is engagement and how users are engaging with the website or app. Engagement is a good thing, but what if users aren't engaging in the way that we want them to? Then the number one metric we should care about is conversions as defined by your organization.

In my experience, no matter what else an organization says it cares about, the conversation eventually comes back to conversions. What counts as a conversion will be different for every organization — here's how I generally think about it by type:

B2B organizations tend to measure conversions in terms of leads through completion of contact forms and phone calls with occasional interest in downloads or content requests for white papers, research, or other documents as well as signups for content like email newsletters.

B2C organizations may also classify conversions in terms of completion of contact forms and phone calls or email signups and otherwise. How conversions are measured is dependent on whether the organization offers e-commerce.

Non-profit organizations may classify conversions in various ways that can include donations or requests for services determinate on what dictates success for the organization.

E-commerce organizations classify conversions as sales but various other key events may also be important in how users use the cart or purchase up-sell and cross-sell opportunities.

Tip: Define Website Success Early

Before building a report, define the website's primary goal. A site designed to drive e-commerce purchases should not be measured the same way as a site designed to generate leads or encourage content consumption.

Taking these concerns one step further, software as a service (SaaS) organizations may also use conversions that mix those of a B2B or B2C organization with those of an e-commerce organization. User-Generated Content based organizations who rely on content creation or usage by users may have key events or conversions related to users generating content or how frequently content is used.

No matter what basic conversions are needed to be set up for the organization, conversions should be the crux of all website analytics. Knowing which channels, sources, and mediums drive conversions is important because understanding how the ups and downs occur must be connected to a general understanding of user behavior. Each marketing channel has a purpose and thus it should be expected that certain sources and mediums will drive conversions and others may drive the first visit to the website but very well may not drive the conversion.

To understand how this works, let's consider the modern marketing and sales funnel. Through marketing theory and research, we know that all consumers no matter the industry must go through a process to arrive at a point in which they purchase goods and services from an organization. First, the user must become aware that you have an offering (awareness). Second, the user/consumer must have interest in your offering (interest). Third, the user then purchases your offering (conversion). Once the consumer has purchased from you, your hope is that you have provided so much value that you have created loyalty followed by advocacy for the consumer to then support you by telling others about your goods and services in a positive way.

Each source that drives traffic to a website or app has a traditional function within this funnel. Some serve to drive awareness and others tend to be used for conversion or loyalty and advocacy. The role each of these sources and mediums plays in your marketing process is important because it helps you know what types of behaviors to expect from each channel. For instance, it's not a surprise that Google Paid Search may drive conversions if done well, whereas referral traffic from public relations efforts, such as news sites, may drive traffic but not frequently drive conversions. This is also true for what we'll call traditional banner and tile online advertising. These channels "sometimes" drive conversions but more often than not they serve as awareness channels to drive awareness and traffic but may not be the final channel the user uses to convert to a lead or sale.

Tip: Track Fewer, Better Conversions

Not every event should become a key event or conversion. Focus on the actions that most clearly reflect organizational value.

To visualize how this works, I've provided the modern sales funnel as well as the sources and mediums that traditionally drive traffic to a website below.

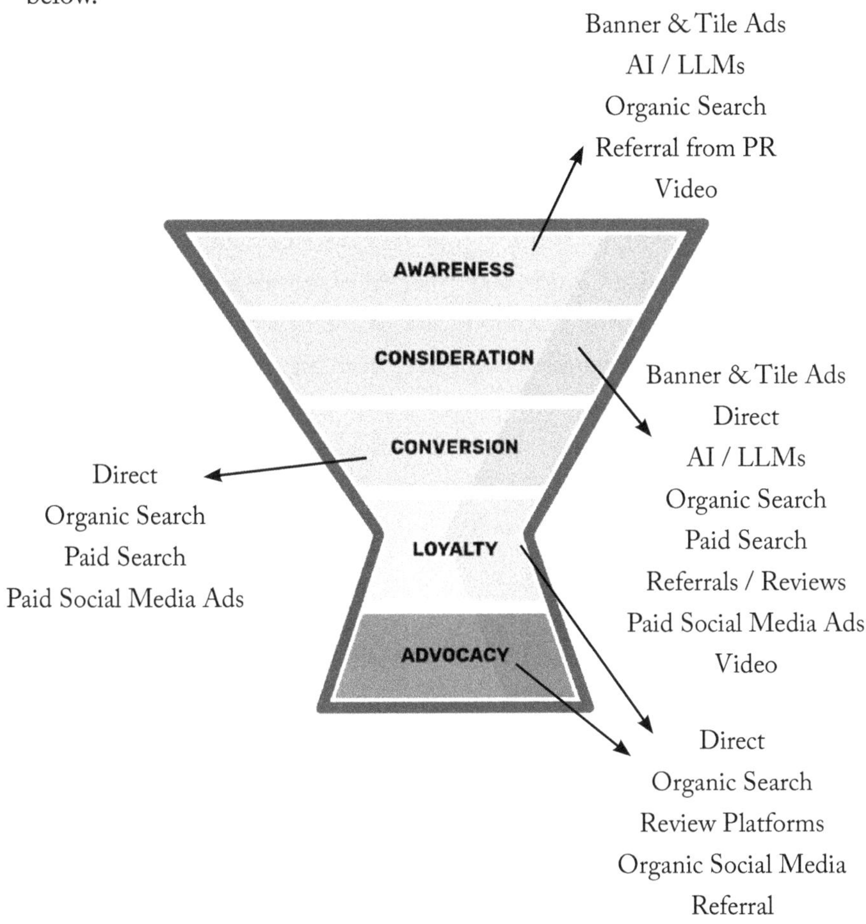

For instance, many website owners use advertising channels as a way to drive awareness, interest, and conversion; however, different advertising channels tend to operate in different areas within this funnel. For instance, many times paid social media ads can both drive initial awareness to a product or service, but, can also serve as a reminder about a product or service that the consumer may already be considering. Also, video is a powerful tool; however, it doesn't always drive traffic to the website from platforms like YouTube. Video sometimes drives consideration and conversion from select social media channels or even if the video is shared from an email in a B2B campaign. Conceptually, there is no exact rule as to which marketing channel falls at which stage of the funnel, but there are some widely accepted norms across industries. Every industry and organization is different, but the alignment of these channels to their typical function in the sales funnel is generally true for most organizations.

As the web has changed, so have the channels that drive conversions. For years marketers have utilized organic search as a way to drive awareness, consideration, and conversion. As Google advances how it shares information with users through its AI Overviews and adoption of ChatGPT, Perplexity, Claude, and other AI platforms advances, data from our research at Forum Communications and beyond points to a clear pattern: a decline in awareness-based traffic from organic search, alongside an increase in higher-intent traffic arriving from those same engines. How so? Users are receiving answers to their questions without the need for visiting a website thus users more frequently visiting websites when they are ready to convert and not before. We'll explore this further in the next chapter on search analytics.

Insight: QR Codes and UTMs: Bridging the Gap Between Physical and Digital Measurement

Two tools every analyst should have in their standard kit are UTM parameters and QR codes. Used together, they solve one of the oldest problems in digital measurement: knowing not just that someone arrived at your website, but exactly where they came from and why. I've used this strategy many times for tracking print or television advertising.

A **UTM parameter** (short for Urchin Tracking Module, named after the company Google acquired to build what became Google Analytics discussed in Chapter 1) is a short piece of code appended to the end of a URL that tells your analytics platform exactly how a visitor arrived. A fully tagged URL contains up to five parameters: Source (the platform or publisher: google, newsletter, instagram), Medium (the type of channel: cpc, email, social), Campaign (the specific initiative:

summer_sale, product_launch), Content (useful for A/B testing different creative or links), and Term (the keyword that triggered a paid ad). When a user clicks a UTM-tagged link, those parameters are captured in your analytics report, letting you compare the behavior and conversion rate of visitors from each campaign individually rather than lumping them all into a single "direct" or "referral" bucket.

A **QR code** is a scannable image that encodes a URL and when that URL is UTM-tagged, a QR code becomes a direct bridge between a physical placement and a digital analytics report. A billboard, a printed mailer, a trade show banner, or a product package can each carry a unique QR code pointing to a uniquely tagged URL, and when someone scans it, your analytics platform records the visit with full campaign attribution — something that would otherwise be invisible to any web analytics tool.

Used properly, the combination answers questions that neither tool can answer alone: not just how many people scanned a QR code, but how many of those visitors converted, what they looked at, how long they stayed, and how that behavior compared to visitors arriving from paid search or email on the same day.

A few practical rules worth following. First, never send a UTM-tagged URL to a page that redirects before landing. The parameters can be dropped in transit. Second, establish a consistent naming convention for your UTM values before a campaign launches and enforce it across every team member building links; a single typo in a source parameter creates a separate, uncombined row in your report that makes campaign data impossible to aggregate cleanly. Free tools like Google's Campaign URL Builder make tagging straightforward, and URL shorteners like Bitly can wrap a long tagged URL into something clean enough to print or display.

Time Marks the Spot

It's important to remember that all website analytics are measured over a time period. If you create a new conversion metric today and want to compare it to past behavior, that's impossible because the conversion didn't exist in the past. Thus, setting up GA4 for the metrics, events and conversions that are most important to you from the beginning is critical. For analysts to understand any metric, it must exist and be comparable across time periods. I only bring this up again because I cannot count the number of times clients have asked us to track something new and then ask us to compare that to the prior year. In many cases it is possible but it requires data to be exported to spreadsheets and manipulated. Plus, it can take significant time to pull together. Because GA4 is so powerful, planning in advance and ensuring that, at a minimum, events or key events are established is critical so they can be tracked.

User Behavior Ups and Downs

Now, we started this discussion about measuring the ups and downs by narrowing our most important metric down to conversions. That wasn't to say that the other items weren't important, just that conversions should be the most important. Historically digital marketers have measured success by an increase or decrease in website traffic. Users, sessions, and page views are broad-stroke metrics that together can provide a great deal of directional information. We can consider this simple metric in a variety of dimensions from source and medium to reviewing traffic to individual pages of the website or sections on the app. It's a very telling metric as it speaks to where users come from and what content users consume. It's simply a measure of popularity and comparing time period over time period we can determine what types of content are the most popular and what sources and mediums drive the most traffic.

The next step up from this basic metric is understanding engagement. For GA4 to classify a session as engaged, the user must spend at least 10 seconds on the site, trigger a key event or conversion, or view at least two pages. These users are "engaged" and affect the site's number of engaged users, and the number of engaged users divided by the total number of users equals the site's engagement rate. If you're historically familiar with bounce rate, bounce rate calculates the percentage of sessions that were not engaged. Consider engagement rate the more valuable metric as it reflects positive behavior whereas bounce rate reflects negative behaviors. Additionally, reviewing average session duration (time on site) tells the story of how engaged users are on the website. Measuring each of these engagement metrics over time tells a story by source, medium, page, and more.

From here, we can do the same sort of metric analysis with events, key events, and conversions, which also tell a significant story. The end goal is for the data to tell such a story that you can make decisions for improvement. If your engagement rate is low, why? What can you discern from the data to inform your next move? So what story does the data tell? To understand the answer to this question, we have to set benchmarks.

Benchmarks

So how do you really *know* if your efforts are good or bad? **Benchmarks** are points of reference that can be used to measure or compare performance for any metric. This allows you to set a baseline for evaluating efforts and for informing future decisions. Benchmarks are traditionally set in three different ways with each providing different value as a comparison tool.

Historical benchmarks are benchmarks set based on your own historical performance. I personally like this set of benchmarks as you're comparing data against your own performance and only your own performance. If your organization buys into the idea that it is unique and that there is value in the way it communicates and works with users, then this type of benchmark provides the most value.

Competitive benchmarks are those that look at competitor performance. These metrics, specifically those related to engagement and conversion can be valuable but must be reviewed carefully. Many times these are collected via second- or third-party platforms like SE Ranking, SpyFu, or SimilarWeb and are estimated, but not always accurate. You don't have direct access to their website or app data so there's a bit of a tradeoff here having some "idea" of their site or app behavior but it won't be entirely accurate. Consider your own conversion rate or your own volume of users and traffic or even your own engagement rate. Because you do things in a way no one else does and the data collected may not be exactly accurate, comparing all of these against others may skew you in the wrong direction if you don't consider your own website's history in addition to competitive benchmarks.

Tip: Historical Benchmarks are Usually the Most Useful

Your own historical performance often provides a better benchmark than industry or competitive benchmarks because it reflects your unique users, messaging, and business model.

Industry benchmarks are those collected by industry or category and are typically built on a standard of some sort. Every industry may be different and are collected in a variety of ways including industry surveys, third party data sources, or by even creating your own industry benchmark using collected competitive benchmarks.

No matter the method to your benchmarking, benchmarks do change over time. It's important to make sure that you're keeping up with global and industry changes to understand how user behavior in your industry may be changing. As of the time of this writing, a review of a number of sources collecting data across all industries provided the following:

Average B2B Conversion Rate - 3.9%

Average B2C Conversion Rate - 3.6%

Average Time on Page - 52 - 54 seconds

Average Session Duration - 2 minutes 17 seconds

Beyond these four metrics, global benchmarks rarely exist. For instance, a brief search for a global average engagement rate provides industry-specific examples ranging from 53% to 83%, all dependent on industry and even sub-industry type. There is also little to no benchmark available for an expectation on the number of users, sessions, or page views to a given site as there are too many variables for this number to be accurate on any average.

The most practical way to manage benchmarks is to create your own based on your own users' behavior. Having taught digital analytics for a number of years, I can tell you the single most reliably hated question on exams is the one where I give students financial or website performance data and ask whether the organization is doing well. Without historical data or exact industry data, there's actually no real way to know whether the organization was performing well. Many would say that if ROI was positive or the number was high, the organization was successful, but comparing it with historical benchmarks would have provided the more exact and accurate response.

Being Practical: An Example

Over this entire chapter we've covered a lot of ground in terms of analytical measures for websites and apps. And, there is still a lot of ground that could be covered in digging into the finer details of web analytics. Given this is THE "Practical Guide to Digital Marketing Analytics" let's be *practical* and really simplify what matters in web analytics.

All website owners should measure traffic in terms of users, sessions, and page views and do so by source / medium and by page location and do so in regular time intervals dependent on your measurement strategy. At a minimum, you should review this data on a monthly basis, if not also quarterly and occasionally weekly. Each should be done comparing year over year data to ensure your time periods aren't skewed by campaigns or seasonal user behavior.

Measuring users, sessions, and page views by source / medium over time is very telling in terms of which channels are driving most of your site or app traffic. In addition, adding to this same report engagement metrics (engagement rate, engaged users, average session duration, key events, and conversions) can provide guidance as to which channels are providing the most valuable users to your website. The report below provides a great example of the power of this particular report.

Session source / medium	Sessions	Engaged sessions	Engagement rate	Average engagement time per session	Events per session	Event count (All events)	Key events (All events)
Total	3,850 vs. 5,190 ↓ -25.82%	2,236 vs. 3,046 ↓ -26.59%	58.08% vs. 58.69% ↓ -1.04%	47s vs. 48s ↓ -1.53%	5.78 vs. 5.79 ↓ -0.06%	22,272 vs. 30,042 ↓ -25.86%	386.00 vs. 560.00 ↓ -31.07%
google / organic							
Apr 1 - Jun 30, 2025	1,598 (41.51%)	1,071 (47.9%)	67.02%	59s	6.26	9,997 (44.89%)	176.00 (45.6%)
Apr 1 - Jun 30, 2024	1,639 (31.58%)	1,165 (38.25%)	71.08%	1m 05s	6.43	10,542 (35.09%)	178.00 (31.79%)
% change	-2.5%	-8.07%	-5.71%	-8.39%	-2.74%	-5.17%	-1.12%
(direct) / (none)							
Apr 1 - Jun 30, 2025	1,014 (26.34%)	408 (18.25%)	40.24%	25s	4.92	4,993 (22.42%)	41.00 (10.62%)
Apr 1 - Jun 30, 2024	1,011 (19.48%)	425 (13.95%)	42.04%	34s	5.15	5,202 (17.32%)	62.00 (11.07%)
% change	0.3%	-4%	-4.28%	-26.28%	-4.3%	-4.02%	-33.87%
google / cpc							
Apr 1 - Jun 30, 2025	814 (21.14%)	524 (23.43%)	64.37%	43s	5.87	4,781 (21.47%)	135.00 (34.97%)
Apr 1 - Jun 30, 2024	1,558 (30.02%)	1,062 (34.87%)	68.16%	51s	6.41	9,992 (33.26%)	281.00 (50.18%)
% change	-47.75%	-50.66%	-5.56%	-15.99%	-8.42%	-52.15%	-51.96%
bing / organic							
Apr 1 - Jun 30, 2025	98 (2.55%)	69 (3.09%)	70.41%	1m 23s	7.36	721 (3.24%)	8.00 (2.07%)
Apr 1 - Jun 30, 2024	160 (3.08%)	94 (3.09%)	58.75%	1m 00s	6.06	970 (3.23%)	10.00 (1.79%)

Source: Google Analytics 4, 2026

This report is a review from time period to time period (using historical benchmarks) of the primary source / medium channels that drove traffic to this particular website. At a cursory view it looks as if we are down slightly in organic search traffic from Google, roughly flat in traffic from Direct (those that are typing in the URL to the browser directly), down significantly in sessions from Google CPC or Paid Search and down in organic search traffic from Bing. These behaviors are roughly the same for engaged sessions with significant engagement rate growth from Bing organic search. We also see significant declines in key events from Direct and Paid Google Search. This would generally be viewed as negative at first glance but let's pay attention to the details.

Over this time period, the site overall generated only 3,850 sessions compared to 5,190 sessions during the prior measured period. But, Google Paid Search / Google Ads traffic loss represents 56% of the total loss in traffic. You could assume the keywords they are advertising for have become much more competitive if the budget did not change OR the budget has been reduced. The chart alone cannot tell you which. At some stage, every real analysis requires you to close the dashboard and ask a real question. If you ask the question, you may find the latter is true so reduction in paid search traffic is due to a reduction in budget. Considering this and the loss in traffic, that loss is also likely negatively affecting visibility and brand awareness which likely is leading to the decline in sessions and key events across the board. While that seems like such a simple thing, connecting the dots to understand exactly what's happening takes time, experience, and thought.

Think: Reviewing a Report

If organic search traffic declines, but conversions remain stable or improve, is that automatically a negative result?

What might this suggest about user behavior?

In comparing industry benchmarks for this particular site, the site remains at the industry average for site engagement with a decline in engagement rate against the average industry benchmark in direct traffic. This could mean a lot of different things: users are finding what they are looking for quickly, direct traffic could represent a higher volume of bot traffic, or a variety of other reasons. Similar data is available for page-specific metrics as well. I've used the channel and source/medium reports here because they apply to any website on the web. Once you move into page-level reporting, you're in the specifics of your own organization — and I can't do that part for you. Reviewing page specific reporting is helpful in knowing what pages drive the most traffic but also looking specifically at engagement to understand where pages may be letting users down. Cross tabulating a report with pages and screens as your primary dimension and source / medium as a secondary dimension can also provide information on where the traffic for those pages is coming from initially if that was the user's first landing page. No matter the report or metric being considered, making sure that you are setting aside time to complete analysis—not just a cursory look—of your website or app analytics is critical to truly understanding your users' behavior.

Tip: Review Reports Consistently

Website analytics are most useful when reviewed at regular intervals.

Monthly and quarterly reviews are often more meaningful than occasional spot checks.

Many times throughout this chapter, we've referred to search traffic, whether paid or organic, and its impact on the website or app. In the next chapter, let's dive into the details of search analytics and how search impacts the entirety of our digital analytics plan.

References

[GA4] About Events. (n.d.). Google. https://support.google.com/analytics/answer/9322688

[GA4] Automatically collected events. (n.d.). Google. https://support.google.com/analytics/answer/9234069

[GA4] Conversions vs. key events in Google Analytics. (n.d.). Google. https://support.google.com/analytics/answer/13965727

[GA4] Custom events. (n.d.). Google. https://support.google.com/analytics/answer/12229021

Average Time Spent on Website: And Why It Matters Even More in 2025. (n.d.). Spectrum Infinite. https://spectruminfinite.com/blogs/average-time-spent-on-website-2025/

Allen, K. (n.d.). *What is Web Analytics? How It Works in 2024.* Woopra. https://www.woopra.com/learn/web-analytics

Bailyn, E. (2025, March 7). *Average Website Visitor Conversion Rate Benchmarks for 2025.* FirstPageSage. https://firstpagesage.com/seo-blog/average-website-visitor-conversion-rate-benchmarks-for-2025/

Belcic, I. (2020, July 16). *A Complete Guide to Web Tracking (And How To Avoid It).* Avast. https://www.avast.com/c-web-tracking

Cardillo, A. (2025, May 28). *How Many Websites Are On The Internet? (2025).* Exploding Topics. https://explodingtopics.com/blog/how-many-websites-on-the-internet

Chatterjee, S. (2023, November 2). *Google Analytics 4 Dimensions: What You Need to Know.* SEMRush. https://www.semrush.com/blog/google-analytics-dimensions/

Chia, A. (2023, July 10). *Web Analytics 101: A Comprehensive Guide*. Splunk. https://www.splunk.com/en_us/blog/learn/web-analytics.html

Fedorovicious, J. (2025, April 1). *A Guide to Custom Dimensions in Google Analytics 4*. Analytics Mania. https://www.analyticsmania.com/post/a-guide-to-custom-dimensions-in-google-analytics-4/

Google Analytics Alternatives. (n.d.). Gartner. https://www.gartner.com/reviews/market/web-product-and-digital-experience-analytics/vendor/google/product/google-analytics/alternatives

Google Marketing Platform. (n.d.). https://marketingplatform.google.com/about/analytics-360/

Hazarika, T. (2026, April 6). *50+ QR Code Usage Statistics 2026: Consumer & Marketing Data*. Uniqode. https://www.uniqode.com/blog/qr-code-insights/qr-code-statistics

How do GA4 data streams work?. (2023, June 22). Webgarh. https://reflect.webgarh.com/how-do-ga4-data-streams-work/

How To Use UTM Parameters (and When To Use Them). (2026, April 13). Shopify. https://www.shopify.com/blog/utm-parameters

Marketing KPIs & Benchmarks for 2025. (2025, February 18). Launch Team Incorporated. https://www.launchteaminc.com/blog/predictions-setting-kpis-benchmarks-2025

McGaw, D. (2026, February 5). *What Is UTM Tracking? UTM Codes Explained*. UTM.io. https://web.utm.io/blog/what-is-utm-tracking/

Montag, J. (2025, May 30). *Is Your Bounce Rate Too High? What the Average Bounce Rate Really Means*. Leadpages. https://www.leadpages.com/blog/average-bounce-rate

Pattoli, M. (2026, February 28). *Offline Marketing Attribution: Complete Guide 2026*. Cometly. https://www.cometly.com/post/offline-marketing-attribution

QR Code Trends for 2026: What to Expect. (2026, January 13). QR Code KIT. https://qrcodekit.com/news/qr-code-trends/

Rudan, N. (2025, July 1). *Content Marketing Benchmarks by Industry for 2025*. Databox. https://databox.com/content-marketing-benchmarks-by-industry

Sharma, H. (2025, January 30). *GA4 Attribution Models Explained: How to Choose the Right One.* Optimize Smart. https://www.optimizesmart.com/attribution-models-in-ga4/

Southern, M. (2024, June 12). *Google Launches Custom Event Data Import for GA4*. Search Engine Journal. https://www.searchenginejournal.com/google-launches-custom-event-data-import-for-ga4/519341/

Tracy, S. (2024, December 2). *Understanding The 3 Types of Analytical Benchmarks*. Analythical. https://analythical.com/blog/how-to-benchmark-success

Understanding Data Streams in Google Analytics 4. (n.d.). Rudderstack. https://www.rudderstack.com/learn/GA4/understanding-data-streams-in-google-analytics-4/

UTM Parameters. (n.d.). Wikipedia. https://en.wikipedia.org/wiki/UTM_parameters

UTM Parameters: The Complete Guide to Campaign Tracking (2026). (2026, May 15). Nextutils. https://www.nextutils.com/blog/utm-parameters-guide

Vakulski, I. (2024, April 13). *GA4 Data Streams: In-Depth Guide*. Vakulski Group. https://www.vakulski-group.com/blog/post/ga4-data-streams/
Google Analytics 4 Stats 2025 (n.d.). GA4.com. https://ga4.com/ga4-stats

Zaric, S. (2025, June 26). *The 11 Most-Tracked Google Analytics Metrics in GA4*. Databox. https://databox.com/the-most-tracked-google-analytics-metrics

Chapter 5
Organic & AI Search Analytics

Unless your user base has memorized your website's URL or knows exactly how to access your app, they need a way to find you. Since the advent of the web, search engines have been a primary driver of traffic to organizations — whether searching in Google for a product or service or searching in the App Store for the name or type of an application. In addition, users now utilize platforms like ChatGPT, Claude, Google Gemini, and others for information and for conversational queries. This makes search and AI response analytics a subset of website analytics, but also another set of important elements to consider when measuring success or failure in digital analytics.

Many digital analysts who have little experience in search engine optimization (SEO), generative engine optimization (GEO), or paid search (which I'll define shortly and cover fully in the next chapter) may simply look at search analytics as a measure of the website traffic from search engines — whether organic or paid and its related engagement once the user is on the site. This is problematic for a few reasons. First, understanding the user's experience before they arrive on the website or app is critical to understand the user's expectation once they arrive. Second, understanding how the website or app competes before the user arrives on the site within the search engine results page or in their query is important as a gauge of your organization's ability to compete. And, third, search engine behavior is actively changing. For instance, during the summer of 2025, the entirety of organic search shifted as Google expanded its use of AI Overviews and AI Mode to all users. With these AI-based responses in search engine results — and with new platforms we refer to as **Large Language Models (LLMs)** like ChatGPT, Perplexity, and Claude — users are no longer being handed a list of results to sift through. The platforms are simply answering the question. This is having a direct impact on user behavior and marketing tactics to organically place your organization in these results. No matter the challenge in today's search or AI-driven marketplace, measuring efforts and success is paramount to ensuring that you are not only driving users to your organization from these platforms, but that you are driving the right users to your organization.

Traditionally digital marketers have used the words Do, Go, and Know to describe how users search on the web. Users may have transactional searches like those related to buying something or completing a task so they are "Do"-ing something. They also may be interested in visiting a location on the web or physically "Go"-ing somewhere in a navigational search. The search behavior most impacted by AI and LLMs is the search behavior where users are seeking to learn or "know" something also referred to as an informational search. With this change in search behavior, and users visiting websites for informational searches less frequently, traffic alone is no longer sufficient as a measure of search marketing success. Digital analysts must pay attention to a variety of search engine and generative engine metrics to determine whether the organization is gaining visibility for the brand, since those search engines may no longer drive traffic. To understand these other metrics that can be measured beyond site traffic, let's first consider how search engines operate both from an organic and paid perspective.

Search Engine Basics for Analysts

Search engines like Google began by working through a simple process of crawling, indexing and providing results. Programs that can be referred to as "bots," "crawlers," or "spiders" review or "crawl" websites by visiting from link to link to link (page to page to page) to understand the structure of a website and follow these links from site to site to understand the structure of the entire internet. As these "spiders" visit the page they make note of the text, images, and video content on each page. The information collected during this process is then analyzed and indexed by the search engine. Consider it a giant library of all of the content that should be accessible on the web.

Once the content is indexed, when a user completes a search within the search engine, the search engine reviews the query, the index of all available content to its search engine, and provides a result based on the user's search query, prior search history, and more all based on a complex algorithm to determine what content to show and in what order. The web page or pages where it delivers this information is called the **Search Engine Results Page (SERP)**. Every organization should want to appear as high as possible on the SERP for keywords or phrases that are relevant to their organization and its goals.

The effort digital marketers put forth to optimize websites for search engines is referred to as **search engine optimization (SEO)**. SEO efforts involve:

- The management of a website to improve technical elements ensuring the website's code meets certain standards and loads rapidly on devices;

- Content elements to ensure that content is built for users and search engines can easily read and index content on the site to provide quality content to those users;

- And, usability elements so that users can easily find the content they are seeking to improve the overall user experience.

Marketers tend to refer to these groupings as three different categories of SEO: **technical SEO** (code cleanliness and site speed), **on-page SEO** (quality content and usability), and **off-page SEO** (popularity, public relations, and trustworthiness). These items seem very straightforward, but because marketers continually work to take advantage of the algorithm, things do change. Search engines continuously update their ranking criteria to prevent marketers from gaming the system in ways that degrade the user experience. We'll discuss some of these updated tactical elements throughout the remainder of this chapter.

In addition to SEO, search marketers also actively work to drive visibility in Google's AI Overviews, ChatGPT, Claude, Perplexity, and more. Actively working to influence these results is referred to in this text as **generative engine optimization (GEO)**. You may also hear it referred to in industry as AI optimization (AIO) or answer engine optimization (AEO). The tactics and related metrics to these efforts are still in development, but discussing these measures even at a cursory level is important for today's digital marketing analysts.

Nonetheless, all of these elements as well as even more recent changes related to implementation of SEO and GEO efforts are a multi-faceted and complicated function of digital marketing. These complex efforts lead to trackable metrics which create the basis for what matters in terms of organic SEO and GEO analytics. For search, digital marketers have traditionally measured the volume of traffic from organic search sources, the position at which the organization appears on a search engine results page (SERP), the number of times the brand is visible during a search, metrics related to competitive rankings and **vector embedding** (a method of converting language into data to capture meaning) as well as engagement metrics during the user's visit. These are all used to determine next steps for website improvements to drive more or better traffic from organic sources through higher rankings. Other metrics have also been traditionally considered that relate directly back to this complex algorithm inclusive of metrics related to the website's loading speed on mobile and traditional devices, the number of backlinks, and much more. **Backlinks** are the links from sites you do not own that link to your website. These metrics, as well as a variety of other metrics can play into the ability of an organization to appear in both SERPs and LLM responses (responses from ChatGPT, Google AI Overviews, and others).

While SEO specialists, or "SEOs" as they are referred to in industry, tend to manage and review much of their own data, digital analysts may also be called upon to help review web analytics or search analytics to help determine both results and next step strategies. Analysts may be asked to provide data regarding specific pages, the position at which a search engine results page shows the organization's page, where organic search traffic is coming from, their related engagement by page or by keyword, and even audit results so changes can be made to improve the site's overall user experience and position in search engines.

Organic and AI-related search isn't the only element that is considered in search. For paid search, additional metrics are tracked. In paid search, marketers place a bid on a given keyword or set of keywords and create headlines, descriptions, and other assets to show users during their search. The search engine chooses which ads to show and in which order related to how much the marketer bid on the keyword, the quality of their ad, the quality of the landing page and its relevance to the keyword, and other related factors. Paid search tends to be more direct from an analytical perspective than organic / AI search analytics and tied directly to conversions / key events. Paid search analytics overall do have some similarity to organic search analytics in that the page's quality impacts its results but are slightly different in other areas. We'll cover paid search in full in Chapter 6. For the remainder of this chapter, our focus is organic and AI-driven search.

Organic Search Analytics

Organic search analytics first begins with the tools that are used most frequently in SEO today. To determine success or failure in organic search efforts you must first understand the volume of traffic driven from organic search sources to your website or app and the related engagement that takes place on the site or app from those users.

Google Search Console: What is It, How to Set It Up, & What to Measure

The first tool beyond website analytics is another free Google resource — Google Search Console. Google Search Console, also referred to as GSC, is a free tool that allows you to submit the pages on your website to Google's search engine crawlers. The platform also allows you to review the performance of your website and its ability to communicate effectively with these crawlers. GSC provides valuable information in terms of how Google sees your website, feedback on your website's "Core Web Vitals," the average position where your listing appears in Google search results, and the volume of clicks and impressions received from Google search engine users.

We'll address this idea of Core Web Vitals in a few pages, but average position? Why is that important? SEO as a function is focused primarily on being as high as possible on a given Search Engine Results Page, and not just on any page, but the first page. If a user completes a search for a key phrase that is related to your business, most marketers want to appear at the top of the first SERP so that users will see and potentially choose your organization to learn more or to pursue your products or services. Thus, in the traditional sense **average position** is the average position where you place on the traditional SERP. SEOs primarily aim to rank in the top three positions or higher as those are presented to the user just below paid results in a standard search. Position 1, or an average position of 1, is the most coveted because this position is at the very top of the listing. In fact, research shows that the top 3 organic search results receive more than 68% of all clicks on the Google SERP and that the #1 position receives more clicks than results #3 - #10 combined!

Now, if you've visited a Google search results page in the past few years, you know it is more than just a traditional listing of search results. It may include a map, locations, local service listings, an AI Overviews response, or even other questions users ask, which SEOs refer to as "People Also Ask" or PAA for short. So, yes other "position" measurements matter, but note that **average position** can also refer to other positions as well. We'll address these other positions later in the chapter, but for now, we'll focus on the traditional search engine results page.

Wait, clicks and impressions?

You may want to highlight / notate / flag this paragraph as clicks and impressions are pivotal calculations in all things paid and organic in digital marketing. **Clicks** are the number of times users across a given platform "click" to visit your website. **Impressions** are the number of times users 'see' your listing on that particular platform. Clicks and impressions are metrics that you will see frequently throughout the remainder of this book as valuable metrics to determine success. These two metrics are also used to calculate another powerful metric — **click-through rate** (CTR).

CTR is simply a calculation of the number of clicks divided by the number of impressions. This metric is incredibly helpful in understanding the number of users that find value in your ad / listing / link / etc. and for comparing benchmarks to other advertisers.

$$\text{Click-Through Rate} = \frac{\text{Clicks}}{\text{Impressions}}$$

Clicks, impressions, and CTR are the basics of all organic and paid digital marketing analytics efforts in advertising and driving traffic to a website or app.

Now — let's get back to Google Search Console. To get started with GSC, you will create an account and verify ownership of your website. In creating your account for the first time, you can choose to connect Google Search Console to the entirety of your website's domain (which includes all subdomains) or to a single URL prefix.

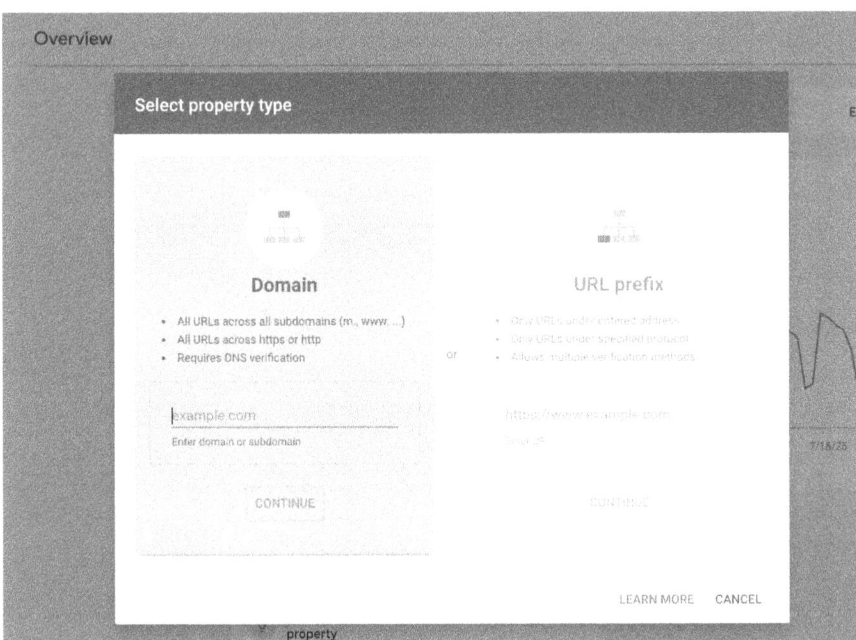

Source: Google Search Console, 2026

Insight: What is a Domain Name?

You may already know this, but a website domain is simply your user-friendly name on the internet (for example, https://www.forumspeaks.com) that points to a numerical internet protocol (IP) address. Domain names make websites easier to find than using a numerical address. Subdomains are like child domains where rather than www at the beginning of your domain, you can branch off to other sections of the site for organization like e-commerce stores, blogs, intranets, and more.

Next, you'll need to verify ownership of the website domain. Domain ownership can be verified by adding a TXT or CNAME record to your domain name provider. If you're not familiar with these records, your IT team may be aware of where they are located. These records can only be added by someone who has access to your website's domain name.

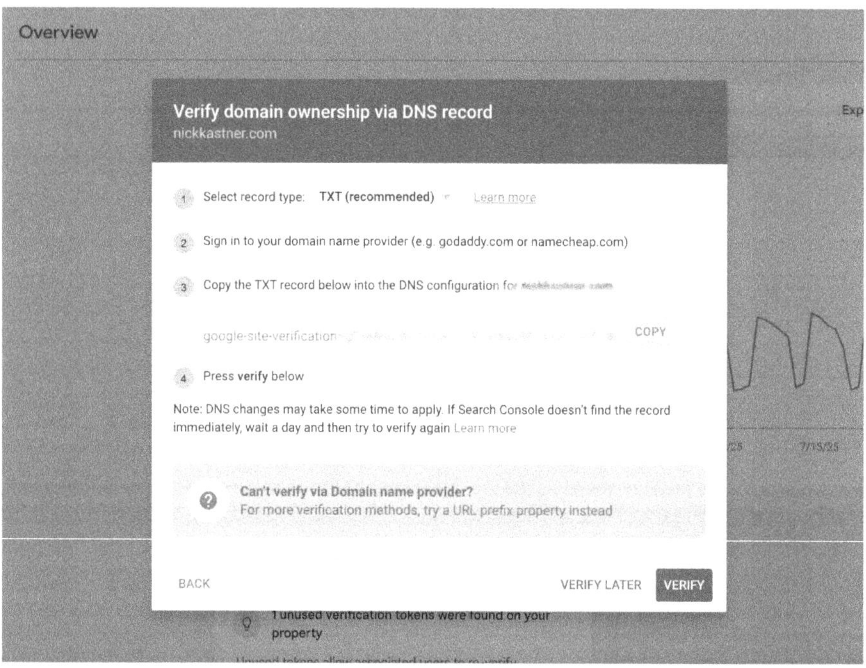

Source: Google Search Console, 2026

Once your account is verified, you can now use Google Search Console. The first step is to link your website's XML sitemap to the tool.

An **XML sitemap** is a file written using Extensible Markup Language (XML) that simply lists all of the pages of a website including guidelines as to which pages should be indexed by search engines and those that should not (for instance, thank you pages once a form is completed — no reason for those to be visible).

Google crawls websites based on the links that its crawlers find available across the web. However, if your website is new or if you want to simplify this process you can tell Google where your website is and the pages available to be part of its index. The XML sitemap accomplishes both of these tasks. This special file provides easy access to all of the pages of your website that you want Google to crawl. Some website content management systems or related plugins will automatically create this XML sitemap. This sitemap, if automatically created, typically exists at: [insertyourwebsiteurl.com]*/sitemap.xml*

Some website content management systems may place this file or file(s) elsewhere. Some websites may also have more than one XML sitemap or you may have to manually create this sitemap. In any case, once you know where this sitemap (or sitemaps) is located, to upload simply navigate to the "Sitemaps" section of Google Search Console and you'll find a screen that looks like this:

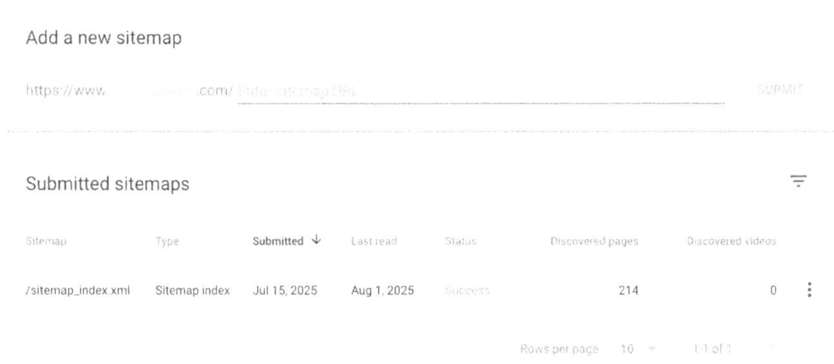

Source: Google Search Console, 2026

The example above shows how the sitemap submission process works as well as what it looks like once an XML sitemap has been added to GSC. Once a sitemap has been added, GSC will provide the most recent submission date, the last time the sitemap has been read, the status as to whether or not the sitemap could be read, and the content that was discovered in the process. Once complete, this isn't something that needs to be done frequently but should be reviewed to ensure that the sitemap is still accessible and content is continually being discovered via the sitemap. An error here will disrupt service to GSC, can negatively affect your search engine visibility and may signify a more significant issue with your website.

Once your Google Search Console account is set up, GSC offers a great deal of features that ensure Google can access your content, provide an understanding of search visibility, and offer simple analysis when problems arise. In simple terms, GSC shows you whether Google can or cannot see content and over time whether you are gaining or losing visibility, clicks, and impressions. GSC also provides details as specific as the number of clicks and impressions by keyword, page, location, date, and more.

Below is a screenshot of the popular Performance report that provides search volume in clicks, impressions, average CTR and average position charted over time in a visual line chart. The example below includes two of these metrics: clicks and impressions. The report can display up to 16 months of data. Because GSC retains only 16 months, anything longer requires exporting data on a rolling basis which I would recommend.

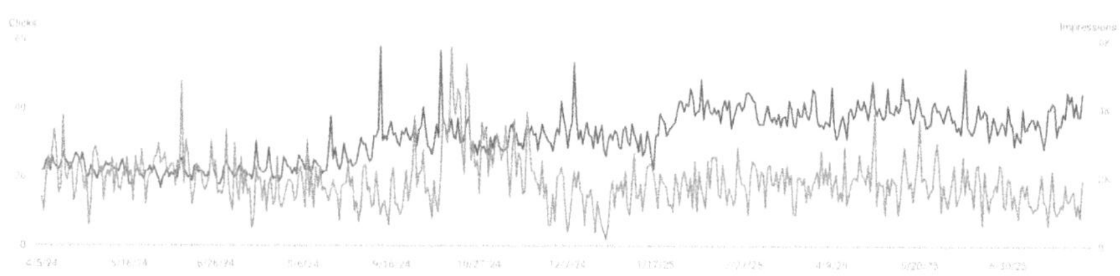

Source: Google Search Console, 2026

Note that historical benchmarking against your own historical data is the most reliable approach. While there are ways to benchmark yourself against competitors, GSC is not the tool to do that. Analytically the focus in

GSC is reviewing changes in click and impression behavior for individual searches, individual pages, as well as data related to Google Core Web Vitals, and confirming your sitemap is uploaded correctly.

Side Quest: The Alligator Graph (2025)

When using any software product, sometimes things change without your approval. In mid-September 2025, SEO professionals around the world noticed some unusual behavior in their GSC accounts. The number of impressions was down and the average position seemed to have improved! The graphs themselves for this action were referred to as "alligator graphs" because the data charts for clicks and impressions looked like an alligator's mouth (see sample image below).

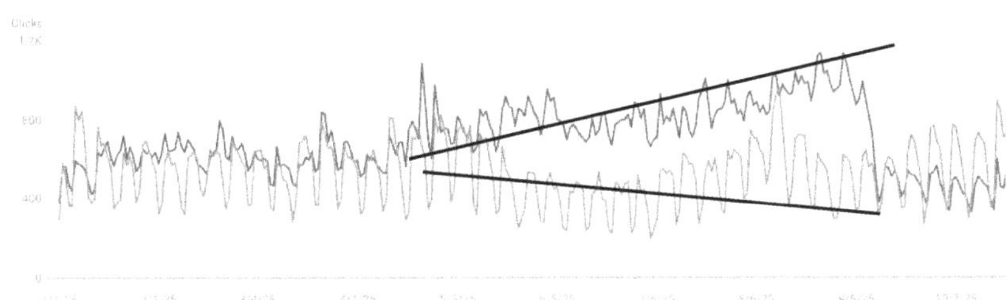

Source: Google Search Console, 2026

SEOs quickly determined that the drop in impressions was related to a change Google made to how it tracked search results data.

For as long as I can personally recall, Google allowed marketers to track web page positions for a given keyword all the way to position #100. Google traditionally has offered 10 search results per page which meant that SEOs and analysts could track all the way to the end of page 10 to determine how they were progressing in their organic search ranking efforts. Consider this — Google had made available all of the data for the top 100 websites for nearly any search possible! That's a LOT OF DATA! The parameter Google used to collect and share this large volume of data is referred to as the "&num=100 parameter."

After the change, Google only shared data for the top 20 rankings for any given keyword or phrase. Data from prior to mid-September 2025 still shows impressions that may be related to positions a website held within the top 100 positions for a given keyword or phrase that the website ranked for, while data after this date only shows impressions for the top 20. In addition, average position for positions held beyond position 20 was no longer shared; therefore, the average position a website may hold across all keywords (or even just a single keyword) could no longer be worse than 20.

For those that tracked every fluctuation, this resulted in an immense data loss. For those that only tracked positions within the top 20, this resulted in little to no data change. I mention this because as you look at data historically, for some websites you may see a dramatic drop in impressions beginning in mid-September 2025. Consider this a cautionary tale as data gaps can sometimes be related to happenings across thc industry — not just in your data set.

While Google continues to allow users to navigate search results after page 2 (or position #20), this data is no longer trackable in Google Search Console.

GSC also provides detailed performance data tied to specific keywords or phrases. You can pull reports that tell you how often a query surfaced your site (impressions), how often users actually clicked, and where you ranked, and whether your page titles and meta descriptions are compelling enough to earn the click. This data is incredibly helpful for SEOs and analysts to determine whether their SEO efforts have been effective, to identify opportunities for optimization, and to better understand how users are discovering the organization through search. It also provides insight into whether the language used in page titles, meta descriptions, and content is compelling enough to drive users to click through to the website. On the next page is an example of the reporting capabilities for individual search queries and how this data can be interpreted in practice.

Top queries	↓ Clicks	Impressions
shower glass atlanta	18	586
shower door installation	18	130
shower doors	17	6,747
glass company atlanta	17	1,081
frameless shower doors	16	930
drexler shower doors	16	797
custom shower doors	15	3,073
custom glass shower doors	14	8,532
frameless glass wine cellar doors	14	1,954

Source: Google Search Console, 2026

All GSC tracking ties back to our core questions regarding analytical strategy: What is the goal? How do we measure progress toward that goal? And why do the ups and downs occur? Utilizing data from GSC alongside other analytical tools provides valuable insight into how Google evaluates an organization's website. For instance, aligning keyword performance reports like those on the prior page along with Google's Core Web Vitals data (shown below) may reveal that a specific page which previously performed well in terms of ranking for a given keyword is now underperforming due to changes in page experience or site performance.

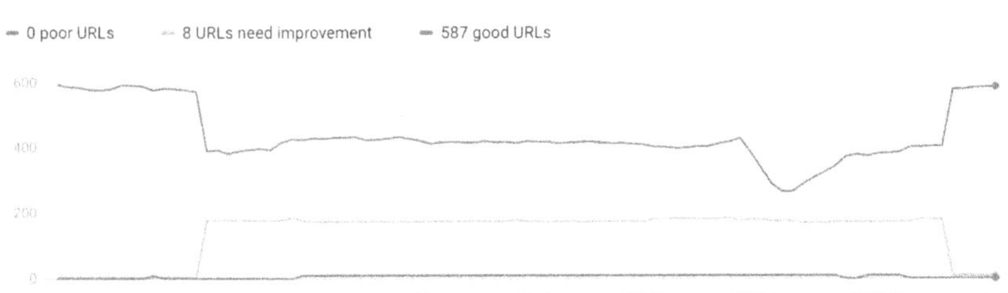

Source: Google Search Console, 2026

Understanding Search Using GSC, Core Web Vitals, & Website Analytics

I purposefully introduced this idea of search analytics using Google Search Console because it's direct. You can easily see the ups and downs so the key from this as a knowledge base is simply sorting out why those ups and downs occur. The tool easily shows an analyst global results as well as individual keyword and page results. The biggest challenge for analysts is understanding why these things occur. Is it related to technical SEO, on-page SEO, or off-page SEO elements? Or, maybe something entirely different?

In May 2020, following a review of Google's own research along with accessible industry research, Google confirmed something digital marketers had known for some time — users prefer websites with great experiences on each page. While this may seem obvious, how to measure "great experiences" isn't easy. Research has shown that the speed at which web pages load or how friendly a website is on a mobile device were all things that were measurable, but what else? With Google's confirmation of the importance of page experience, Google announced new measurements that would allow Google to measure experience. Google referred to these elements as **Core Web Vitals**. This set of metrics would be directly related to site speed, how responsive a given webpage was for mobile use, and visual stability across devices.

The three primary measurements for Core Web Vitals included **Largest Contentful Paint (LCP)**, **First Input Delay (FID)**, and **Cumulative Layout Shift (CLS)**. In simple terms, the LCP measures how long it takes for the largest visible element to load on a page which provides a strong indication of perceived page load speed. If you think of a web page as a painting, what's the largest section of that painting (the "paint") and how long does it take to complete? FID measures interactivity by quantifying the amount of time from a user's first interaction to the moment the browser begins processing that same interaction. To explain FID, think about the first click that you make on an interactive website and how long it takes to load the interaction that you just clicked or tapped on. The last calculation — CLS — quantifies how much elements shift or move during loading which can indicate a poor user experience. Have you ever watched a website load and different elements moved around on the page as it loaded? CLS measures that motion as it is believed if not designed on purpose, that motion creates a negative experience.

Of the measures initially presented in 2020, First Input Delay (FID) was the weakest measurement. FID does provide some guidance on the user experience, however it only measures the "delay" before the event handler runs or the click occurs, not the total time for the action to occur. Thus, it relied on user interaction and not any metrics that might point to the ongoing experience. In March of 2024, Google moved from FID to a new metric called **Interaction to Next Paint (INP)**. This metric assesses a given page's overall responsiveness by observing the latency, or delay, of all interactions (clicks, taps, keyboard interactions, etc.) that happen during the entirety of the user's visit to a given page.

These measurements tell us a number of things about how Google understands search and user behavior. First, with Google utilizing Core Web Vitals as an element of its search algorithm we know that user experience is critical to search success. This has been historically true for website analytics, but now it also impacts search. Second, Google's focus on user experience also speaks to the types of sites that it wants to present to users. Sites that are driven by "word walls" or massive amounts of text with few images or sections to break up content will likely perform worse than those that include more user experience-driven content. And third, Google is providing websites an opportunity to improve by providing this data to users so the expectation is that search marketers should pay attention to the user experience across the site and other experiences.

The Core Web Vitals report shown earlier showed that 587 URLs, or pages, on that particular site perform well in these categories. However, 8 pages need additional work. Reviewing those pages to determine what Core Web Vitals issues exist and comparing those pages to your ranked keywords may point directly to an issue that can be addressed. Paying attention to the requirements of each of the Core Web Vitals and expectations can provide a great deal of insight as to how to correct the issue.

Insight: What's in a Click?

It's important to note that the number of clicks in Google Search Console does not always align with data in Google Analytics 4. These don't align as GSC and GA4 track users differently. GSC focuses strictly on clicks from Google Search results, while GA4 tracks sessions initiated by users on a website, which can be influenced by various factors like JavaScript execution, cookie consent, and ad blocking.

For example, your web pages all pass Core Web Vitals; however, across the board your web pages perform poorly in search. You have completed all elements of known technical SEO. Your on-page content meets the "requirement" of quality and off-page your marketing team has done a wonderful job of getting mentions across the web of your site and backlinks pointing to the quality of your content. What could be the problem? Google is looking for sites that create great experiences and generally speaking, your website has few photos, no videos, and few opportunities for interaction. You're creating a poor user experience. Understanding how all of these elements align (technical SEO, on-page SEO, off-page SEO, Core Web Vitals, etc.) is a critical element for an analyst to ensure that you are providing quality feedback to your marketing teams — or working closely with them — to meet your organization's marketing goals.

Bing Webmaster Tools

As of February 2026, Google holds almost 90% of global market share for search engines. While other platforms like Bing (4.98% global market share), Yahoo! (1.39% global market share), and DuckDuckGo (0.76% global market share) exist, Google is simply the dominant player in this space. (*Bing Search supplies a substantial portion of the search results for Yahoo! and DuckDuckGo as well.*) And, while Google Search Console is the more dominant platform due to Google's market share, Bing Webmaster Tools provides some added benefit that Google Search Console does not.

First, Bing Webmaster Tools (BWT) offers access to IndexNow, a free, open-source protocol that allows webmasters, or those who manage websites, to notify search engines when URLs or web pages change. This gives webmasters direct access to search engines for updates.

Source: Bing Webmaster Tools, 2026

Second, Site Explorer provides a global view of a website's structure providing data on clicks, impressions, backlink counts for off-page SEO tracking, and more. This tool, along with advanced filtering, provides access to identify not just keywords, but high and low-performing pages as well as direct insight into internal linking strategies.

In addition, BWT provides insight into backlinks to websites including what words were used to link back to the site as well as other common backlink-related metrics. BWT also gives you competitive backlink data, providing direct insight into competitors' link-building strategies. This feature is unique to BWT — at least in terms of free tools.

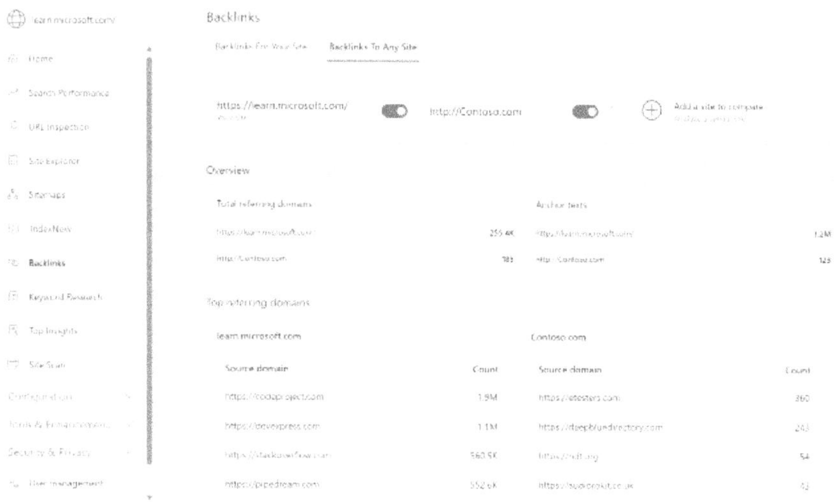

Source: Bing Webmaster Tools, 2026

Tip: Okay, So What Really Matters in Search Analytics?

There's a lot of language that's tossed around by SEOs in terms of what can be tracked to determine success. And while thus far I've explained how to get to this data, what are we actually tracking for organic search?

There are a few metrics that mean more to organic search marketers than others. Those are:

- Impressions
- Click-Through Rate (CTR)
- Backlink-related Metrics
- Bounce Rate
- Pages per Session
- Customer Lifetime Value
- Non-Branded Traffic
- Google Business Profile Metrics
- Clicks
- Keyword Rankings
- Engagement Rate
- Session Duration
- Organic Conversions
- Cost Per Acquisition
- Return on Investment

I'll go over each of these but let's start with a few metrics that we've already discussed and that are easily available in Google Search Console and Bing Webmaster Tools: *impressions and clicks*.

Impressions are part of the broader category of **search visibility**. Search visibility measures how often your website appears in search engine results. This can be any place you appear in search results, whether the user scrolls past or clicks. Remember that search engines are not just basic search in a top 10 list but can include AI Overviews and featured snippets — highlighted boxes pulled out within search results — as well as 'People Also Ask' and other rich results like recipes and shopping listings. These other positions, when visible to the user, can also be listed as impressions. Traditionally, the higher the ranking, the more impressions.

Clicks, in terms of organic search, are related to **organic traffic**. Organic search traffic, as discussed in Chapter 4, refers to visitors who visit your website from unpaid search. This matters — as well as the related click-through rate (CTR) because it shares actual performance from your search impressions.

While impressions show us how frequently users see your website in search engine results, the volume of impressions is driven by your ranking in those results. The higher your website is listed in those rankings, traditionally the more impressions and clicks you'll receive. According to research by popular SEO software provider Ahrefs, roughly 97% of all search clicks occur in the top 20 results. That means only 3% of clicks occur beyond the top 2 search engine results pages! **Keyword rankings** show us where websites appear in those search engine results page for specific terms that are relevant to our organization. Our goal is to rank as high as possible to boost impressions and clicks. All of an SEO's efforts are focused on improving these rankings; thus measuring ranking, impressions, and clicks all tie together.

The remainder of the metrics analysts measure in organic search directly relate to keyword ranking performance. Therein lies the challenge: how do SEO specialists impact metrics to improve these rankings? I've mentioned the importance of technical, on-page, and off-page SEO. In reality, there are reportedly over 200 ranking factors in Google alone driven by machine learning that dictate the position that a given website appears in search engine results. These elements include everything from content relevance to the searched keyword or phrase, whether the site is trustworthy based on backlinks and mentions across social and other media, E-E-A-T (Experience, Expertise, Authoritativeness, Trustworthiness), page speed, Core Web Vitals metrics, the freshness of your content (new content performs better traditionally than older content), location, user's search history (as Google customizes results if a user is logged in based on prior history), and more. It's complicated! But the remainder of the metrics mentioned above cover elements that are easily trackable. "Okay, so what do these metrics tell us?"

Metrics related to backlinks speak to the popularity or trustworthiness of a webpage. To reiterate, backlinks are incoming links from other websites. For instance, the ***total number of backlinks*** tell us the general trustworthiness or authority a page may have. A single website may link to another website's pages multiple times. Thus tracking the ***number of referring domains*** provides value by telling analysts whether they are driving value across sites (which is critical to growing ranking) or if they have a few websites linking to their website multiple times. Analysts also track the ***number of lost backlinks*** — links that have been removed — as well as the number of ***new backlinks earned.*** There is also value in gaining mentions of your brand on social media, or simply mentions on other sites. While these may not result in backlinks, Google's algorithm is smart enough to find value in the number of mentions as a measure of trustworthiness.

Website related metrics like bounce rate and engagement rate are very helpful for analysts especially in looking at these rates related to organic search traffic. While Google and other search engines don't track overall user behavior as part of their search algorithms, they do consider the immediate click that occurs from the search engine. For instance, if users frequently find you on a search engine, visit your website and then click "Back" to go back to the search engine, the search engine could assume that the user did not find what they were looking for. Thus bounce (the number of users that click to visit a page and immediately go back) as well as engagement (users who spend more than 10 seconds on a page, visit more than 2 pages, or convert) show the analyst how frequently users are not finding the information they are seeking. And if a search engine frequently sees that users are not staying on the site and bouncing back to the search engine, this can negatively affect your rankings. These results are directly related to session duration (how long a user stays on your website) and time on page (how long a user stays on a given page). The same is true if you're generating a high number of impressions from traditional search results but few clicks. Again, search engines may see this as a signal that your content isn't as helpful as others. (Quick note: If you see high impressions but low clicks from traditional search, take a look at your website's meta description — the description that you provide to search engines regarding a given page. If you don't have a meta description or even if you do, sometimes search engines will choose to not use your meta description or write their own which may hurt your CTR.)

Non-branded traffic also speaks directly to SEO performance. For instance, your website and its pages should rank for your organization's brand name. Thus, branded organic search traffic is traffic related to your brand name. This traffic can be driven up and down by your marketing efforts regarding brand awareness. Non-branded traffic speaks to your marketing team's ability to help your website rank for keywords that are adjacent to your offering but do not include your brand name. If your non-branded organic search traffic continues to increase, this speaks to the quality of your SEO efforts. If it declines, why? This can be a result of poor efforts by your SEO team, but also can be a result of an algorithm change by a search engine that negatively impacted your website and should be addressed.

SEO specialists and analysts also care about metrics related to the financial element of marketing. Organic conversions speak to the conversions driven from organic search. Remember that conversions can be a variety of things but they measure success in one's marketing efforts. Other related metrics including customer lifetime value, cost per acquisition, and return on investment also relate to the value created by marketing and related channels. When and where possible, if an analyst can begin to point to specific metrics like these by channel then not only is the analyst providing specific value, but SEO specialists can prove value in their efforts.

No matter the metrics tracked for organic search, there is no perfect benchmark based on industry outside of keyword rankings. The benchmark for keyword rankings should be obvious — #1. The other metrics should be tracked for growth over time compared to prior periods of time, typically year over year to account for seasonality.

The other metrics that SEO specialists and analysts believe are important are those related to Google Business Profile. Let's discuss in the next section.

Google Business Profile & Related Mapping Tools

Google Business Profile, or GBP for short, is a free tool provided by Google that allows business owners to manage their online presence in Google Maps and related Search. You may also hear business owners refer to this as Google My Business, or GMB, as this was the tool's previous name. Additional tools also exist that matter in managing map listings like Bing Places for Business, Apple Business Connect, Waze, and others. These platforms are important for all organizations, but specifically for those whose customers visit their locations. While each have their own algorithm to determine list order, I'm going to focus specifically on GBP because it is the most prominent.

With GBP, organizations can create or claim their own profile and then manage the profile accordingly. This includes the ability to complete their profile inclusive of product and service offerings, read and respond to reviews, upload posts and photos, and even manage bookings or leads. This platform is very powerful and can be very beneficial when managed appropriately.

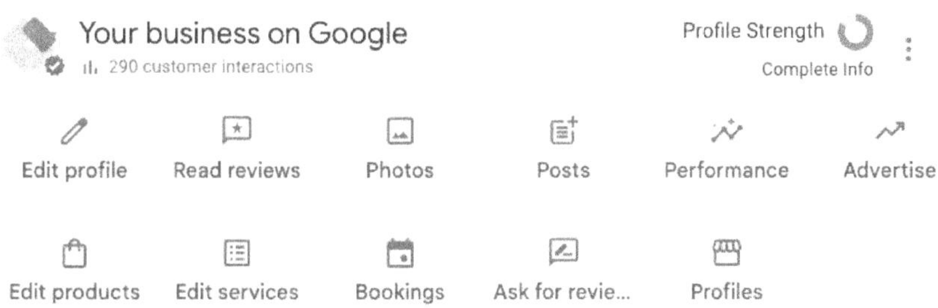

Source: Google Business Profile, 2026

Optimizing your GBP account could be a book in and of itself. Frequency of posting photos or posts, frequency and quality of reviews, completion level of your profile, user's location, click volume and engagement, and more all play into one's ability to rank well when users search for a service in a local area. There are also challenges created by GBP and its algorithm for organizations where users don't visit their physical location but the organization provides services across a service area. The algorithm is built to benefit brands where users visit their physical location. For organizations in service industries like pest control, heating and air, plumbing, and others, the algorithm can actually hurt their ability to rank or perform well if they work out of their home. GBP requires businesses to prove their location is for business which is very difficult for businesses based in someone's home. There are ways to work within the system, but it can be complicated. I'll end this paragraph where we started — GBP management could be its own text. Luckily, our focus isn't how to rank well in Google Maps (or any other platform). The focus is measurement and what these metrics mean to the organization.

With Google Business Profile, analysts can track reviews (both volume and score, on a range from 1 to 5, with 5 being the best) as well as how frequently users interact with the profile, click, call, book appointments (if the feature is being used), or ask for directions. These metrics and reports are simple and can be incredibly meaningful for organizations where users visit their physical location. They speak to the quality of your services (reviews), profile views (search visibility), clicks, calls, direction requests, and bookings (conversions).

Below and on the following page are samples of the reports from a live account:

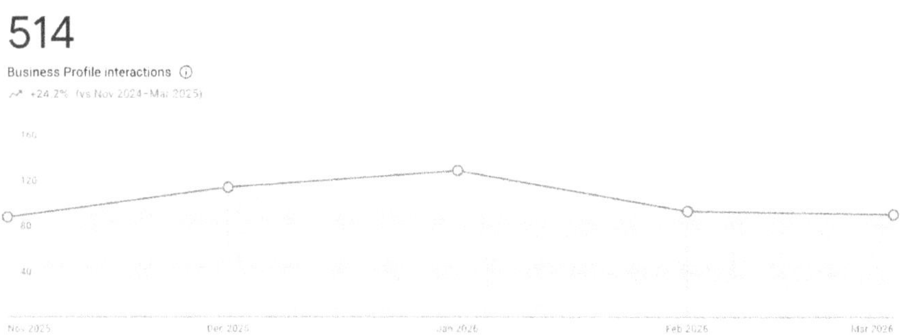

Source: Google Business Profile, 2026

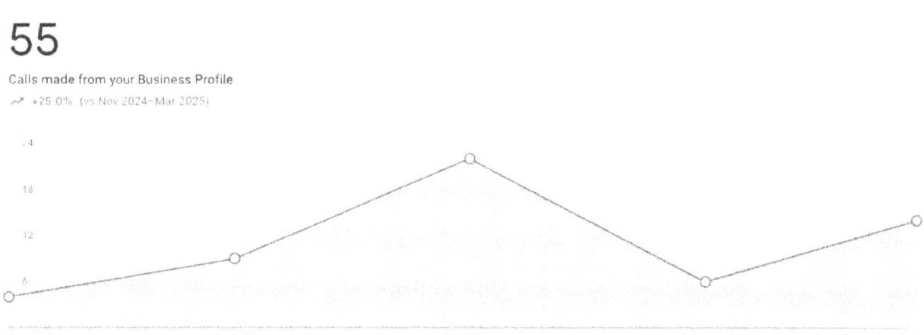

Source: Google Business Profile, 2026

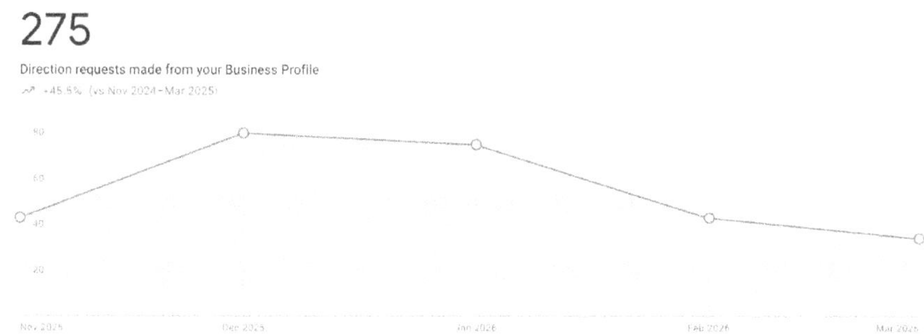

Source: Google Business Profile, 2026

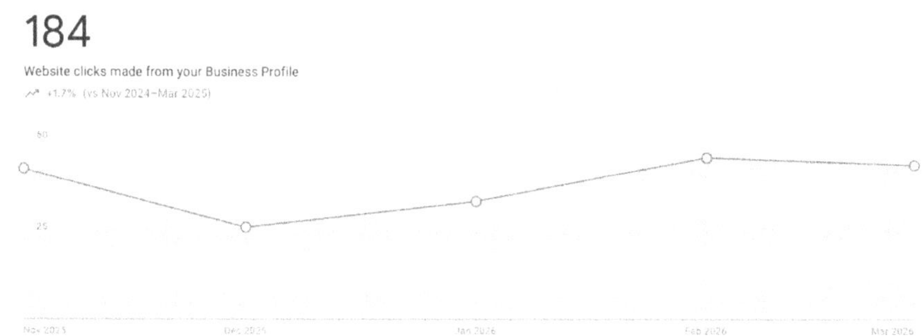

Source: Google Business Profile, 2026

Each of these metrics points to specific behaviors or activities that are positively or negatively affecting your Google Business Profile success. The metrics provided in the dashboard are more results-driven than explanatory on how to improve position or visibility on the platform.

For instance, if you complete a search for "Gainesville, GA dentist," does the dental practice you are marketing for appear? If not, why not? The data provided from GBP can speak to whether you're achieving visibility or if visibility is improving, but it does not speak to why the ups and downs occur. Specifically, one measure that you don't see in your GBP account is where you actually rank in the map results or for individual keywords.

For that information, you have three options. The first is to manually search for the keyword and see where the organization ranks. Unfortunately, this isn't very telling as your own location and search history affect those results thus can show incorrect information if the organization isn't near you or the results are skewed by your own prior search behaviors. The second option is to complete a search utilizing VPN software or ISearchFrom.com that allows you to simulate Google results from other locations. The third option is to utilize software that can display these results.

With the first two options, in order to collect all of the information needed, you'll need to complete multiple searches. For instance, below is a search for a key phrase based in Tampa, Florida as well as the results. This is the ranking of this key phrase on a given Thursday night.

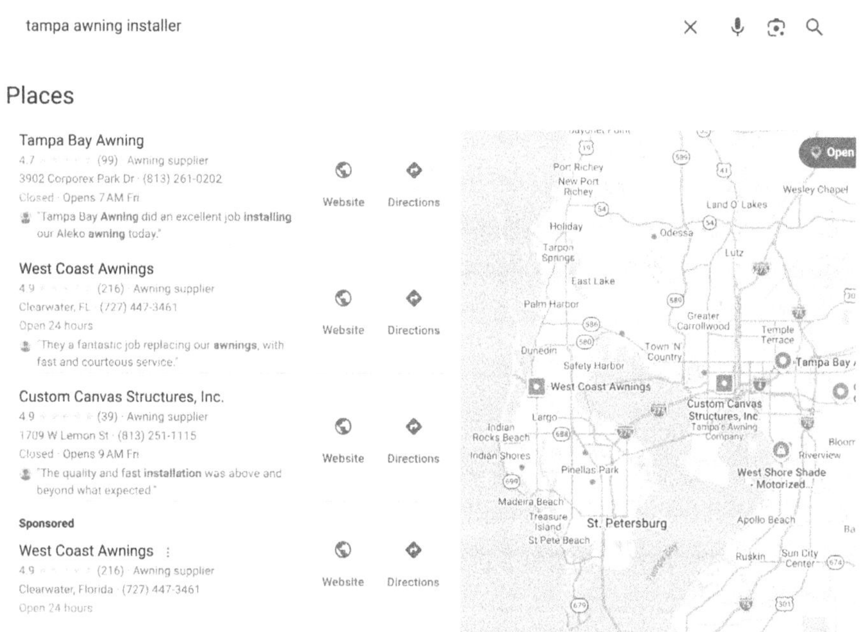

Source: Google Search, 2026

To keep track of ranking results, this same search — along with other key phrases you are tracking — would need to be completed at similar intervals either every day, week, or month. Frankly, this is a lot of manual work!

The third option — separate software — is the ideal option especially for organizations that rely on location-based business. This may include organizations in healthcare, localized services, brick and mortar retail, restaurants, and more. Tools like SE Ranking's Local Marketing Tool or Local Falcon, another software platform, provide valuable rank tracking capabilities. One of the most valuable tools visualizes rankings across a grid so you can see over time how rankings change. The tool utilizes a business location's ranking position in Google Maps over the geographical location selected. Users can specify which key phrases to track and dictate what areas on a map to review. This map view allows search marketers focused on local search to see where they rank and how rankings change over time with limited costs. Below is a sample of SE Ranking's Local Marketing tool.

Source: SE Ranking

A combination of GBP and an alternative software like SE Ranking, Local Falcon, or otherwise provides comprehensive coverage of rankings inside of Google Maps. Just remember that Google Maps is not the only localized search results platform where rankings matter. Bing Maps, Apple Maps, and others also have impact in overall visibility. Both SE Ranking and Local Falcon can provide data for Bing Maps. Other tools like BrightLocal, and Nightwatch offer similar capabilities. All SEOs have a preferred platform for tracking so finding the platform that works best for your organization's budget and needs is important.

Just like tracking of Google Maps / GBP listings, there are other additional SEO tracking tools that can provide significant value in tracking beyond just Google Search Console.

Other Search Analytics Tools

For overall search visibility in Google, Google Search Console provides significant value simply due to its cost and capabilities. Alongside data from Google Analytics 4, analysts can learn a great deal of information. However, what neither of these platforms do is provide detailed information on ranking position in search across platforms, changes over time, or other valuable data that can help SEOs improve performance.

These other platforms can provide a variety of additional valuable information such as:

- The estimated number of monthly searches for a given keyword;
- A measure of how difficult the keyword is to rank for based on search volume, competition, and other metrics;
- Ranking position of your website for a given keyword over time typically tracked daily;
- Competitor position in rankings as well as related traffic;
- Volume of external links, linking domains, and anchor text for your website as well as competitors;
- SERP feature tracking including featured snippets, maps (also called local packs), People Also Ask, or other features that appear in the search;
- Technical audit tools providing details of errors and opportunities for correction to meet technical SEO requirements;
- And, ranking position data from other platforms like Bing and Yahoo!

There are a variety of options for SEO analysts in terms of software platforms. The most popular platforms due to their depth and market presence are Semrush and Ahrefs. However, other platforms provide benefits as well including SE Ranking, Moz Pro, Surfer SEO, BrightEdge, Morningscore, Nightwatch, and many others. Selecting the right SEO software for your organization comes down to your organization's needs.

These other platforms provide a wide variety of additional data. Below are screenshots and explanations of the data provided by popular SEO analytics software Semrush.

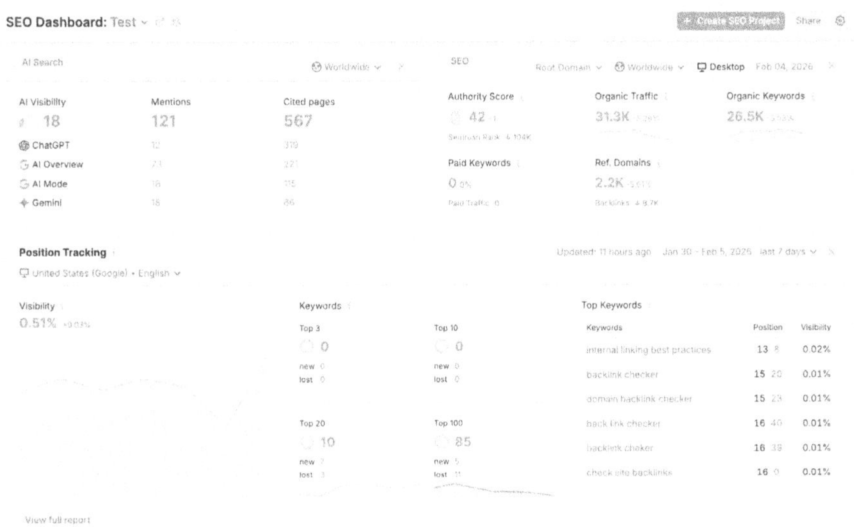

Source: Semrush

Most SEO platforms begin with a dashboard. Some dashboards are customizable where others are set for you. As you can see from the screenshot above Semrush offers data regarding AI search, standard SEO, and position tracking.

There are some new metrics here that we've yet to discuss. All SEO software platforms are different but follow the same general principles. We'll address AI search and related metrics shortly, but for now let's focus on basic SEO. Starting in the panel at the top right:

- **Authority Score:** many platforms offer a similar metric, but generally speaking authority score is a measure of how much authority your website has. Most platforms have a proprietary way this is measured. It is typically on a scale from 0 - 100 with 100 being the highest possible score. It takes into account the domain's overall reputation based on the number and quality of backlinks, site quality, search influence, volume of organic traffic, and more. It is meant to be a predictive score on the ease of ranking for a given keyword or a measure of competitiveness for ranking in comparison to other websites. Semrush also takes into account prospective "spam" factors. Spam — as defined here — refers to patterns that would indicate the domain is working to manipulate search bots or algorithms to improve credibility but is truly unworthy of said credibility. Think of spam as trash or efforts to trick the system. We also call these behaviors "black-hat techniques" in SEO circles.

- **Organic Traffic** has already been defined but as a reminder, organic traffic is the volume of traffic measured in users or sessions to your website from search engines that was unpaid.

- **Organic Keywords** is simply the number of individual keywords that drive traffic to your website from organic traffic.

- **Referring Domains** refers to the number of domains, or individual websites, that link to your website. This is considered a signal of authority because websites link to other websites when they find value in their content. Note that referring domains and referring links are different. A domain, or website, may have multiple pages that link to the same site thus a single domain can link to a website's pages multiple times.

- **Visibility** is another metric that is different across different platforms. In Semrush, this is placed in the "Position Tracking" section of the report. This metric is traditionally based on percentage (0 - 100%) that serves as an estimate of how often your domain appears in the top 100 organic search results for the keywords that are tracked. A score of 100% would mean that you rank #1 for all keywords that you are currently tracking. Beside visibility in this particular report are notation of 'Top 3,' 'Top 10,' etc. This is related to the visibility score as it is simply a count of how many keywords are listed in the top 3, top 10, etc. of search results. Remember that a primary metric of SEO is position, or where the keyword ranks on a basic search for a keyword.

- **Top Keywords** in the case of the Semrush report are the keywords that a webpage on your website currently holds the highest rankings for. In other platforms, this can also be the keywords that drive the highest volume of traffic. Because this is different per platform, you need to be aware of how the platform works and how to relay this message back to your internal team.

Insight: Tracking Rankings is Weird

In its simplest terms, SEO is a race to see what webpage can be at the top of a given keyword search. When SEO began as a marketing discipline, this effort could be directly attributed to the success of certain SEO strategies. Now, we still focus on visibility, however, because of the number of attributing factors, visibility reporting provides data assuming the device and the browser are from a new IP address in a specific location (as prior behavior and location impact search results). In reality, this sort of behavior is rare. True search results would include additional factors including a user's prior search history, prior interactions with the website in question, or even visits to web pages that also rank for a given keyword (including potential competitors). For instance, if a user frequents a competitor's web pages primarily from Google Search results, it's likely that the competitor will show higher in the individual's search results and your site will be positioned lower. So, visibility reporting may show you at a certain position, but that position will not be the same for all users based on their own prior search behavior. This is an important note as many times clients or staff members have asked me why the report shows that the webpage holds one position in search results but their browser or another person in the office shows that they hold a different position. The answer is simply that their behavior has impacted their own search results.

Most SEO platforms provide similar dashboard reports and they are incredibly helpful in seeing the general direction of rankings, impact of recent SEO efforts, or even how a recent update by a search engine may have positively or negatively impacted your global rankings. However, more telling, or impactful, for SEOs are reports that become more prescriptive and provide data that leads to decision making and change. Remember that the end goal in SEO is to improve rankings which improves visibility which should improve volume of traffic to your website. If the consumer finds the content they are seeking on your site, you should then see conversions on your site from this traffic either immediately or over time dependent on your audience.

Let's take a look at some of the more specific reports from Semrush and see how this works.

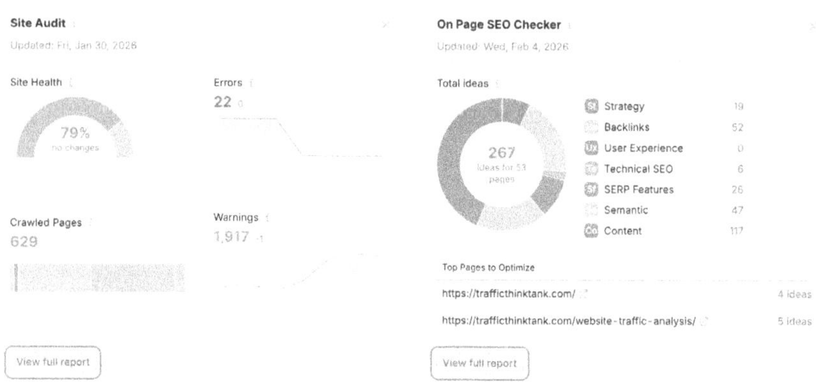

Source: Semrush

First is the site audit. The site audit from any platform focuses on improvements from a technical SEO perspective. This can include a variety of things from code errors and warnings to server errors. The goal is to limit the number of errors and warnings, or "clean up the code," to improve site speed and make it easier for search engine bots to parse and see what matters most.

You'll also note from Semrush the "On Page SEO Checker." This provides direct feedback on ideas that could improve the way search engines see your website. This is different for every platform and may be presented in a variety of ways. Also, with widespread adoption of AI, some platforms are utilizing AI to provide this feedback to improve sites for search engines and consumers.

Source: Semrush

Above is a position tracking report. Position tracking is one of the most critical parts of SEO analytics because it shows us how we are performing and where we rank for given terms. Now, it is very important to remember that this report shows what I would refer to as a "flat" search from a given location. When I say "flat" search, this assumes that the user has never used Google before and the data is only taking into account the geolocation of the user and the user's query. However, that's not typically how users search. Each user's prior search history, especially if logged in to their Google account, is taken into account. This may also include travel history or geolocation changes. Thus, when a user searches for a given keyword, their results may not be the same as another user's results. In addition, this also means that your reporting and an individual's own search results may show different rankings.

Considering individual keyword performance is important as it tells us a number of things. First, individual keyword performance tells us how we are performing in search engines for each individual term. Improved rankings can indicate successful efforts over time. Declining rankings can indicate algorithm changes, new competition, or poor SEO efforts. Second, individual keyword performance can provide guidance on whether we are cannibalizing our own terms. Sometimes, we can accidentally rank two pages for the same keyword and must determine which page is the correct page to rank for a given term.

Insight: Flat Search Example

An analyst provides reporting to marketing leadership for a company. Members of leadership do the same search and get different results. What do you do?

Well, first, of course this is true. Leadership's search results are going to be dependent on their own browser and account history — not just their search and their geolocation. Reporting is accurate if we understand that we are looking at the results of a "flat" search from a geolocation.

This is important to note because the leadership can easily become convinced that these reports are not accurate —which is not the case.

Just as important as individual keyword performance is overall keyword performance. The report below from Semrush shows the overall performance for organic traffic and keyword improvements and declines for a website. An overall performance report for organic traffic can explain both improvements and declines in search traffic, but can also indicate global behavior changes in user behavior.

For instance, a decline in organic traffic can indicate poor performance in search or a change in the algorithm that may negatively impact search rankings. This is visible in the example provided as organic search traffic declines as well as keywords rankings decrease. But if ranking improvements are found and traffic is still declining it can indicate a change in global behavior for your search terms. This can be due to changes in keyword popularity, or also can indicate a change in search functionality. For instance, at the launch of Google AI Overviews, sites globally saw a decline in organic search traffic as users began getting more information directly from search engines than ever before.

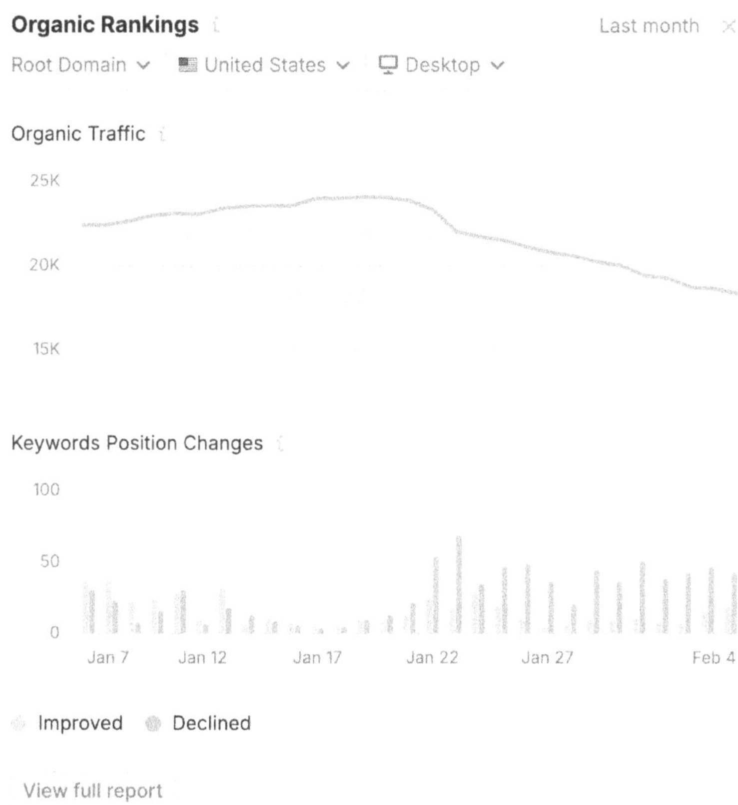

Source: Semrush

And, the last major report provided by most SEO analytics platforms is the backlinks report. I've provided an example of this report on the following page.

While there are differences in how each SEO analytics platform provides the backlinks report, the general idea is this report provides an overview of the number of backlinks linking to the site. In addition, an idea of the authority of these pages is provided. Higher authority sites are those that tend to have their own high volume of backlinks or are thought of highly across the web. Websites like The New York Times, Google, or Apple all have incredibly high authority. Links from these sites provide very high value where smaller and more localized sites tend to provide lower authority but can be very important especially to prove importance in local markets. The more backlinks from higher quality sites, the more authority your own site can have.

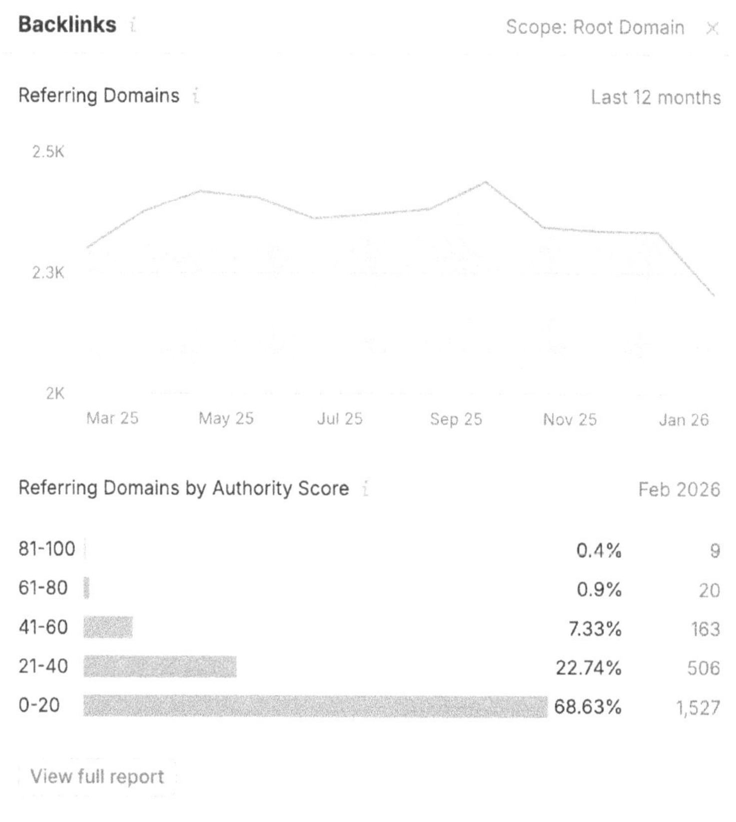

Source: Semrush

If you analyze the two reports — the backlinks report and the overall keyword performance report — from the prior two pages, you'll note that as this given site saw a loss in backlinks, the site also saw a decrease in keyword positions and thus organic traffic. As has been stated throughout this chapter, technical SEO, on-page SEO, and off-page SEO all work together. Thus, each of these reports provide insight as to how to improve SEO performance which is the end goal of our reporting in this marketing channel.

AI-Related (GEO) Metrics and Their Connection to Organic Search

With the launch of Google's AI Overviews as well as the popularity of platforms like ChatGPT and Claude, search marketers and analysts are rapidly working to find ways to track AI platforms and their related "rankings." However, these platforms are very new. Thus, related data and its accuracy are difficult to ascertain.

For instance, in Google Search Console, if a user completes a search and receives the answer to their question in the AI Overview, there is currently no simple way to know that an AI Overviews response was provided to the user. Industry data seems to indicate that AI Overviews' responses are shown to users in Google 60-80% of the time for certain query types based on the query set. For many informational queries, the user is more likely than not to get the answer they seek directly on the results page. There is no filter or dimension that can be filtered to determine if an AI Overview appeared. Thus, this creates a new challenge for SEO analysts. Analysts may even see a large increase in impressions for a given keyword but a major decline in click-through rate. Why? Users are searching but they aren't clicking because search engines are providing the answer.

This is the current "Wild, Wild West" of digital analysis. In addition to this lack of specific data, analysts are actively trying to determine how to measure how frequently their brands are being cited in AI responses ranging from Google to Claude, Perplexity to ChatGPT. New platforms are being developed, existing SEO platforms are adding new functionality to track these mentions, and new tools are being released frequently. There are also manual ways to create new tracking — writing your own code to track mentions in a way that works for your organization.

Unlike SEO and search engine results pages, when a user asks a question of a Large Language Model (LLM) like ChatGPT, there is no second page of results. The platform provides a direct response. How do you track those results? And when you do, what do you track? This is a priority for nearly every marketing team I talk to. Unlike the platforms discussed thus far, determining how to measure what could be referred to as the "word of mouth" response from an LLM is difficult.

Tip: Tracking Google AI Overviews Impressions

Given my goal in this text is to remain practical, if you're curious about writing your own code to track Google AI Overviews impressions and clicks, see the references for this chapter and the article entitled "*Google AI Overviews: How to Measure Impressions & Track Visibility*." Some platforms now exist that can help with this, however many are choosing to build their own. I'm not going to belabor this topic, but what I do want to cover is what we do need to track across platforms.

What is Zero-click?

The adoption of AI in search has produced a new user behavior worth naming. **Zero-click search** and related behaviors is simply a search completed by a user that does not result in an actual click to a website or other platform. Users find their responses via Google's map, knowledge panel, featured snippets, direct answer boxes, or AI Overviews. In 2019 (prior to AI Overviews' launch), SparkToro conducted an initial study with Jumpshot regarding user behavior and search. In 2024, a followup study was done in partnership with Datos that found that 58.5% of US searches resulted in zero-click behavior. By 2026, additional studies put the US figure at roughly 65% or higher meaning roughly than one in three Google searches now send a click anywhere at all.

According to DigitalApplied, there are two distinct forces driving zero-click search. First, search engine results pages (SERPs) utilize a number of new features from maps to Google's People Also Ask (PAA) which have been absorbing clicks for a decade. These tools allow Google to continue to monetize users by keeping them on-platform. Second, AI Overviews and other AI platforms have restructured the way users are using the internet compressing what should have been years of change into a single year. As an analyst, these facts create new challenges in determining how to attribute actions and conversions to marketing channels. If a user receives their information from search engines but it doesn't result in a click or conversion to something on the web, how do we track it? And, how do we attribute sales to the right source?

Attribution in Zero-click Environments

As you've probably sorted out by now, the internet changed everything about how we track analytics in marketing. However, the shift driven by AI platforms has created new challenges in how we track results — and, frankly, is pushing us back toward traditional metrics that are difficult to measure. Let's take a second and explain how attribution models work.

Side Quest: Attribution Models

One of the primary questions digital marketers have to wrestle with is which platform or marketing channel receives the credit for a conversion. While this seems like it should be easy, that's far from true. For instance, do we want to give credit for the conversion to the first ad a user clicks on or the last? Or, do they all receive some element of credit? There is no "best" way to sort out attribution as it all depends on your organization and your strategy. You may choose your attribution model based on how long it takes to drive a conversion (the length of your sales cycle), your marketing channel mix, your infrastructure, or even just what your team is capable of. No matter which methodology you choose, there are two real options: a **single-touch attribution** where one channel gets 100% of the credit or a **multi-touch attribution** where all channels get some percentage of the credit.

If you choose single-touch attribution there are two primary choices: first-touch or last-touch.

With **first-touch attribution**, your organization is likely focused on elements that are at the top of the sales funnel. So if your primary goal is to understand which channels do the best job of introducing new customers to your brand, first-touch attribution can do just that. For example, a user searches for "loudspeakers" in a Google search and visits your website for the first time. They then see retargeting ads on social media, go to YouTube and watch videos about your brand on your channel and search for you two other times to visit your website before they convert. None of those other brand touches will count for anything but the first search will receive credit for the conversion.

Last-touch attribution tends to be a popular choice as it gives credit to the last marketing channel used by the customer to get to you. That's great if your organization is focused on direct-response efforts like paid search, retargeting, or even Shopping ads. However, this also means that your advertising efforts near the top of the funnel (brand awareness efforts) will never be given any credit for the work they do to drive business. Another example: a user watches a YouTube video on your channel, finds your social media accounts and follows you, searches for your brand and visits your website twice, receives a retargeting ad, and then converts to business. The retargeting ad will receive the credit for the conversion.

Either single-touch attribution model makes it very clear as to who gets the credit no matter if it's for the introduction or the one that closed the deal. This makes single-attribution modeling very appealing as you can explain to an executive which channels work in seconds. What you can't easily do is explain the work of the channels in the other areas of the funnel. The channels in the middle receive no credit for the work that they do to drive the conversion.

Multi-touch attribution models solve this problem by giving credit to the multiple touchpoints across the customer journey. So instead of just giving credit to the first or last touch, all touchpoints receive some element of credit. There are four primary multi-touch attribution models: linear, time-decay, position-based, and data-driven models.

For **linear attribution** models, every touchpoint along the way receives the same amount of credit. At first glance giving the same amount of credit to each touchpoint makes sense, but we all know that not every touchpoint does the same amount of work. For instance, that retargeting ad that was on screen for 2 seconds that they didn't see versus the email that they re-opened 5 times before responding. It's clear that one did more work than the other.
With **time-decay attribution**, this is addressed on the basis of time. For instance, the more time has passed since the touchpoint, the less value it receives. So although their first touchpoint may have been a direct mail piece sent to them, they converted 6 weeks later following an email; thus, the email will receive more credit. That may work for your organization, but it limits the value of that first touchpoint.

Position-based attribution attempts to fix the problems with time-decay by providing the majority of the credit to the first- and last-touchpoints and leaving the remainder for the channels in the middle. This is typically divided as 40% for the first, 20% for those in the middle, and 40% for the last touchpoint. This assumes the value created in marketing is at the beginning and the end and focuses on optimization at those phases. But, if selling your goods and services requires education, then are we undervaluing that effort as well?

The final multi-touch attribution model is **data-driven**. This approach doesn't use as many rules, but uses machine learning to determine which touchpoints correlate with conversions. This is the most accurate view of attribution but also likely the most costly and may not be feasible for small businesses.

No matter the attribution model, determining how zero-click behavior impacts attribution is important. All of these models rely heavily on accessible digital data to operate. What these models cannot account for are broad advertising channels like magazine advertising, billboards, traditional television advertising, etc. They also cannot account for untrackable metrics like if the user "saw" your name mentioned in an AI response from Claude or in a citation in a Google AI Overviews search response.

In digital analytics, we've traditionally utilized the last-touch attribution model as it provided the cleanest alternative to track who gets credit for a given conversion or click. We've also frequently used any of the multi-touch attribution models based on the organization type (position-based is great for B2B so we invest in the top and bottom of the funnel / time-decay can be great for e-commerce, etc.) With the widespread adoption of AI, last-click has become practically obsolete as we have little to no insight as to how AI responses may have impacted the user forcing marketers to utilize more qualitative metrics in determining how well their search engine efforts are performing. That's not to say that you don't continue to track what's been presented in this chapter thus far, but it does mean that other metrics must also be considered. Thus, understanding how AI impacts not just search, but all channels, is critical.

Tip: But, which SEO software should I use?

I've already addressed some of the critical pieces of any SEO analytics marketing technology stack — Google Search Console, Bing Webmaster Tools, and an analytics platform. However, there's more needed. As I mentioned, the additional software platform you choose is entirely dependent on what your organization needs.

Some platforms are perfect for beginners as they are self-explanatory and easy to use. Other platforms fit the needs of a seasoned SEO pro a bit more as they provide details that other platforms simply do not. It all depends on how your team utilizes data and what resources they need to improve rankings. While you would think that by now someone would perfect the software — there is no perfect platform and each have pros and cons. Some may be more expensive while others are feature-rich but difficult to use. The list below is not exhaustive, but from my experience here are the pros and cons for some of the most prominent platforms.

Platform	Pro	Con
Semrush	Most complete platform that covers SEO, PPC, AI, & content	Expensive and can be difficult to learn
Ahrefs	Best database for backlinks and strong tools for keyword research	Weak in PPC and social & expensive to scale for agencies
SE Ranking	Best value for the cost and full-stack capabilities	Backlink analysis not as detailed as other platforms
BrightEdge	Enterprise-level platform & AI-driven SEO	Very expensive & may be too much for some
Moz Pro	Beginner-friendly & trusted	Limited depth in data and innovation
Surfer SEO	Best-in-class on-page optimization	Not a full SEO suite
Nightwatch	Best rank tracking	Focused on rank tracking
Morningscore	Simple	Lacks depth

Foundational Metrics for GEO

Now that we understand how traditional digital attribution models work, what do we do in this new era of zero-click? Marketers cannot track user behavior on platforms that they do not own no matter if it is single-touch or multi-touch. So when asked by finance or any member of leadership what channel drove the lead to conversion, the answer is simply all of them. As we've already discussed, brand awareness can be difficult to track and unfortunately, AI platform mentions and efforts put forth into Generative Engine Optimization (GEO) are just that — brand awareness.

Now, GEO and related measurements and analytics are entirely new to market. New tools are being developed daily and no platform has this entirely right. Most of what is being tracked by SEO / GEO / AI tracking platforms are the following:

- **Brand Mentions**: how frequently is your brand name mentioned in target prompts?

- **Citations**: how frequently is your brand name or website being cited as a source for information in target prompts?

- **Link Acquisition**: If provided a citation, is the AI engine simply mentioning you or linking back to your website?
- **Citation Prominence / Top-Cited Sources**: If your brand is mentioned, is it mentioned in the deeper response or as a main source for information?

- **Competitive Benchmarking**: How much of the share of available mentions for your target prompts are you or your competitors?

Ethan Crump of SEO / GEO / content marketing agency Foundation believes that the solution to GEO metrics revolves around three primary pillars: visibility, citation, and sentiment. Visibility as a metric shows how frequently you appear in AI results. Citation shows whether AI sees you as a credible source and worth quoting. Sentiment shows whether that visibility hurts or benefits your organization.

Each of these categories has related metrics that can be manually calculated or eventually calculated by AI tracking platforms. They also include the aforementioned analytical metrics as a count of mentions, citations, and competitive benchmarking. Let's break down Crump's metrics based on category and how each of them work.

In Visibility, Crump states that we should measure **Share of Model (SoM), Generative Position**, and **Query Coverage**. To track SoM, a marketer would need to use an AI tracking tool like that provided by SE Ranking or otherwise to measure the percentage of responses where your brand appears across priority prompts.

Competitors ↓	ChatGPT	Google AI Mode	Google AI Overviews	Google Gemini	Microsoft Copilot	Perplexity
Clio Selected	32.9%	46.6%	46.8%	47.8%	34%	39.9%
Google	20%	17.3%	20.4%	20.8%	13.4%	17.2%
MyCase	9.7%	17%	17.3%	22.7%	13.8%	10.3%
PracticePanther	11%	11.7%	10.9%	14.4%	6.7%	6.3%
LawRank	4.3%	9.4%	10.2%	17.7%	5.6%	7.7%
Filevine	5%	8%	8.7%	11.2%	7%	7.8%
Lawmatics	8.5%	7.3%	7.5%	9.6%	6.8%	6.2%
Microsoft	6.2%	7.9%	6.3%	9.8%	4.8%	6.9%
Rankings.io	2.3%	6.3%	7.8%	12.2%	6.6%	5.2%
HubSpot	6.9%	6.6%	6.5%	7%	7%	5.3%

Source: Foundation

Even though these tools are needed to help gather the information, I've provided how some of these calculations work as we go throughout the remainder of this topic. Here's the calculation for SoM.

$$\text{Share of Model (SoM)} = \frac{\text{Responses mentioning your brand}}{\text{Total responses across target prompts}}$$

Once complete, you can see where your brand may be performing as compared to your competitors. Generative position is similar to search ranking but rather than tracking for keyword position, you're tracking AI answers from target prompts. Much like SEO, the goal is to be the first mentioned brand for a given phrase.

Insight: What is Query Fanout?

When an AI platform like ChatGPT or Claude is asked a question, it analyzes the question and then breaks the question into multiple, contextually-related subqueries. We refer to this as **query fanout**. These subqueries are run as simultaneous searches to help the platform determine the answer. Thus, a single question asked in a prompt actually results in multiple queries being completed simultaneously for the platform to generate a response.

Query coverage is a measure that determines whether your brand shows across all potential prompts where a high-value buyer may be seeking your product or service. According to Crump, you would track this metric using the top 15-20 questions that may be asked by AI regarding your offering. Then, map the query fanouts to see how the AI platform is determining the answer to your primary question. From there, you can identify content gaps where you may not appear but hope to. It's calculated as a percentage.

$$\text{Query Coverage} = \frac{\text{Target prompts where your brand appears}}{\text{Total target prompts tracked}}$$

Tip: Target Prompts Matter

Because AI platforms are so variable, it is impossible to know every query that your brand may be mentioned for. When setting up AI tracking, you have to decide what queries you want to track for your brand name. These are referred to as **target prompts** both in this text and on the platforms you'll be using to track visibility and citations.

The next metrics category is Citations. **Citations** are directly related to how frequently your brand is not just mentioned, but cited with a link as an authority. These are critical as they provide value both in driving traffic back to your website but also in that citations can add to your overall brand's authority on the web.

The first of these metrics is a simple calculation: **Citation frequency**. This calculation simply is how many times your brand and its related web pages are cited and include a clickable link or footnote back to those pages for your target prompts.

Source authority is the second of these metrics for Citations. Now it is possible that the source is your website. However, it's also possible that it's a third-party site that mentions your brand. If it is a third-party site, referencing the site's authority score — or your own understanding of that site's authority — is important. Being cited in an article by Fortune Magazine and being cited in another company's blog are two different levels of authority.

The last metric mentioned is Citation drift. **Citation drift** is how frequently your brand's coverage fluctuates or is replaced by a competitor or another source as the AI model utilizes different sources. This can help you as an analyst understand how much value the model places in your site or the content that you provide.

The third and final category mentioned is Sentiment. Sentiment has become an area of interest since the invention of social media as marketers seek to not just understand how frequently their brand is mentioned but to understand how consumers feel about the brand. Crump suggests three primary metrics here: sentiment score, hallucination rate, and comparative positioning.

Sentiment score is simply a measure of the tone used to describe the brand. Does the LLM describe the brand in a positive, neutral, or negative light? This is likely related directly to other brand mentions across the web including reviews which are becoming critical to the fabric of any organization's sentiment score across platforms. To track sentiment score, categories must be created and a determination of how your brand classifies positive, neutral, and negative tone to determine a score. This is typically scored on a range from -1 to +1 (or as a percentage -100% to +100%). Neutral mentions means the brand could trend toward zero which also is an interesting finding.

$$\text{Sentiment Score} = \frac{(\text{Positive mentions - Negative mentions})}{\text{Total mentions}}$$

Hallucination rate is how frequently information is incorrect. While many times it seems that AI platforms are capturing factual information from the web, that's not always true. In 2025, our agency received a phone call from a client discussing how a local newspaper had run a story about an upcoming event that they were holding that was not true. The event had been held two years prior; however, in a ChatGPT search, the LLM told the reporter it was an annual event and even provided the date for the current year! To determine hallucination rate, one simply needs to log how frequently data is incorrect and track over time. Updating content on your website or deleting old content that is no longer relevant can decrease the rate of hallucination.

Last is **competitive positioning**. When your organization and a competitor both appear in a response, who is mentioned first? To track, simply review the number of times you appear first and the number of times your competitor appears first.

Insight: Google Search Console Adds Social Reporting

Just days before sending this book to print, Google announced a new feature in Google Search Console that allows creators and publishers to see the performance or rankability of social posts inside of the platform. The initial release stated that this includes posts from Instagram, TikTok, X, and YouTube. This is a major addition to GSC and reflects how much weight Google gives relevant content and social media — and emphasizes the value citations and social mentions carry in its algorithm.

While none of these metrics result in direct attribution or provide tracking in a way that drives direct conversion, they are important as they are becoming a major part of digital analytics and how marketers and analysts look at success on the web.

As you've read, AI platforms are driving a lot of interest on the web, paid search has been a mainstay in how brands drive direct demand, and it deserves more room than a closing paragraph can give it. We'll take it up in full in Chapter 6.

References

Bellin, K. (2025, October 23). *Why Google Search Console Impressions fell (and why that's not good)*. Search Engine Land. https://searchengineland.com/why-google-search-console-impressions-dropped-interpret-data-463677

Bing Webmaster Tools or Google Search Console: A Comparison. (2024, August 20). Microsoft Bing Blogs. https://blogs.bing.com/webmaster/August-2024/Bing-Webmaster-Tools-or-Google-Search-Console-A-Comparison

Crump, E. (2026, May 30). *GEO Metrics: How to Measure Visibility, Trust, and Brand Presence in AI Search*. Foundation. https://foundationinc.co/lab/geo-metrics

Digital Applied Team (2026, April 5). *Zero-Click Search Statistics 2026: Complete Data Guide*. DigitalApplied. https://www.digitalapplied.com/blog/zero-click-search-statistics-2026-complete-data

Evaluating page experience for a better web. (2020, May 28). Google Search Central. https://developers.google.com/search/blog/2020/05/evaluating-page-experience

Google Click-Through Rates (CTRs) by Ranking Position in 2026. (2025, May 28). First Page Sage. https://firstpagesage.com/reports/google-click-through-rates-ctrs-by-ranking-position/

In-Depth guide to how Google Search works. (n.d.). Google Search Central. https://developers.google.com/search/docs/fundamentals/how-search-works

Introducing INP to Core Web Vitals. (2023, May 10). Google Search Central. https://developers.google.com/search/blog/2023/05/introducing-inp

King, M. (2022, September 6). *Why Google Search Console & Google Analytics Data Never Matches*. iPullRank. https://ipullrank.com/why-google-search-console-google-analytics-data-never-matches

Law, R. & Guan, X. (2025, October 22). 96.98% of Clicks Happen in the Top 20 Search Results. Ahrefs. https://www.ahrefs.com/blog/almost-all-clicks-happen-in-the-top-10-results/

Mmeje, C. (2024, November 21). *What is an XML Sitemap? SEO Benefits and Examples*. Moz. https://moz.com/learn/seo/xml-sitemaps

Pattoli, M. (2026, February 8). *Marketing Attribution Frameworks: A Complete Guide to Measuring What Actually Drives Revenue*. Cometly. https://www.cometly.com/post/marketing-attribution-frameworks-complete-guide

Postol, A. (2024, November 20). SE Ranking's Local Marketing Tool: How to get your business on the map. SE Ranking. https://www.seranking.com/blog/local-marketing-tool/

Ranking Results. (n.d.). Google Search. https://www.google.com/intl/en_us/search/howsearchworks/how-search-works/ranking-results

SEO Dashboard. (n.d.). SEMRush. https://www.semrush.com/kb/1195-seo-dashboard

Southern, M. (2026, July 7). *Google Search Console Adds Reports For Social Posts*. Search Engine Journal. https://www.searchenginejournal.com/google-search-console-adds-social-video-platform-properties/581634/

Sullivan, A., Song, H., & Moreno, N. (n.d.) *Towards a better responsiveness metric*. web.dev. https://web.dev/blog/better-responsiveness-metric

Wagner, J. & Pollard, B. (2025, September 2). *Interaction to Next Paint (INP)*. web.dev. https://web.dev/articles/inp

Chapter 6
Paid Search Analytics

Where organic search is a long-term strategy, paid search is built for quick return. Organic SEO and GEO require patience, consistent effort, and time before you see meaningful results. Paid search, on the other hand, can put your organization in front of consumers looking for your offerings quickly. That speed and precision are exactly why paid search advertising and its related analytics is one of the most scrutinized channels in digital marketing.

Paid search, most commonly referred to as pay-per-click advertising or PPC, is the practice of placing advertisements on search engines and paying each time a user clicks on your advertisement. Below is a sample of what the basic PPC ads look like when on Google.

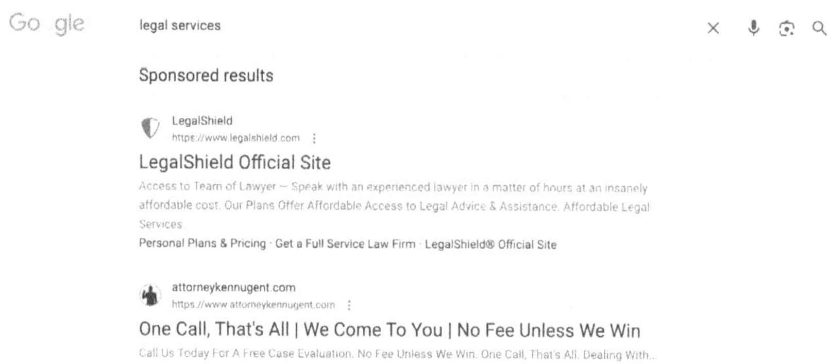

Source: Google

Google Ads (seen above) is the dominant platform for paid search by a wide margin in market share, followed by Microsoft Advertising (which serves ads across Bing, Yahoo!, and DuckDuckGo). Beyond these traditional search engines, paid search has expanded into other platforms including retail sites and what has come to be known as retail media. Retail media is a rapidly growing channel where advertisers place paid ads including search-style ads directly within e-commerce platforms like Amazon as well as directly on retail sites like Walmart, Target, Costco, and more. In addition, platforms like Criteo allow for advertisements to be placed across retailers, grocers, and — as of 2026 — even ChatGPT. Each of these platforms has its own set of metrics, nuances, and best practices, all of which we will cover in this chapter.

Understanding paid search analytics is critical not just for analysts and media buyers running these campaigns, but for anyone responsible for measuring marketing performance. These platforms are incredibly data-rich, and that data is available almost in real time. If your campaigns are performing poorly, you will know quickly. If they are outperforming your benchmarks, you'll know just as quickly. The challenge is knowing which metrics matter, what they are telling you, and how to connect them to the financial metrics from Chapter 2 and the goals framework from Chapter 3.

Before diving into the metrics themselves, it is worth taking a minute to understand how paid search platforms are structured. Whether you are working in Google Ads, Microsoft Advertising, or Amazon's ad console, the organizational hierarchy is nearly identical. This hierarchy matters because it determines where each metric lives — and therefore where problems can be diagnosed.

At the top of the structure of these platforms is the **account**. The account is your organization's relationship with the platform. It holds your billing information, your conversion tracking settings, and your overall performance history. Account-level data gives you the broadest possible view of performance including total spend, total conversions, and overall return on ad spend (ROAS which we'll discuss later), but it is rarely where you make decisions. It is where you take stock of your results across the platform.

Below the account level are **campaigns**. A campaign is where you set your budget, your geographic targeting, your bidding strategy, and your campaign type. Think of a campaign as a bucket of budget with a specific purpose. A retail brand might have one campaign targeting branded search terms, another targeting non-branded product searches, and a third running a seasonal promotion. Each has its own daily budget and its own strategic intent. When analysts talk about budget allocation in paid search, they are almost always talking at the campaign level.

Within each campaign are **ad groups**. An ad group contains a tightly related set of keywords and the ads that will appear when those keywords are triggered. The relationship between your keywords and your ad copy within an ad group directly affects your **Quality Score** which, as we will discuss shortly, has a meaningful impact on both your cost per click and your ad placement. Keeping ad groups tightly themed, meaning the keywords within a group are closely related to one another and to the ads being served, is one of the foundational best practices of paid search management and one of the most common areas where poorly structured accounts lose efficiency and effectiveness.

At the lowest level of the hierarchy are the **keywords** and **ads** themselves. Keywords define the search queries that can trigger your ads. Ads are what the user actually sees. Dependent on the platform, ads can include headlines, descriptions, images, AI creations, videos, callouts and more. Performance data then flows up through all of these levels. A single keyword's clicks, impressions, and conversions roll up into the ad group, into the campaign, and ultimately into account-level totals. This is why segmenting your analysis by campaign and ad group, rather than looking only at account-wide numbers, is so important. A struggling keyword buried inside a large account can quietly drain budget for months if no one is reviewing performance at the right level. I've seen this in a number of larger Google Ads accounts, especially accounts that have sat unmanaged for long periods of time.

Now that you understand some of the basics of paid search structure, let's start with the fundamentals.

The Basics of Paid Search Metrics

Paid search platforms are among the most metric-dense environments in all of digital marketing. When you log into Google Ads or Microsoft Advertising for the first time, the sheer number of columns, reports, and dashboards can be overwhelming. The goal of this section is not to walk you through every single metric available (that would take an entire book of its own), but to give you a practical command of the metrics that actually drive decisions.

At its core, paid search analytics builds on the same foundational concepts introduced in Chapter 5: clicks, impressions, and click-through rate. As a quick refresher, an impression is counted every time your advertisement is shown to a user. A click is counted every time that user clicks on your ad. Click-through rate, or CTR, is simply clicks divided by impressions. These three metrics are the starting point for everything else in paid search, and they will appear in virtually every report you pull. Frankly, these three metrics also show up in any paid advertisement on the web in some form or fashion.

What makes paid search different from organic search analytics is that every click comes with a cost. That financial reality introduces a set of metrics (and challenges) that do not exist in organic search and that connect directly to the financial concepts from Chapter 2.

Insight: Quality Score as a Secret Weapon

A higher Quality Score doesn't just improve your ad ranking — it directly reduces what you pay-per-click. Two advertisers bidding on the same keyword can pay very different CPCs based on the quality of their ads and landing pages. Optimizing for Quality Score is one of the highest-return activities in paid search management.

Cost Per Click (CPC)

Cost per click, or CPC, is one of the most important metrics in paid search. It represents the average amount your organization pays each time a user clicks on one of your ads. CPC is not a fixed number. It fluctuates based on the competitiveness of the keyword you are bidding on, the quality of your ad, the quality of your landing page, your bid strategy, and the time of day or week.

Both Google and Microsoft use an auction system to determine which ads appear and in what order. In this auction, your bid is just one factor. Both platforms also evaluate what is known as your **Quality Score** — a rating from 1 to 10 that reflects the relevance of your keyword, the quality of your ad copy, and the user experience on the landing page the ad points to. A high Quality Score can actually reduce your CPC because the platform rewards relevance and user experience. A low Quality Score means you may have to pay more than a competitor with a better-written, more relevant ad to achieve the same position. All Quality Scores are relative to your competition so when you consider Quality Score as a measure, the goal is to beat your competition in every category to generate the highest relevance for the end user (and the lowest prospective ad cost for the given keyword).

CPC is calculated simply as total spend divided by total clicks. Analysts look at the CPC metric in averages over given periods of time. Tracking CPC over time and by keyword is important because rising CPCs without a corresponding rise in conversions are a red flag as you are paying more for the same results. Conversely, if your CPC is declining while conversions remain steady or grow, that is a signal that your optimization efforts are working. This can even happen in the same ad group with different keywords!

$$\text{Cost Per Click (CPC)} = \frac{\text{Total Ad Spend}}{\text{Total Clicks}}$$

Increases in competition can also affect CPC. Consider this: an organization has maintained top positions and low CPC in a market. A competitor enters the market and CPCs rise. The competitor's landing pages are better and their ads are more relevant. The analyst notes that CPC is rising but how would they know how competition is doing? There are impression share reports, covered later in this chapter, that address this. but in addition, competitive data platforms like SpyFu can show you competitive ads and provide additional insight. I've watched clients' costs climb year over year, driven almost entirely by new competition entering the auction.

Tip: Negative Keywords

Historically when dealing with PPC efforts, my primary focus has always been improvement of CPC and Quality Score. Part of that effort is ensuring that the keywords in any ad group are relevant to the ads and landing pages they are sending users to after the click. In addition to keywords, marketers have controls that allow them to do all sorts of things: add other creative assets (depending on the platform) from images to brand callouts, and designate what are referred to as negative keywords — keywords you do NOT want to appear for. Given many of these platforms see your keywords as general ideas of what you want to rank for (not exact representation of your keyword selection), can improve Quality Score and CPC by filtering out irrelevant searches.

Cost Per Acquisition (CPA)

While CPC tells you what you paid for an individual click, **cost per acquisition** — also called cost per conversion or CPA — tells you what you paid for an actual result. CPA is calculated by dividing your total ad spend by the number of conversions generated.

$$\text{Cost Per Acquisition (CPA)} = \frac{\text{Total Ad Spend}}{\text{Conversions}}$$

This is one of the most financially meaningful metrics in paid search because it connects advertising spend directly to the outcomes your organization cares about, whether those are leads, purchases, sign-ups, or phone calls.

A low CPA is generally favorable, but "low" is relative. To determine whether your CPA is acceptable, you have to go back to the financial metrics from Chapter 2. Specifically, your CPA should be evaluated in relation to your customer lifetime value (CLV). If your CLV is $5,000 and your CPA is $200, that is an excellent return. If your CLV is $250 and your CPA is $200, your margins are dangerously thin. This is why analysts cannot evaluate paid search metrics in isolation — they must be grounded in financial reality.

Tip: CPA is more valuable with CLV

A $50 CPA sounds great until you realize your average order value is $40. Always evaluate your cost per acquisition against average order value when possible. Measuring CPA against customer lifetime value and gross margin is even better.

Return on Ad Spend (ROAS)

Return on ad spend, or ROAS, is the paid search equivalent of the return on marketing investment (ROMI) calculation introduced in Chapter 2. ROAS measures how much revenue is generated for every dollar spent on advertising. It is calculated as total revenue from ads divided by total ad spend.

$$\text{Return on Ad Spend (ROAS)} = \frac{\text{Total Ad Revenue}}{\text{Total Advertising Spend}}$$

For example, if you spend $1,000 on a Google Ads campaign and generate $6,500 in revenue, your ROAS is 6.5, meaning you generated $6.50 in revenue for every $1.00 spent.

ROAS is the primary efficiency metric for most paid search campaigns, particularly in e-commerce where revenue can be tracked directly. B2B organizations or service businesses where conversions are leads rather than transactions will find ROAS more difficult to calculate because the revenue value of a lead isn't always immediately known. Utilizing industry benchmarks — or better, baselines set by your own data — is great when possible. When it's not possible, assign an estimated value to conversions based on average close rate and average deal size — a practical workaround that allows you to still use ROAS as a decision-making tool.

It is also worth noting the difference between ROAS and ROMI. ROAS looks only at revenue relative to ad spend. ROMI, as discussed in Chapter 2, considers total profit relative to the full cost of the marketing campaign. ROAS is a faster, more commonly used metric in paid search reporting, but ROMI gives you a truer picture of profitability.

Conversion Rate

Conversion rate in paid search is calculated the same way as it is across all digital channels: conversions divided by clicks. However, in paid search it carries additional weight because you are paying for every click that enters the funnel. A low conversion rate in paid search can mean a lot of different things. It doesn't always mean your landing pages are struggling — but it always means you are spending money on clicks that aren't generating results.

$$\text{Conversion Rate} = \frac{\text{Conversions}}{\text{Clicks}}$$

When reviewing conversion rates by keyword, ad group, and campaign, you will often find variation. Some keywords may convert at 10% or higher while others convert at less than 1%. This data is useful because it allows you to shift budget toward higher-converting terms and pause or revise lower-performing ones. Sometimes those low-converting keywords can still play a strategic role as well. Industry conversion rate benchmarks can vary significantly. Commonly reported e-commerce campaigns often see average rates between 2% and 4%, while B2B lead generation campaigns can range from 4% to 8% depending on the offer and the audience.

Think: Conversion Rate Discrepancy

A campaign shows strong CTR and healthy click volume, but conversion rate is well below the industry benchmark. The ad spend is significant. **What are the first three things you would investigate, and in what order?**

Keyword Match Types and the Search Terms Report

One of the most common misunderstandings in paid search is the belief that a keyword is an instruction to be followed. "I've given you this keyword, now I want to rank for it and it alone." It is not. A keyword is a signal, and how literally the platform interprets that signal depends on the match type you assign to it. There are three match types: broad match, phrase match, and exact match.

Broad match gives the ad platform the most latitude. A broad match keyword allows for the keyword to be in your keyword set as well as keywords that are adjacent to it. For instance, using the keyword "running shoes" in broad match can trigger ads for "jogging sneakers", "marathon training gear", or "best shoes for flat feet". Broad match casts the widest net and, left unmanaged, wastes the most money as it extends past your primary keyword.

Phrase match requires the meaning of your keyword or the keyword itself to be present in the query. "Running shoes" in phrase match can trigger on "buy running shoes online" or "running shoes in blue" but should not trigger on "walking shoes".

Exact match is the tightest control, triggering only on your keyword and its close variants — plurals, misspellings, and queries the platform judges to carry the same intent. "Running shoes" simply means "running shoes" or its close variants.

Notice that even exact match includes "close variants." There is no match type that guarantees your ad appears only for the literal string you typed. This is why the search terms report exists, and why I would argue it is the single most useful report in a paid search account.

The search terms report shows the actual queries users typed that triggered your ads — as opposed to the keywords you bid on. A plumbing contractor bidding on emergency plumber may discover they are paying for clicks on emergency plumber salary and how to become an emergency plumber. Neither of those searches will generate a lead.

Reviewing the search terms report on a regular cadence and adding irrelevant queries as negative keywords is the most reliable — and least glamorous — way to lower CPA in a search account. In my experience, it is also the task most likely to be skipped. When our agency audits a neglected account, the search terms report is the first place we look, and it is almost always where we find poorly converting terms and wasted spend quickly.

Bidding Strategies

Every discussion of CPC, CPA, and ROAS eventually runs into a question we have been quietly stepping around: who is actually setting these bids?

In the early years of paid search, the answer was you. Manual CPC bidding meant a marketer set a maximum bid at the keyword level and adjusted it based on performance. That approach still exists, and it still has a place. But much of the spend on both Google Ads and Microsoft Advertising now flows through automated bidding — what Google calls **Smart Bidding**. The strategies you will encounter most often:

- **Manual CPC**: you set the maximum bid for each keyword. This is an approach I've relied on for years, but it is labor intensive.

- **Enhanced CPC (eCPC)**: your manual bid, with the platform permitted to adjust it up or down based on the estimated likelihood of a conversion.

- **Maximize Clicks**: the platform spends your budget to generate as many clicks as it can. Useful for gathering baseline data in a brand-new account. Dangerous as a long-term strategy, because clicks are not typically the goal for the account.

- **Maximize Conversions / Target CPA (tCPA)**: the platform bids to produce the most conversions within your budget, or to hit a cost per acquisition you specify.

- **Maximize Conversion Value / Target ROAS (tROAS)**: the platform bids to maximize total conversion value, or to hit a return on ad spend target you specify. This is the strategy of choice for e-commerce accounts with reliable revenue tracking.

Here is the part that matters most for analysts, and it connects directly to everything Chapter 3 said about data quality: automated bidding is only as good as the conversion data you provide it. If your conversion tracking counts a newsletter signup and a $4,000 purchase as the same event, target ROAS has nothing meaningful to optimize toward. If half your conversions are duplicate form fills, the algorithm will learn to buy more duplicate form fills. The platform is not evaluating whether a conversion was any good. It is optimizing toward the definition you handed it. Unfortunately, we've had to correct this missteps in accounts before. They typically happen when the account is given entirely to AI, and P-Max (which we'll discuss later), to manage.

Automated bidding also requires volume. A campaign generating three conversions a month gives the algorithm almost nothing to learn from, and target CPA in a low-volume account frequently performs worse than a competently managed manual bid. Google's guidance has historically pointed to roughly 30 conversions in a 30-day window as a working floor for target CPA, and more for target ROAS. Below that, your bid strategy is making decisions without enough information to make good decisions.

Finally, remember that changing a bid strategy triggers a learning period, typically one to two weeks, during which performance is unstable and should not be judged. I have watched analysts change bid strategies weekly and then report on the results. They were not measuring the strategy. They were measuring the learning period, over and over.

Ad Position and Ad Rank

In the early days of paid search, ad position was straightforward — you bid higher, you ranked higher. Today, both Google and Microsoft use a more nuanced ad rank calculation that considers your maximum bid, your Quality Score, the context of the user's search, and the expected impact of your ad assets. The result is that two advertisers with very different bids can end up in similar positions if one has a significantly stronger Quality Score.

Average position as a standalone metric was actually deprecated by Google in 2019 precisely because it was misleading. Appearing in "position 1" meant nothing if your ad was appearing at the bottom of the page rather than the top. In its place, Google introduced a set of metrics that more accurately describe where your ads are physically appearing on the page, which connects directly to the next major concept in this chapter: impression share.

An Understanding of Impression Share

Impression share is one of the most strategically important and most underutilized metrics in all of paid search analytics. If you take nothing else from this chapter, understand impression share. It has the potential to change how you think about campaign performance entirely. Impression share is the number of impressions your ads received divided by the number of impressions your ads were eligible to receive and displayed as a percentage.

$$\text{Impression Share} = \frac{\text{Impressions You Received}}{\text{Impressions You Were Eligible to Receive}}$$

In other words, it answers the question: of all the times someone searched for a keyword you were targeting, what percentage of those searches actually triggered your ad? If there were 1,000 eligible searches and your ad appeared 600 times, your impression share is 60%. The gap between your impression share and 100% represents opportunity and potential visibility you are currently not capturing. The platform will then tell you why you are missing that impression share, and this is where the metric becomes truly actionable. It is worth noting that the denominator in this equation (impressions you were eligible to receive) is an estimate produced by the ad platform based on targeting, quality, and auction data.

Insight: Impression Share Reframes Performance

A campaign with a 5% CTR sounds strong until you learn the impression share is 20%. That means your ad never appeared for 80% of the searches it was eligible to appear for. Impression share forces analysts to evaluate not just how well a campaign performs when it shows, but how often it shows at all.

Lost Impression Share: Budget vs. Rank

Both Google Ads and Microsoft Advertising break down lost impression share into two primary causes: lost due to budget and lost due to rank. Understanding which category is driving your impression share loss is critical because the solutions are entirely different.

Lost impression share due to budget means your ads are being limited because your daily budget runs out before all eligible searches have occurred. This is a common issue for organizations running campaigns with conservative budgets in competitive markets. If you are losing 30% of your impression share to budget, it means your ads are going dark for a portion of the day and during that time, your competitors' ads are the only ones showing. The fix here is straightforward: increase your budget, reduce your bids to make your budget last longer, or narrow your keyword targeting to focus spend where it matters most.

Lost impression share due to rank means your ads are eligible to appear but are losing the auction to competitors. This is a Quality Score and bid problem. Your ad relevance, landing page experience, or bid level is not competitive enough to earn placement for all eligible searches. The solutions here involve improving ad copy, refining landing pages, reviewing keyword-to-ad alignment, or adjusting bids on specific terms.

Absolute Top Impression Share

Beyond general impression share, Google Ads provides a metric called **absolute top impression share**, which measures the percentage of time your ad appeared in the very first position above all other ads and organic results. This is distinct from **top impression share**, which measures how often your ad appeared anywhere in the block of ads above the organic results — a block that can hold up to four ads on a desktop search, though often fewer.

For highly competitive branded terms or conversion-critical keywords, absolute top impression share is worth monitoring. Losing the absolute top position on your own brand name to a competitor is a scenario that should trigger an immediate response. It is also a useful diagnostic tool when you are trying to understand why a high-performing campaign suddenly sees a dip in conversions: if your absolute top impression share has declined, a competitor may have aggressively increased their bids against your terms. For instance, our agency frequently sees new competitors enter a client's market aggressively, and absolute top impression share is the first metric to show it. We also frequently see brands, specifically those in B2B service or installation-related industries, struggle with competitors creating bidding wars for keywords.

Search Impression Share for Brand vs. Non-Brand

Like the distinction between branded and non-branded traffic in organic search from Chapter 5, impression share in paid search should also be reviewed separately for branded and non-branded campaigns. Your branded impression share (how often you appear when someone searches your company name) should ideally be very high, close to 100%. If it is not, a competitor is likely bidding on your brand terms and capturing customers who were already looking for you specifically.

Non-branded impression share tells a different story. It reflects your competitive standing in the broader market. Growing your non-branded impression share over time, even incrementally, signals that your paid search program is expanding its reach to audiences who may not yet know your organization. Combined with conversion rate data by campaign type, this gives analysts a powerful view of both acquisition and demand-capture activity within a single channel.

Tip: Set Impression Share Benchmarks Early

Before making budget recommendations, establish a baseline for your impression share by campaign type. Documenting this number monthly allows you to clearly demonstrate whether budget changes, bid adjustments, or competitive shifts are expanding or contracting your visibility in the market.

Microsoft Advertising vs. Google Ads

When most people think about paid search, they think about Google. That makes sense — as noted in Chapter 5, Google commands roughly 90% of global search market share as of early 2026. But dismissing Microsoft Advertising and the Bing network entirely is a mistake that costs organizations meaningful reach, often at a lower cost.

Microsoft Advertising serves ads across Bing, Yahoo!, DuckDuckGo, and Microsoft's own properties including MSN and the Edge browser's new tab page. The combined audience reach is significant, particularly in specific demographics that skew toward higher household incomes and older users. Microsoft's own audience research has long characterized the Bing user as older and more affluent than the average internet user, with a meaningfully higher propensity to shop online. For e-commerce advertisers and B2B marketers targeting decision-makers, this audience profile is worth paying attention to.

Insight: Import, Then Optimize

Microsoft Advertising allows you to import campaigns directly from Google Ads. This makes launching on Bing fast and practical. However, campaigns imported from Google should not simply be left to run on auto-pilot. CPCs, audience behavior, and performance patterns differ enough that Bing campaigns benefit from their own review and optimization cadence over time.

Where the Platforms Diverge

At a high level, Google Ads and Microsoft Advertising share the same foundational mechanics: keyword bidding, auction-based ad placement, Quality Score, CPC pricing, and conversion tracking. If you understand one, you can navigate the other. However, there are meaningful differences that affect both strategy and analytics.

The first difference is cost. CPC on Microsoft Advertising is generally lower than on Google Ads across most industries and keyword categories. This is primarily a function of less competition. Fewer advertisers are bidding on Bing, which means the auction is less intense and clicks are cheaper. For organizations with limited budgets, this means Microsoft Advertising can often deliver more clicks and sometimes more conversions per dollar spent than Google. That said, the total volume available on Bing is substantially lower, so Microsoft Advertising typically serves as a complement to Google rather than a replacement.

The second is audience targeting. Microsoft Advertising has a native integration with LinkedIn that Google does not offer. This integration allows B2B advertisers to layer LinkedIn profile data including job function, industry, company name, and seniority directly onto their Bing search campaigns. For a B2B marketer trying to reach CFOs or IT directors through paid search, this capability is genuinely powerful and has no equivalent in Google Ads.

The third is interface and reporting. Google Ads is more sophisticated, updated more frequently, and supported by a significantly larger ecosystem. Microsoft Advertising's interface is simpler and somewhat less feature-rich, though it has improved substantially in recent years. From an analytics perspective, both platforms offer comparable core reporting with some differences in how metrics are labeled and organized.

Tip: Audit Conversion Tracking on Both Platforms

Before presenting paid search performance data that spans both Google and Bing, confirm that conversion actions are identically defined on both platforms. Mismatched definitions — a "purchase" on Google versus a "thank you page view" on Bing — will produce data that cannot be meaningfully compared.

Metrics That Matter on Each Platform

The core metrics (impressions, clicks, CTR, CPC, conversions, CPA, ROAS, and impression share) exist on both platforms and should be reviewed consistently across both. Where analysts sometimes get tripped up is in how conversion tracking is set up differently across the two. Google Ads conversion tracking integrates tightly with Google Analytics 4, which is an advantage if your GA4 implementation is solid. Microsoft Advertising has its own Universal Event Tracking (UET) tag that must be installed separately on your website and configured independently.

If your organization is running campaigns on both platforms and you are reviewing aggregate performance in a dashboard, make sure your attribution methodology is consistent. A conversion in Google Ads and a conversion in Microsoft Advertising should be defined the same way and measured by the same standard. Inconsistencies in conversion tracking between platforms are one of the most common sources of reporting confusion in paid search analytics.

Which Platform Deserves More Budget?

The honest answer is: it depends, and the data should tell you. There is no universal rule that Google deserves 90% of your paid search budget simply because it holds 90% of search volume. If your Microsoft Advertising campaigns consistently deliver a lower CPA and comparable ROAS, that data is an argument for increasing Bing's share of budget. The goal is efficient conversion, not platform loyalty.

In practice, most organizations that use both platforms allocate the majority of their budget to Google while using Microsoft Advertising as a secondary channel to capture incremental reach and serve the Bing audience. Reviewing platform-level ROAS and CPA on a monthly basis and adjusting budget allocation accordingly is a reasonable and practical approach for most teams. The key is understanding your audience. If you find that a significant portion of your audience has a high proclivity to use Bing, then know that not advertising on Bing could be a mistake. At the same time, if your audience does not typically use Bing, then Bing may not warrant a meaningful share of budget. Be wise in how you manage the allocation, and you can find success on either platform.

Tip: Offline Conversion Tracking

Both Google Ads and Microsoft Advertising support offline conversion imports, which allow you to upload CRM data on closed deals back into the ad platform.

When configured correctly, this allows Google's and Microsoft's bidding algorithms to optimize toward closed revenue rather than just initial lead volume. For B2B advertisers with longer sales cycles, this capability can dramatically improve the efficiency of automated bidding strategies.

Google's P-Max: An Overview

If you have spent any time in Google Ads in the past few years, you have almost certainly encountered Performance Max campaigns, commonly referred to as **P-Max**. Launched broadly in 2021 and made the default campaign type for many use cases by 2022, P-Max represents a significant shift in how Google approaches paid advertising — and a significant challenge for anyone trying to understand what is actually happening inside a campaign.

P-Max is a single campaign type that uses Google's machine learning to serve ads across every Google-owned surface simultaneously: Search, Display, YouTube, Gmail, Discover, and Google Maps. Rather than creating separate campaigns for each channel, advertisers provide Google with a set of assets — headlines, descriptions, images, videos, and audience signals — and Google's algorithm determines where to show them, to whom, and when. The stated goal is to maximize conversions or conversion value across all of Google's inventory at once. In using P-Max, you are handing some, if not all, of the keys to your campaign to machine learning and Google.

What P-Max Changes for Analytics

From a pure performance standpoint, P-Max campaigns often "look" impressive. Conversion numbers are frequently high, and ROAS can appear strong. The historic problem, from an analyst's perspective, was that P-Max was a black box. The transparency available in a traditional search campaign — where you can see exactly which keywords triggered your ads, which ad copy performed best, and which placements drove conversions — simply did not exist. That criticism was loud enough, and sustained enough, that Google responded. Through 2024 and 2025, P-Max reporting improved substantially:

- **Search terms reporting** now surfaces the actual queries that triggered your Search and Shopping placements within a P-Max campaign.

- **Channel performance reporting**, found under Insights and Reports, shows how impressions, clicks, cost, and conversions are distributed across Search, Shopping, Display, YouTube, Discover, Gmail, and Maps. This was the single question advertisers had been asking since launch. One practical note: the data does not backfill to the beginning of your campaign, so early P-Max history remains dark.

- **Campaign-level negative keywords** are now available at meaningful scale, where P-Max originally offered no keyword exclusions whatsoever.

- **Asset-level reporting** now includes impression, cost, and conversion data alongside the older "Low," "Good," and "Best" ratings.

This is a real improvement, and it changes the analyst's job. P-Max is no longer a black box. While it's not a transparent window quite yet, I'd consider it to be like 'illegally tinted windows' on a car. With that said, caution should be taken in two specific areas.

First, visibility is not control. You can now see that Display is consuming forty percent of your budget and producing twelve percent of your conversions. You still cannot simply move that budget to Search. The reporting tells you what happened. It just does not hand you the levers to change anything.

Second, Google is incentivized to drive conversions — not to drive good ones. This is where my own experience is strongest, and it is not something the new reporting fixes. In B2B accounts especially, I have repeatedly seen P-Max deliver a high volume of conversions of genuinely poor quality. The algorithm is optimizing toward the definition of a conversion you gave it. If that definition is loose, or if you've allowed P-Max to run uncontrolled and its definition of a conversion has been trained, P-Max will exploit the looseness, at scale, and the dashboard will look terrific while your lead quality has collapsed.

There is also a well-documented concern about P-Max cannibalizing branded search traffic. Because P-Max can serve across Search inventory, it can bid on your own brand terms — terms that would have converted anyway, at a far lower CPC, through a standard search campaign. If your branded campaign and a P-Max campaign are both active, P-Max may claim credit for branded conversions it did not meaningfully influence, inflating its apparent ROAS and hiding the cannibalization inside a number that looks like growth.

Side Quest: Brand Exclusions in P-Max

In 2024, Google began allowing advertisers to add brand exclusions to P-Max campaigns, preventing P-Max from triggering on your own brand terms. This is a critical configuration step that is easy to miss during setup. If you are running both a branded search campaign and a P-Max campaign simultaneously, adding your brand name and common brand variations as exclusions in P-Max ensures that your branded traffic is captured by the dedicated branded campaign where you have more control and typically a lower CPC rather than being absorbed into P-Max's broader conversion count.

Always verify this setting when auditing a P-Max campaign.

To add brand exclusions: In Google Ads, navigate to your P-Max campaign, select Campaign Settings, and look for Brand Exclusions under the Automated Settings section.

As of 2025, P-Max now supports campaign-level negative keywords at scale: a control that did not exist at launch. Brand exclusions and negative keywords do different jobs: exclusions protect your brand terms; negatives filter irrelevant queries. Use both.

How to Analyze P-Max Performance Responsibly

Given P-Max's limited transparency, analysts need to be deliberate about how they evaluate these campaigns. Rather than reviewing P-Max in isolation, compare its performance alongside your other active campaigns. Look at overall account-level conversion trends before and after P-Max was introduced. If branded conversion volume shifted from your search campaigns to P-Max after launch, that is a signal of cannibalization rather than incremental growth. Experiment with asset group segmentation to understand which creative combinations are driving performance within the campaign. While you cannot see the full keyword data, reviewing the search themes report and the audience insights panel in Google Ads can give you directional information about who is seeing your ads and what they are searching for. It is also worth running structured experiments — available within Google Ads' Experiments tool — to test whether P-Max is driving genuinely incremental conversions or primarily capturing conversions that would have occurred through your standard search campaigns anyway. This kind of experiment takes time to run meaningfully, typically several weeks with sufficient conversion volume, but it provides the clearest evidence of whether P-Max is truly additive to your results.

When P-Max Makes Sense — and When It Doesn't

Our agency was recently approached by a client whose prior agency ran nearly all of their ads through P-Max. Once we gained access to the account, we found that P-Max was driving 'conversions' — but the quality of those leads was awful. Just by pausing the P-Max campaigns and creating new campaigns we managed, we immediately reduced wasted spend and drove higher quality conversions. Why did this happen and why didn't P-Max work for this client the way it should?

P-Max is best suited for organizations that have strong conversion tracking in place, a meaningful volume of historical conversion data for Google's algorithm to learn from, consistent management of the account, and a diverse asset library including video. E-commerce businesses with product feeds and well-organized Google Merchant Center accounts often see strong results from P-Max because the algorithm has rich product data to work with alongside audience and search data.P-Max is a more difficult fit for small budgets, new accounts with limited conversion history, or campaigns where granular keyword control is important. I've seen this poor fit more often than not, as B2B tends to require control, and agency clients expect agencies to manage keywords closely. The same is true for highly regulated industries where specific terms must or must not trigger ads. In those cases, traditional search campaigns with manual or enhanced CPC bidding often provide better control and more interpretable analytics. To be clear: P-Max can work for the right organizations — but ensuring things are set up correctly is critical.

Tip: Managing P-Max Campaigns Effectively

Early on in any Google Ads campaign, there is a period of time referred to as "learning" where Google and its related AI are working to determine what exactly you are hoping to accomplish. Make sure during this period that you closely monitor the types of searches you are appearing in as well as the value of conversions that may occur during this period. The information that Google collects during this period defines the type of customer and search behavior that will define the P-Max campaign over the long term. Early mistakes at this point in a campaign can lead to poor results over the longer term. So, while P-Max helps in "managing" your campaigns, just like the work of an analyst in general, complete data and accurate feedback can ensure P-Max is successful — if it's managed effectively from day one. If it is not, P-Max campaigns can blow up a budget, and drive poor quality conversions, very quickly.

Think: Evaluating P-Max

A client's Google Ads account shows a 40% increase in reported conversions after launching a P-Max campaign. Overall website conversion volume in GA4 has not changed. **What are the most likely explanations, and how would you investigate?**

Retail Media and Paid Search

One of the fastest-growing segments of digital advertising is retail media and thus it deserves its own serious discussion in any modern treatment of paid search analytics. **Retail media** refers to advertising placed directly on e-commerce platforms and retailer-owned digital properties, where shoppers are actively browsing and purchasing. Amazon Advertising is by far the largest player in this space, but Walmart Connect, Target's Roundel, Kroger Precision Marketing, Home Depot's Orange Apron Media, and dozens of other retailers have built their own media networks as well. Even advertising through Instacart — a platform spanning multiple retailers — is considered retail media. The reason retail media belongs in a chapter about paid search is straightforward: the mechanics are nearly identical. Advertisers bid on keywords, ads appear when users search within the platform, and they pay when users click. The core metrics (impressions, clicks, CTR, CPC, conversions, and ROAS) map almost directly to what we have already discussed. What makes retail media distinct is context. Users searching within Amazon or Walmart are not researching options in the early stages of the funnel. They are actively shopping. Their intent to purchase is often significantly higher than that of a user running the same search in Google, which fundamentally changes how you evaluate performance.

Insight: Retail Media is the Closest Platform to the Purchase

When a user searches "wireless earbuds" on Amazon, they are likely moments away from adding a product to their cart. That same search on Google could represent a user who is weeks away from making a decision. The proximity to purchase in retail media changes your expectations for conversion rate, CPC, and ROAS and those expectations should be set accordingly before any campaign launches.

Amazon Advertising: The Dominant Retail Media Platform

Amazon Advertising is the third-largest digital advertising platform in the world behind Google and Meta. Amazon offers several paid search ad formats, but the most relevant for this discussion are Sponsored Products, Sponsored Brands, and Sponsored Display. Of these, Sponsored Products are the closest analog to traditional paid search. They appear directly in Amazon search results when a shopper's query matches a keyword you are targeting, and you pay-per-click.

In Amazon's ecosystem, keyword match types work similarly to Google Ads: broad match, phrase match, and exact match each control how closely a user's search must align with your target keyword. If you skipped ahead, the discussion of match types earlier in this chapter applies almost directly here. What Amazon adds is **automatic targeting**, where Amazon's algorithm matches your ads to relevant searches without you specifying individual keywords.

Automatic campaigns are useful for discovery by identifying which search terms are converting so you can add them as exact match keywords in a manual campaign, but they require careful negative keyword management to prevent irrelevant spend. The metrics in Amazon Advertising should feel familiar: impressions, clicks, CTR, CPC, and orders (conversions). Amazon adds its own version of ROAS called **Advertising Cost of Sale, or ACoS**. ACoS is calculated as total ad spend divided by total attributed sales, expressed as a percentage.

$$\text{Advertising Cost of Sale (ACoS)} = \frac{\text{Total Ad Spend}}{\text{Total Attributed Sales}}$$

A lower ACoS means you are spending a smaller percentage of revenue on advertising, which is generally favorable. ACoS is the inverse of ROAS: a ROAS of 4 is equivalent to an ACoS of 25%.

Tip: Know Your Target ACoS Before Launch

Your target ACoS should be derived from your product's gross margin. If your gross margin on a product is 40%, an ACoS above 40% means you are losing money on every ad-driven sale. Establish your break-even ACoS from the product economics first, then set a target ACoS below that threshold to ensure profitability.

Amazon also offers a metric called **Total ACoS**, or TACoS, which divides total ad spend by total sales including both ad-attributed and organic sales.

$$\text{Total Advertising Cost of Sale (TACoS)} = \frac{\text{Total Ad Spend}}{\text{Total Sales}}$$

TACoS provides a more complete picture of how advertising is supporting overall business performance on the platform, particularly for brands that are using advertising investment to grow organic rank and reviews over time.

Walmart Connect, Target Roundel, and More

Beyond Amazon, Walmart Connect has emerged as the second most significant retail media platform for consumer packaged goods and general merchandise advertisers. Walmart's paid search product, Sponsored Products, operates similarly to Amazon's: keyword-targeted ads appearing within Walmart.com search results, with CPC pricing and conversion tracking tied to Walmart purchases. Walmart's first-party data is particularly valuable because it encompasses both online and in-store purchase behavior, giving advertisers insight into how digital advertising influences physical retail sales.

Target's Roundel and other retailer media networks follow the same general framework. The key difference across these platforms is the audience. Each retailer's shoppers have distinct demographic and behavioral profiles, and purchase data from their loyalty programs provides a level of targeting precision that general search platforms cannot match. A diaper brand advertising on a platform like Kroger Precision Marketing can target known parents who have purchased baby products recently, combining the intent signal of a search query with the behavioral signal of actual purchase history.

Criteo provides a single platform utilized by a number of retailers, giving marketers a 'one-stop shop' to place ads across numerous retailer websites. Criteo was also selected as one of the first partners to run ChatGPT advertisements, adding further credibility to the network.

Retail Media Analytics vs. Traditional Paid Search Analytics

While the mechanics are similar, there are important analytical differences between retail media and traditional paid search that analysts should understand. The most significant is attribution. In traditional paid search, you rely on website analytics (primarily GA4) to track what happens after the click. In retail media, you are advertising within a walled garden. Amazon, Walmart, and other retail platforms control the data, and your visibility into the post-click experience is limited to what they choose to share through their own reporting interfaces. There is no GA4 tag running inside Amazon's product pages.

This means retail media analytics is largely self-reported by the platform, which creates its own challenges. Consider Amazon's attribution window — the period of time after a click during which a sale can be credited to an ad. It is not a single number, and this trips up more analysts than almost anything else on the platform.

For Sponsored Products, the window is seven days for Seller Central (third-party) accounts and fourteen days for Vendor Central (first-party) accounts. Sponsored Brands and Sponsored Display use a fourteen-day window for both account types. That means two advertisers running an identical Sponsored Products campaign can report meaningfully different ACoS figures purely because of the type of account they hold. A sale that occurs ten days after a click will be credited to the ad in a vendor account and will be invisible in a seller account.

Also, because attribution accrues across the window, the data you pull today for last week's campaigns is incomplete. Sales are attributed back to the date of the click, which means a report you run on Tuesday will show fewer sales for last Monday than the same report run ten days later. Analysts who make bid decisions on data that has not yet had time to mature are not reacting to performance. They are reacting to an artifact of the attribution window usually by cutting bids on a campaign that was working.

As a practical rule: do not judge a Sponsored Products campaign on data younger than the attribution window that applies to your account. And when you compare Amazon performance to Google performance, remember that a seven-day Amazon window and a thirty-day Google Ads window are not measuring the same thing. Understanding the attribution window on each platform you work with is essential for interpreting conversion data accurately — and for comparing platforms honestly.

Another distinction is the concept of share of voice within retail media. Because these platforms are closed ecosystems, analysts can track how prominently a brand appears in search results for relevant terms over time: a metric that functions similarly to impression share. Some third-party analytics tools, including Helium 10 for Amazon and similar platforms for other retailers, provide share of voice reporting that can help analysts benchmark competitive positioning within retail search environments.

Think: Comparing Retail Media to Google Ads

Your organization sells a consumer product on both your own website (supported by Google Ads) and on Amazon (supported by Sponsored Products). Both channels report strong ROAS.

How would you determine which channel deserves incremental budget, and what data would you need to make that recommendation confidently?

Paid Search in AI Surfaces

Every metric in this chapter assumes a results page: a query is typed, a list is returned, and ads appear alongside it. That assumption is now under pressure in a major way. Google has begun placing ads inside AI Overviews. And as noted earlier, Criteo became the first advertising technology partner inside OpenAI's advertising pilot in ChatGPT in March 2026. Both are connecting brandsto a new platform that did not sell advertising at all a year before, and one that expanded to additional markets within months of launch.

I am not going to pretend to know where this settles. Anyone who tells you they do is selling something. What I will tell you is that the analytical fundamentals in this chapter do not change. You will still pay for attention. You will still need to know what an acquisition costs. You will still need to measure that cost against customer lifetime value and gross margin, exactly as we discussed in Chapter 2. What changes is the visibility. Early AI ad surfaces report far less than Google Ads does, and the discipline of asking "what is this platform not telling me?" — the same discipline this chapter has asked of P-Max, and of retail media walled gardens — becomes more important, not less.

Treat these placements the way you would treat any new channel: as an experiment, with a defined budget and a defined question. Do not move meaningful spend into a channel you cannot yet measure.

Making Data-Driven Decisions

All of the metrics discussed in this chapter are only useful if they inform action. Paid search analytics generates more data than almost any other digital marketing channel, and the risk of drowning in that data — reviewing report after report without arriving at a clear next step — is real. The discipline of data-driven decision making in paid search comes down to a few principles that experienced analysts develop over time.

Start with Goals, Not Metrics

Before opening a campaign report, you should know what question you are trying to answer. Are you evaluating whether the campaign's overall investment is justified? Are you trying to identify underperforming keywords to pause or optimize? Are you building a case for increasing budget in Q4? The question you are trying to answer determines which metrics you need to look at. Starting with the data and working backward to a conclusion is a common trap — one that often leads to cherry-picking metrics that tell a convenient story rather than an accurate one.

Connect your paid search metrics to the goals framework introduced in Chapter 3. If the organizational goal is revenue growth, your primary paid search metrics should be ROAS, total conversion value, and conversion rate. If the goal is new customer acquisition, CPA and impression share on non-branded terms become more relevant. The metrics should follow the goal, not the other way around.

Review Relative Performance, Not Absolute Numbers

A campaign generating 200 conversions this month is not inherently good or bad. It is only meaningful in context. Compared to 150 conversions last month, it represents growth. Compared to 400 conversions during the same month last year, it represents a significant decline. Paid search performance should always be reviewed against historical benchmarks (ideally year-over-year to account for seasonality) and against the account's own trajectory.

Beyond historical comparison, benchmark against your own campaigns. If one ad group is converting at 8% and another is converting at 1.5% for closely related keywords, that gap is an analytical insight and not just a data point. Investigate why the disparity exists. Is it the keyword match type? The ad copy? The landing page experience? The bid strategy? These questions are what separate reporting from genuine analysis.

Segment Before You Conclude

Aggregate paid search data can be deceptive. An account-level ROAS of 5 sounds strong, but that number can mask enormous variation underneath. When you segment by campaign, ad group, keyword, device, day of week, and geography, you will almost always find that a small number of keywords or campaigns are driving the majority of results and that other segments are actively dragging performance down.

This principle, which mirrors the Pareto principle, is nearly universal in paid search. Roughly 20% of keywords will drive 80% of conversions in most accounts. Identifying those high-performing terms, protecting them with appropriate budgets and bids, and either optimizing or eliminating low performers is the practical application of everything we have covered in this chapter.

Connect Paid Search Data to the Full Funnel

One of the most important analytical steps that is frequently skipped is connecting paid search performance data to your website analytics in GA4 and, where possible, to downstream CRM data. Paid search platforms report on what happens up to the point of the click and the initial conversion. But if your conversion is a lead rather than a sale, the story does not end there. Leads close at different rates. Some keywords produce high lead volume but poor close rates. Others produce fewer leads that close at a much higher percentage. And in some industries, sales cycles are simply longer, so leads take longer to close.

If your organization has a CRM system that tracks leads through to close, building a reporting bridge between your paid search data and your CRM data can transform how you allocate paid search budget. Rather than optimizing toward the cheapest lead, you can optimize toward the lead most likely to become a profitable customer. That is a fundamentally different and more financially impactful objective.

This type of integration is more technically complex and may require support from your IT or data team. But even a simplified version — where closed deals are manually tagged with their original traffic source and close rates are compared by campaign — provides actionable data that most organizations never have access to.

Insight: Paid Search Analytics is Continuous, Not Periodic

Unlike many digital marketing channels where monthly reporting is sufficient, paid search benefits from frequent review. At a minimum weekly reviews if not more frequently for active campaigns.

Budgets deplete daily. Competitors adjust bids continuously. Quality Scores change. The faster you identify a performance shift and respond, the less wasted spend accumulates. Set up automated alerts in Google Ads and Microsoft Advertising for significant changes in CTR, CPA, or conversion volume to ensure issues surface quickly.

Reporting Paid Search to Leadership

The final skill in paid search analytics, and arguably the most important for your career, is translating this data into language that resonates with organizational leadership. Finance and executive leadership do not care about impression share or Quality Score. They care about whether the money spent on paid search is generating a return, whether that return is growing, and whether the budget is being invested wisely.

Build paid search reports for leadership around a small number of financially grounded metrics: total spend, total revenue or lead value attributed to paid search, ROAS or ROMI, CPA, and year-over-year trend. Provide clear, brief context for any significant changes. If ROAS declined this quarter, tell the reader why — not with jargon, but with a plain-language explanation. "Increased competition drove up CPCs on our primary keywords, which reduced efficiency. Here is what we are doing about it."

That kind of reporting builds trust. And in the long run, building trust between the marketing team and organizational leadership is what ensures paid search programs continue to receive the investment they need to grow.

Paid search — whether on Google, Microsoft, or retail media platforms — remains one of the most measurable and financially accountable channels in digital marketing. The data is rich, the feedback is fast, and the connection between spend and result is clearer here than almost anywhere else in the digital marketing mix. But paid search is not the only channel where that kind of performance accountability is possible. As video continues to grow as both an awareness and a conversion driver across platforms like YouTube, connected television, and social media, measuring its impact has become one of the more pressing analytical challenges for today's marketers. In the next chapter, we will explore video analytics: what to measure, where to find the data, and how to connect video performance to the broader goals of your organization.

References

About ad rank. (n.d.). Google Ads Help. https://support.google.com/google-ads/answer/1752122

About impression share. (n.d.). Google Ads Help. https://support.google.com/google-ads/answer/2497703

About offline conversion imports. (n.d.). Google Ads Help. https://support.google.com/google-ads/answer/2998031

About Performance Max campaigns. (n.d.). Google Ads Help. https://support.google.com/google-ads/answer/10724817

About Quality Score. (n.d.). Google Ads Help. https://support.google.com/google-ads/answer/6167118

About target ROAS bidding. (n.d.). Google Ads Help. https://support.google.com/google-ads/answer/6268637

Amazon Advertising — Sponsored Products. (n.d.). Amazon Advertising. https://advertising.amazon.com/solutions/products/sponsored-products

Amin, S. (2024, March 12). *Retail media advertising: What it is and why it matters.* Nielsen. https://www.nielsen.com/insights/2024/retail-media-advertising-what-it-is-and-why-it-matters/

Coppola, M. (2024, September 5). *What is ACoS? Amazon Advertising Cost of Sale explained.* Jungle Scout. https://www.junglescout.com/blog/amazon-acos/

Criteo joins OpenAI advertising pilot in ChatGPT [Press release]. (2026, March 2). Criteo. https://www.criteo.com/news/press-releases/2026/03/criteo-joins-openai-advertising-pilot-in-chatgpt/

Google Query "Legal Services" (2026, May 26). https://www.google.com/search?q=legal+services&oq=legal+services

Goodwin, D. (2023, October 18). *Google Performance Max: What you need to know.* Search Engine Journal. https://www.searchenginejournal.com/google-performance-max/

Irvine, M. (2026, July 6). *Google Ads benchmarks for your industry.* WordStream. https://www.wordstream.com/blog/ws/2016/02/29/google-ads-industry-benchmarks

LinkedIn Profile Targeting. (n.d.). Microsoft Advertising. https://about.ads.microsoft.com/en-us/solutions/audience-solutions/linkedin-profile-targeting

Petersen, A. (2024, January 22). Retail media networks: A complete guide for 2024. Skai. https://skai.io/blog/retail-media-networks-guide/

Sponsored Products. (n.d.). Walmart Connect.https://www.walmartconnect.com/sponsored-products

Universal Event Tracking. (n.d.). Microsoft Advertising. https://about.ads.microsoft.com/en-us/solutions/tools/universal-event-tracking

Williams, R. (2024, August 14). *P-Max brand exclusions: How to set them up and why they matter.* Search Engine Land. https://searchengineland.com/pmax-brand-exclusions-setup-444321

Chapter 7
Social Media Analytics

A local salon posts a thirty-second video of the perfect styling for a Renaissance-style wedding. Within four days the video has 14 million views, 600,000 shares, and a wave of duets and stitches from accounts the brand has never heard of. The same salon spends three weeks and a real production budget on a polished campaign video about their services and new stylist. It is well-lit, well-scripted, on brand, and it earns 4,200 views.

Every social media manager or digital marketing director has lived some version of this story. Sometimes this behavior is easy to explain and other times, it's not. Social media analytics is one of the few areas of digital marketing where the gap between effort and outcome can be enormous, and where leadership most often asks a question that has no clean analytical answer: why did that one go viral? We will get to that question directly in this chapter, because it deserves a direct answer, but most of social media analytics is far less mysterious. It is the disciplined measurement of two related but distinct activities: organic content, which is posted for free and distributed to your followers — and, increasingly, to non-followers the algorithm judges likely to be interested.

This chapter will walk through the metrics that matter for both organic and paid social, platform by platform, (focusing primarily on organic) and will spend time on the question of virality not because chasing virality should be anyone's primary strategy, but because new marketers are asked about it constantly and deserve an honest, evidence-based answer.

Organic vs. Paid: Two Different Games, Two Different Scoreboards

Before looking at platform-specific metrics, it is worth being precise about a distinction that gets blurred constantly in social media reporting. Organic social media is content posted from a brand's own account that reaches an audience without any media spend behind it. Distribution depends entirely on the platform's algorithm, the size and engagement of the existing follower base, and increasingly, the algorithm's judgment about whether non-followers will enjoy the content too. Paid social media is content distributed because an advertiser is paying for impressions, clicks, or some other guaranteed unit of delivery, regardless of how an algorithm might otherwise treat it.

These two activities are often run by the same team, sometimes using the same piece of creative, but they should almost never be evaluated with the same scorecard. A paid post is bought attention; its core question is efficiency: what did that attention cost, and what did it produce? An organic post is earned attention; its core question is resonance: did this content connect strongly enough with an audience that the algorithm chose to extend its reach? Conflating the two leads to bad decisions, such as judging an organic post a failure because it didn't perform like a paid post with a media budget behind it, or judging a paid ad a success because it generated a lot of likes without ever calculating its cost per result.

Insight: Organic Reach Has Quietly Collapsed

Across most platforms, organic reach for brand accounts has declined for more than a decade as algorithms increasingly favor paid placements and content from friends and family over content from businesses. Hootsuite's 2026 benchmarks put organic engagement rates for Facebook brand pages in the range of a few tenths of one percent, with organic reach typically capping out at roughly 2 to 5 percent of a page's followers. This does not mean organic social is worthless. Organic social media remains essential for community, customer service, and credibility. But treating organic posting alone as a growth strategy on Facebook in particular is no longer realistic for most brands. Growth increasingly depends on partnering with influencers, or on turning individual staff members and corporate leaders into influencers themselves.

The Metrics That Apply Across (Almost) Every Platform

Before getting into platform-specific dashboards, there is a shared vocabulary that shows up everywhere, even though each platform calculates it slightly differently.

Impressions

What It Is: the total number of times a piece of content was displayed on a screen, including multiple views by the same person. In social media terms, this is the number of times a post, reel, story, etc. has been seen.

Views

What It Is: the total number of times a user actively engages with viewing your content. It's very similar, but slightly different from impressions on some platforms. For instance, on YouTube, an impression counts if someone sees the thumbnail of your video but a view means someone watched it for a period of time. On Instagram, the distinction largely disappeared in 2025, when the platform replaced 'impressions' with 'views' as its primary metric across Reels, Stories, and feed posts. On LinkedIn, an impression is counted when your post appears as someone scrolls their feed; a view requires them to expand or interact with it (watching a video for more than three seconds, expanding an article, or viewing your profile).

Reach

What It Is: the number of unique accounts that saw a piece of content at least once. If a post earns 10,000 views but only 5,000 reach, the average viewer saw it roughly twice.

Frequency

What It Is: the average number of times each person who saw your content was exposed to it. If a post earns 10,000 impressions against 5,000 reach, frequency is 2 — the average person saw it twice.

$$\text{Frequency} = \frac{\text{Impressions}}{\text{Reach}}$$

Engagement Rate

What It Is: the percentage of an audience that interacted with a post, typically measured one of two ways depending on the goal: engagement rate by reach (engagements divided by reach) for organic content, or engagement rate by impressions for paid campaigns. Engagements generally include likes, comments, shares, and saves, but exclude passive views. The formula for paid content is shown below.

$$\text{Engagement Rate} = \frac{\text{Likes} + \text{Comments} + \text{Shares} + \text{Saves}}{\text{Impressions}}$$

A post earning 320 likes, 40 comments, 25 shares, and 15 saves against 12,000 impressions has 400 total engagements. 400 ÷ 12,000 = 0.033, or a 3.3% engagement rate.

Click-Through Rate (CTR)

What It Is: the percentage of people who saw a post or ad and clicked on a link within it, most relevant for paid campaigns or organic posts with a clear call to action.

$$\text{Click Through Rate (CTR)} = \frac{\text{Clicks}}{\text{Impressions}}$$

Cost per Mille (CPM)

What It Is: the cost an advertiser pays per 1,000 impressions on a paid post. CPM is the foundational efficiency metric for paid social because nearly every other paid metric (CPC, CPA) is a downstream function of how cheaply a platform can deliver impressions.

$$\text{Cost Per Mille (CPM)} = \frac{\text{Total Spend}}{\text{Impressions}} \text{ X } 1{,}000$$

Cost per Click (CPC) and Cost per Acquisition (CPA)

What It Is: We defined these two metrics in the last chapter. As a reminder, CPC measures what an advertiser pays for each click; CPA measures what an advertiser pays for each completed goal (a purchase, a lead form, an app install). CPC tells you the price of a click; CPA tells you whether that attention was worth buying in the first place.

Social Mentions and Social Share of Voice (SSoV)

What It Is: Social mentions are simply the number of times a brand is mentioned across social platforms, whether tagged directly ("@brand") or referenced indirectly by name, and how that volume compares to competitors mentioned in the same conversation. Share of voice (or "social" share of voice) turns raw mention counts into a competitive metric: how much of the total conversation in your category is actually about you. It is measured as a percentage.

$$\text{Social Share of Voice (SSoV)} = \frac{\text{Your Brand Mentions}}{\text{Total Category Mentions (including competitors)}}$$

Virality Rate

What It Is: the rate at which people who see a piece of content go on to share it, expressed as shares relative to either impressions or reach. Unlike engagement rate, which blends several types of interaction together, virality rate isolates the one action that actually extends a post's distribution beyond the audience it started with. It is shown as a percentage.

$$\text{Virality Rate} = \frac{\text{Shares}}{\text{Impressions}}$$

A post with 900 shares against 60,000 impressions has a virality rate of 0.015, or 1.5%. Substitute reach for impressions when you want to know what share of unique viewers shared the post rather than what share of total exposures produced a share.

Tip: Save Rate and Share Rate Deserve a Shared Seat at the Table

For years, likes and comments dominated engagement reporting because they were the easiest metrics to see at a glance. By 2026, platforms themselves have signaled that saves and shares carry more algorithmic weight than likes, because a save means a user wants to find the content again and a share means a user is willing to put their own name behind it. A creator with a high save-to-like or share-to-like ratio is producing content that travels; a creator who only collects likes is producing content people enjoy but don't act on. When reviewing a content report, look at the ratio between these metrics, not just their raw totals.

Insight: Social Mentions May Now Matter More Than Backlinks

For two decades, search engine optimization ran on a simple currency: backlinks. The more high-authority websites that linked to your page, the more Google trusted it. Generative engine optimization (GEO) runs on a different and, in some ways, more social currency: brand mentions. Multiple 2026 industry analyses report that large language models weigh unlinked brand mentions on platforms like Reddit, LinkedIn, and YouTube heavily when deciding what to cite, even when no hyperlink is present at all, and several note that Reddit, LinkedIn, and YouTube already rank among the most-referenced domains by major LLMs.

This is precisely why social mentions and share of voice, introduced above, deserve a place in a modern analytics report rather than being treated as a vanity metric left over from the era of social listening. A brand that is frequently and positively mentioned across social platforms is building the same kind of distributed authority that used to require a backlink to prove. Virality rate matters here too: content that gets shared widely doesn't just reach more people in the moment, it seeds more of the unlinked, conversational mentions that generative engines increasingly use to decide who to cite. In other words, a strong social media program is no longer just a brand awareness or engagement play. It is quietly becoming part of the off-page SEO and GEO stack, and marketers who only track mentions for sentiment purposes are likely under-reporting their actual value to the organization.

Platform-by-Platform: What to Actually Measure

Each major platform was built around a different behavior, and that shapes both how content performs on it and which metrics matter most. Note that these platforms frequently change, and content performance can shift with them in a moment's notice. The table on the following page offers a starting orientation, and the sections that follow go deeper on each platform's organic and paid analytics.

Platform	Best for Organic	Best for Paid	Defining Metric
Facebook	Community groups, customer service, longer-form updates	Broad reach, lower-cost and retargeting options at scale	Reach and CPM / organic engagement rate is now minimal without virality
Instagram	Visual storytelling, carousels, reels for discovery	Mid-funnel consideration; strong creative-led targeting	Shares and saves / reach follows shareability
TikTok	Algorithmic discovery that is independent of follower count	Low-cost reach and high engagement with younger audiences	Watch time / completion rates / these two metrics drive the algorithm
X (Twitter)	Real-time commentary, customer service, trends	Lowest-cost reach of major social platforms; weak for sustained growth	Impressions and reply / quote activity
LinkedIn	Creating individual influence as business leaders	Reaching targeted business audiences by title, role, or industry	Engagement rate, click-through rate

Facebook

Facebook's organic and paid data both live inside Meta Business Suite and Ads Manager. Organically, Facebook now functions less like a discovery platform and more like a community and customer-service hub; brand pages that post twice a week in a relevant, conversational tone tend to outperform pages that post daily with generic content, because Facebook's algorithm rewards relevance over volume. Video, particularly Reels, is one of the few organic formats still earning meaningful reach on the platform. On the paid side, Facebook remains one of the most cost-efficient channels for broad-reach awareness and retargeting, with CPMs typically in the range of $7 to $8 and click-through rates between roughly 0.7% and 1.5% which is healthy by historical paid-social standards even as organic performance has declined.

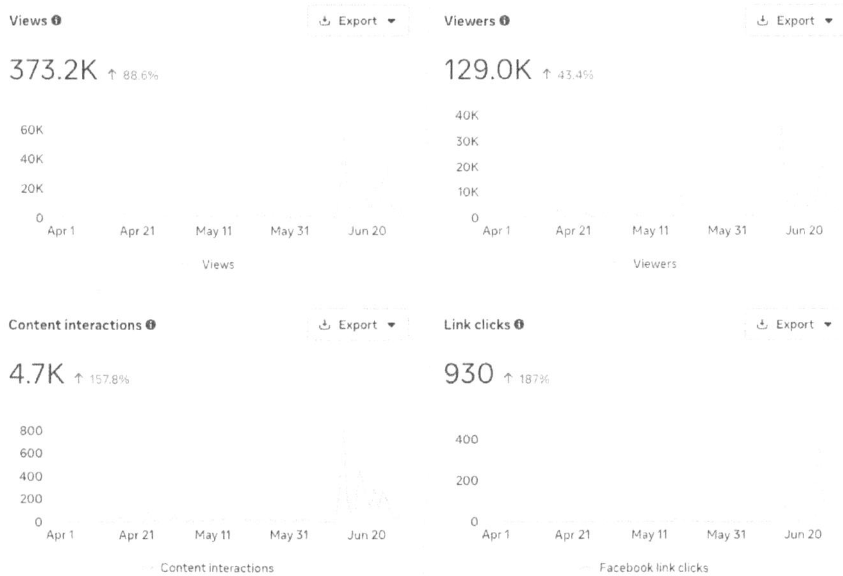

Source: Meta Business Suite

As seen above, additional metrics like views (how many times a post has been viewed), viewers (how many different people saw these posts), content interactions (likes, comments, and shares of content), link clicks (number of users who click links) and more are all seen in the platform. Remember that Facebook, and all social media platforms, want users to stay on platform. Why? Social media platforms make money through user engagement on the platform, not off of the platform, so the algorithm purposefully limits posts that include links or drive users off the platform unless through paid placement.

Instagram

Instagram Insights tracks performance at both the post and profile level, and as of 2025 the platform shifted its primary organic metric from "impressions" to "views" across Reels, Stories, and feed posts, unifying measurement the way TikTok already counted video views.

Organically, Instagram reach increasingly follows shareability rather than follower count: a post that gets saved and sent in direct messages will be shown to more non-followers than one that only collects likes, which is why carousels (often outperforming Reels on save rate) and short, high-value Reels both remain strong organic formats. The image below shows you how simplified reporting works in Instagram. Note that within the Instagram app, you can only track back history to 90 days so if you're manually collecting data, make sure to do so at least every 60 days to limit any data gaps that could occur. If you're using a third-party tool to track, sometimes these tools can hold your historical data on your behalf so just confirm what the platform is capable of before trusting that it's saving historical data.

Source: Instagram

On the paid side, Instagram tends to carry the highest cost-per-click among the major consumer platforms, often $2 to $3.50 depending on placement. Stories placements are typically cheaper than feed placements for the same campaign. It's important to note that outside of "boosting" posts (promoting a given post to both followers or non-followers of your account), paid media or advertising on Instagram typically takes place within Meta Business Suite.

Insight: Meta Business What?

During the pandemic, Facebook launched Facebook Business Suite, renamed Meta Business Suite in 2022, a centralized platform that allowed businesses to manage Facebook Pages, Instagram profiles, and other messaging tools (Facebook Messenger, Whatsapp) as well as their advertising all in one platform. Users can create and schedule posts, manage responses to messages, track analytics, etc. all in Meta Business Suite. If you're looking to start an advertising campaign in any Meta platform (Facebook, Instagram, etc.), it will start in your Business Suite. I'd be remiss if I didn't note that if you are using older Facebook or Instagram accounts for a business, you will need to work to merge these into a single Meta Business Suite account. This process can be very difficult because unfortunately many companies didn't do a good job of managing ownership, thus finding who has access to these accounts and who "owns" them can be an adventure. I can say from experience that it can take months to get these accounts sorted out if the business did a poor job of managing ownership.

TikTok

TikTok Analytics is built around the platform's central organizing principle: distribution is driven almost entirely by content performance, not follower count or social graph. A brand-new account with zero followers can outperform an account with a million followers if the content holds attention. That is why TikTok's defining metric is watch time and completion rate rather than reach — a video watched in full by 1,000 people will be pushed to a far larger audience than a video that reaches 10,000 people who scroll away after two seconds. TikTok consistently posts the highest engagement rates of the major platforms, and by a meaningful margin. With industry medians often in the high single digits to low double digits, TikTok ads typically deliver lower CPMs than Meta platforms. This makes TikTok one of the more efficient channels for both reach and engagement, provided the creative is built natively for the format rather than repurposed from another platform. The only challenge with TikTok is the content requires video and consistency for success. If the organization struggles with video content, there is no one on staff to manage the account, or their audience isn't on this platform as frequently, some brands choose not to use TikTok for organic or paid efforts. With that said, a lot of brands find a great deal of success on TikTok, it's just a matter of understanding your audience and ensuring they are present on the platform.

Insight: TikTok Shop is Collapsing the Funnel into a Single Scroll

TikTok Shop, the platform's native e-commerce feature that lets creators and brands sell products directly inside the TikTok app without a user ever visiting an external website, represents one of the most significant structural shifts in digital commerce analytics in recent years. Because the entire path from product discovery to completed purchase happens inside TikTok, a sale attributed to TikTok Shop will frequently never appear in a website analytics report at all as there is no landing page visit, no add-to-cart event, no checkout conversion tracked in GA4 or any other web analytics tool covered in Chapter 4. And, it's all occurring at scale as the platform grew from $9 billion in U.S. sales in 2024 to $15.1 billion in 2025, a 68% increase, with global projections toward $23 billion or more in 2026.

For a brand running both a traditional e-commerce site and a TikTok Shop simultaneously, this creates a real measurement gap: total revenue may be growing while website conversion rate appears to hold flat or decline, simply because an increasing share of transactions bypassed the website entirely. The practical implication for an analyst is to track TikTok Shop revenue as its own channel in whatever system of record the organization uses keeping it clearly separated from both website-attributed revenue and broader social media engagement metrics and to resist the temptation to judge a TikTok program's performance solely from a web analytics dashboard that was never built to see it. TikTok Shop's own Seller Center provides GMV (gross merchandise value), units sold, video-attributed versus LIVE-attributed sales, and conversion rates at the product and creator level, and these should be treated as the source of truth for in-app commerce the same way a retail media platform's dashboard (Chapter 10) is the source of truth for on-platform purchase attribution.

X (formerly Twitter)

X's analytics dashboard centers on impressions rather than reach, along with engagement actions specific to the platform: replies, reposts (formerly retweets), quote posts, and link clicks. Organically, X rewards real-time relevance — commentary on a trending topic, a live event, or a cultural moment will significantly outperform evergreen content, and the half-life of a post is measured in hours, not days. On the paid side, X consistently shows the lowest CPMs among major platforms, making it an inexpensive way to buy impressions, but follower growth and sustained organic reach have been flat to negative for many brand accounts in recent years. Most marketing teams treat X as a tactical channel for real-time conversation, customer service, and PR rather than a primary growth engine.

LinkedIn

LinkedIn occupies a category of its own among the platforms in this chapter because it is the only major social network where a professional identity, not a personal or entertainment one, is the primary context. A user scrolling LinkedIn is, at least in theory, in a professional mindset which is why the platform consistently outperforms every other social network for B2B lead generation and why its organic and paid analytics look almost nothing like what's been described in the sections above.

Organic content on LinkedIn benefits from a distribution model that still rewards text-based thought leadership posts and document carousels (native PDFs uploaded directly to the platform) at engagement rates meaningfully higher than most other platform-format combinations commonly between 1.5% and 2%, roughly five to seven times what a brand page would expect from a comparable Facebook post. LinkedIn's algorithm has explicitly and repeatedly prioritized content that drives comments and shares over content that only collects likes, which means conversational, opinion-driven posts from individual employee accounts tend to outperform polished brand-page content by a wide margin. This is a phenomenon commonly described as creator-led distribution.

On the paid side, LinkedIn's targeting capabilities are unmatched for B2B: job title, seniority, company size, industry, and skills are all targetable with a precision no other major platform offers, but that precision comes at a cost that surprises most new paid social buyers. LinkedIn CPMs routinely run $60 to $120 or higher (often ten to fifteen times the CPMs available on Meta) which means a campaign that would be efficient on Facebook at a given budget can be dramatically more expensive on LinkedIn for the same number of impressions. The trade-off is audience quality: a $90 CPM that reaches exactly the right VP of Engineering at a target account is often a better business investment than a $7 CPM that reaches a broad audience with a much lower percentage of genuine buying-intent users. LinkedIn's primary metrics follow the same organic/paid split described throughout this section: impressions, reach, engagement rate, and follower growth for organic; CPM, CTR, cost per lead, and conversion rate for paid. However, the platform also surfaces two metrics worth tracking that are largely specific to it: Follower-to-Connection Ratio on personal profiles used for thought leadership (a signal of how effectively an individual creator is building an audience beyond their existing network) and Content Download Rate for document carousels, which functions similarly to save rate on Instagram as a proxy for high-value, bookmark-worthy content.

Insight: Employee Advocacy Outperforms Brand Pages on LinkedIn

One of the most consistently documented patterns in LinkedIn analytics is that content published by individual employees, especially executives and subject-matter experts, reliably reaches a larger percentage of its target audience than the same content published from a company brand page. LinkedIn's own internal data has suggested that employees' combined network is typically ten to twenty times larger than a brand's follower count, and that content shared by employees generates meaningfully higher engagement rates than brand-page equivalents. This has practical implications for how an analyst measures a LinkedIn program's health: if organic brand-page reach is flat but employee-shared content is growing in reach and engagement, the program may be performing very well even while the most obvious dashboard number looks stagnant.

Influencer Marketing

No discussion of social media analytics is complete without influencer marketing, which industry estimates now put at more than $32 billion. At its core, influencer marketing is paid or gifted partnership with a creator who has built a trusted audience, and it sits at an unusual intersection in this chapter: the content itself is organic in feel (it looks like a normal post from someone the audience already follows) even though the relationship behind it is paid. That hybrid nature is exactly why influencer content needs its own measurement approach rather than being folded into either the organic or paid buckets we've used so far.

Influencers are typically segmented into tiers by follower count, and the tiers matter enormously for both cost and performance: nano-influencers (roughly 1,000 to 10,000 followers), micro-influencers (10,000 to 100,000), macro-influencers (100,000 to 1 million), and mega-influencers (over 1 million, often including celebrities). The data on these tiers tells a remarkably consistent story across nearly every platform: engagement rate moves in the opposite direction of follower count.

Nano- and micro-influencers commonly post engagement rates several times higher than macro- and mega-influencers, because their audiences are smaller, more self-selected, and more likely to feel like the creator is a peer rather than a celebrity. The tradeoff is reach: a single mega-influencer post can still outperform any individual micro-influencer post in raw exposure, which is why many of the most effective programs deliberately blend tiers rather than picking one.

Influencers can be hired by either reaching out to them directly or through agents (especially for macro- and mega-influencers) while influencers across all spectrums can be hired through platforms like JoinBrands, Cohley, CreatorIQ, Collabstr, Skeepers, Favikon, and many more. These platforms operate almost like a paid media platform where you can buy from multiple platforms, but all built to help you keep track of, and manage, relationships with creators and influencers.

Influencer Metrics

Engagement Rate (Influencer Content)

What It Is: The same engagement rate concept used elsewhere in this chapter, but benchmarked against influencer tier rather than against a brand's own historical performance, since a 2% engagement rate is unremarkable for a micro-influencer but may be strong for a macro-influencer on the same platform.

$$\text{Engagement Rate} = \frac{\text{Likes} + \text{Comments} + \text{Shares} + \text{Saves}}{\text{Impressions}}$$

Earned Media Value (EMV)

What It Is: An estimated dollar value assigned to the organic reach and engagement an influencer post generates, calculated by modeling what equivalent paid media would have cost to produce the same exposure. EMV is most useful for brand-awareness campaigns where a direct sale isn't the goal and a dollar figure is still needed to justify the spend to leadership. No single universal formula; most platforms and agencies model it from a blend of impressions, engagement actions, and estimated paid-media equivalent rates by platform and format. We'll come back to EMV in the chapter on Earned Media later in the book.

Cost per Engagement (CPE)

What It Is: The total cost of an influencer partnership divided by the number of engagements it generated. This calculation is used to compare efficiency across creators and tiers more fairly than comparing raw follower counts or flat fees.

$$\text{Cost Per Engagement (CPE)} = \frac{\text{Total Cost}}{\text{Total Engagements (Likes + Comments + Shares + Saves)}}$$

Let's say a $5,000 partnership that generated 2,400 likes, 180 comments, 95 shares, and 60 saves produced 2,735 engagements. $5,000 ÷ 2,735 = a CPE of $1.83.

Influencer-Driven Conversion Rate / ROAS

What It Is: These are two different calculations but related. Influencer-driven conversion rate is the percentage of an influencer's audience who complete a desired action (a purchase, a signup) after exposure, almost always tracked through a unique promo code, affiliate link, or tagged URL specific to that creator, since influencer content doesn't generate a trackable click the way an ad does. We defined ROAS in Chapter 6; here it is applied only to the tracked URL or code assigned to a specific creator.

Insight: Why Smaller Often Outperforms Bigger

Multiple 2026 industry benchmarks have found the same pattern: micro-influence commonly outperforms mega-influence several times over in engagement rate. That means a lower cost per engagement and frequently a higher conversion rate. It's sometimes called the "big sister effect" because recommendations coming from a creator who feels like a peer simply feel more authentic than those from celebrities. That doesn't mean that influencers with large followers are useless; it just means that your campaigns need to have goals. It could be you focus on reach per post with macro- and mega-influencers and engagement / conversion from smaller ones. For major product launches, usually reach is the goal so the higher the reach the better. The practical implication for an analyst is to never compare an influencer program's success purely on follower count or on blended average. Accurate measurement should be broken out by tier, the same way you would never judge a paid search campaign without segmenting by keyword intent.

Going Viral: An Honest Answer to the Question Everyone Asks

At some point, nearly every marketer is asked by a boss, a client, or a colleague: "Can you make this go viral?" That's a tough question because in my experience virality is roughly 80% luck and 20% quality effort. The luck portion is real and should not be downplayed: timing, cultural relevance, who happens to see and share the content in its first hour, whether a larger account picks it up, and the platform's algorithmic mood that particular week are all variables a marketer cannot control. The same video posted on a Tuesday versus a Thursday, or one day before versus one day after a relevant news event, can produce wildly different outcomes despite identical content. Most attempts to engineer virality on command fail, and the content that does go viral is disproportionately content nobody predicted would. I recently led a campaign with nearly 90 pieces of social content produced before and after a major international conference. Both the client and I thought that the major product launch would be the driving element for virality with their audience. We had spent thousands on developing content from product animations to video, interviews and more. However, I spent 20 minutes editing a short video from those animations for just one element of the product launch that we thought would be a "gap filler" content piece compared to the majority of the campaign. It went viral and that wasn't the intent! We couldn't have predicted the popularity of the post! That said, the piece was well done and it met the requirement for quality content. So, the 20 percent that is within a marketer's control is not nothing, and it is what separates organizations that occasionally produce viral content from organizations that never do. Good practice does not guarantee a viral outcome on any single post, but it dramatically increases the number of times a brand is positioned to catch the luck when it arrives.

Side Quest: Spotting a Fake Audience Before You Pay for It

Just because you see a high follower count does not mean the followers are real. Influencers sometimes inflate follower counts with bots or to drive engagement (or even purchase engagement). This is an industry-wide problem with some reports placing global losses from fraudulent partnerships and inflated follower counts in the billions of dollars every year. So, as you're preparing a campaign, here are a few things to look for: sudden spikes in follower count with no spike in engagement; generic, low-effort phrases in the comments repeated across a creator's posts; and, follower-to-engagement ratio well below benchmarks for the tier or compared to other creators. Audience authenticity is important and tools do exist that can check these signals if you're running a large campaign. Sometimes just a quick scroll through the comments section can catch the problem before the campaign starts.

The Content Styles That Go Viral Most Often

While no formula guarantees virality, certain styles of content tend to drive virality disproportionately among posts that travel far beyond a brand's existing audience:

- **Authentic, unscripted moments.** Content that looks and feels accidental (a genuine reaction, a behind-the-scenes mistake, an unpolished customer interaction) consistently outperforms polished, clearly scripted brand content. Audiences are highly attuned to detecting when something is manufactured to seem authentic, and they reward the real thing disproportionately.

- **High-arousal emotional content.** Psychological research on virality consistently finds that content triggering strong emotional arousal — humor, awe, sadness, surprise, outrage, or warmth — spreads further than content that is merely informative or pleasant. Low-arousal positive emotions like contentment rarely drive sharing; high-arousal emotions, positive or negative, do.

- **Useful, save-worthy formats.** Lists, how-to breakdowns, and document-style carousels travel because people save and revisit them, which signals strong value to the algorithm even when the content itself is unglamorous.

- **Trend and sound participation, especially on TikTok.** Content built on a currently trending audio, format, or meme inherits some of that trend's existing distribution momentum, giving brand-new accounts a way to be discovered without an existing audience.

- **Timely cultural or news-adjacent commentary, especially on X.** Being among the first relevant voices in a real-time conversation can produce outsized reach that has nothing to do with production quality and everything to do with timing.

Side Quest: How to actually Measure for Viral Success

If a piece of content does take off, don't just celebrate the view count and measure it like any other campaign. Track reach versus impressions to see how far it traveled beyond your existing audience. A high reach-to-follower ratio is the real signature of virality, not raw views. Track how the engagement works: a viral post driven by shares and saves builds a durable, repeatable asset where one driven mostly by passive views or controversial comments may have just generated negative noise. Track follower growth in the 48 to 72 hours after the spike since a true viral moment should convert some percentage of new viewers into followers. Also track downstream behavior to your other brand assets: website traffic, branded search volume, and (if applicable) sales, for the week following the spike, not just the week of. A video with 10 million views and zero measurable change in any of those numbers was attention without value — entertaining, perhaps, but not something to build a strategy around.

None of these guarantee a result. But a brand that consistently produces authentic, emotionally resonant, save-worthy, trend-aware content is simply rolling the dice far more often (and with better odds!) than a brand that posts polished, low-arousal, generic updates and hopes.

We've seen clients create virality on Instagram with real-time trends and well planned campaigns. But, as we mentioned it is 80% luck. One example: a major celebrity pop star's security team called a client and asked for a private tour. The client called our agency's social media manager for advice. The client said "I told them no because we don't do private tours. I didn't know who she was." Our team responded and told them to call back! They did and the pop star created a small viral moment for their social media account. It didn't drive conversion but it certainly drove reach! It does go to show, however, that understanding the cultural zeitgeist and the importance of knowing who / what is trending in the moment is part of analysis and social success.

Think: Chasing Virality or Building a System

Some social teams focus on trying to create virality and others focus on engaging their audience. Remember that on most platforms, organic posts are seen by your followers, not non-followers unless you create virality. So, if going viral is mostly luck, what should a marketing team optimize for day to day? Is it better to occasionally produce a viral hit or to consistently produce content that performs above the benchmark?

How would you explain to a client or executive why you can't promise a video will go viral without sounding like you're lowering expectations or making excuses?

Being Practical: An Example

Consider a mid-sized apparel brand running both organic and paid social in the same month. Organically, their Instagram account posts a behind-the-scenes reel of a warehouse employee dancing while fulfilling orders. It costs nothing beyond the time to film and edit, earns 2.1 million views, an exceptional 5% save rate, and drives a measurable spike in branded search and a 4% increase in followers over the following week. This is a textbook example of the 20% of good practice (authentic, unscripted, emotionally warm) meeting a piece of the 80% that is luck (the right algorithmic moment).

In the same month, the brand runs a paid Meta campaign promoting a new product line spending $8,000 at a $7.40 CPM buying roughly 1,081,000 impressions. A 1.1% CTR on those impressions produces about 11,900 clicks. At a $22 CPA, the campaign delivered roughly 364 purchases. No one expects or needs that campaign to go viral. Its job is to reliably and efficiently turn a known budget into a known number of sales, and by that measure, it succeeds completely without a single share or comment.

Reporting on these two efforts with the same scorecard would do a disservice to both. The reel should be evaluated on reach, save rate, and follower growth. Those are the hallmarks of earned social media attention. The paid campaign should be evaluated on CPM, CTR, and CPA. Those elements are the language of bought efficiency. A marketing analyst who can clearly explain both halves of that story, in the right vocabulary, is doing the job correctly even in a month where nothing the brand posted went viral.

In the next chapter, we shift from social platforms broadly to video specifically. In today's digital environment, video is increasingly responsible for the highest-performing organic and paid content across nearly every platform we've discussed here as well as YouTube and others.

References

Anjana, V. (2026, June 19). *Influencer Marketing Growth Statistics for 2026*. Socioapt. https://socioapt.com/blog/influencer-marketing-growth-statistics/

Babber, A. (2026, June 8). *Influencer Marketing Statistics 2026: ROI, Spend, and Performance Data*. BloggersIdeas. https://www.bloggersideas.com/influencer-marketing-statistics/

Beaton, J. (2026, March 27). *Influencer Benchmarks: Instagram Creator Stats for 2026*. Dash Social. https://www.dashsocial.com/blog/influencer-benchmarks

Cintra, J. (2025, October 22). *TikTok Shop Analytics 2026: KPIs, Attribution & Reporting Guide*. Dataslayer. https://www.dataslayer.ai/blog/tiktok-shop-analytics-2025-tracking-the-fastest-growing-retailer

Clark, P. (2026, April 2). *FAQ on GEO and AEO: Where AI search and SEO overlap in 2026*. EMARKETER. https://www.emarketer.com/content/faq-on-geo-aeo--where-ai-search-seo-overlap-2026

Crabb, J. (2026, June 4). *The Science Behind Viral Content: How to Go Viral.* Disrupt. https://disruptmarketing.co/blog/the-science-behind-viral-content/

Cucu, E. (2026, March 15). *LinkedIn organic and paid benchmarks 2026*. Socialinsider. https://www.socialinsider.io/blog/linkedin-benchmarks/

Eisenhauer, T. (2026, June 10). *Social Media Benchmarks 2026: Engagement Rates by Industry.* Apaya. https://apaya.com/blog/social-media-benchmarks

Generative Engine Optimization (GEO): The 2026 Guide to AI Search Visibility. (n.d.). LLMrefs. https://llmrefs.com/generative-engine-optimization

Going Viral on Social Media: How 2025 Algorithms Really Work. (2025, October 19). Orhun Ajans. https://orhunajans.com/en/blog/category-marketing/going-viral-on-social-media-how-2025-algorithms-really-work

Hill, C. (2025, June 26). *The social media metrics to track in 2026 (and why).* Sprout Social. https://sproutsocial.com/insights/social-media-metrics/

How to navigate Shop analytics in Seller Center. (2025, November 12). TikTok Seller University. https://seller-us.tiktok.com/universityessay?knowledge_id=813364865828654

Hu, N. & Newberry, C. (2026, April 14). *Social media benchmarks: 2026 data + tips*. Hootsuite. https://blog.hootsuite.com/social-media-benchmarks/

Influencer Engagement Rates By Follower Tier (2026): Exact Platform & Niche Benchmarks. (2026, April 14). Nowadays Media. https://nowadays.media/blog/influencer-engagement-rate-benchmarks-2026-by-platform-niche-follower-tier/

Influencer Marketing Statistics 2026: 150+ Data Points. (2026, April 6). Digital Applied. https://www.digitalapplied.com/blog/influencer-marketing-statistics-2026-data-points

LaTorraca, D. (n.d.). *What does Meta's Shift to Views From Impressions Mean for Your Social Reporting?*. Zoomph. https://zoomph.com/blog/instagrams-shift-from-impressions-to-views-what-it-means-for-sports-sponsorship-social-media-reporting/

Lauron, S. (2024, Sept 13). *The Complete Guide to LinkedIn Analytics.* Hootsuite. https://blog.hootsuite.com/linkedin-analytics/

LinkedIn Impressions vs Views: The Metrics That Can Make or Break Your Content Strategy. (2025, August 8). ContentIn. https://contentin.io/blog/linkedin-impressions-vs-views/

Lukes, J. (n.d.). *The social media benchmarks to guide your 2026 strategy*. Emplifi. https://emplifi.io/resources/social-media-benchmarks/

Martin, M. (2026, May 7). *Social media algorithms in 2026: How they rank content*. Hootsuite. https://blog.hootsuite.com/social-media-algorithm/

Meta Business Suite (n.d.). Buffer. https://buffer.com/social-media-terms/meta-business-suite

Mirkovic, G. (2026, June 18). *GEO vs. SEO: Everything to Know in 2026*. WordStream. https://www.wordstream.com/blog/generative-engine-optimization

Mohtasham, H. (2026, May 18). *What Is Social Media Reach? The Definitive Guide for 2026*. CUFinder. https://cufinder.io/blog/wiki/marketing-metrics/social-media-reach/

Moons, D. (2025, June 13). *27 Google Ads Benchmarks (2025)*. Store Growers. https://www.storegrowers.com/google-ads-benchmarks/

Newberry, C. (2026, June 16). *How to calculate engagement rate: 2026 formulas & benchmarks*. Hootsuite. https://blog.hootsuite.com/calculate-engagement-rate/

Ngugi, L. (2025, November 12). *Meta Marketing Benchmarks for Facebook & Instagram in 2026*. WebFX. https://www.webfx.com/blog/social-media/meta-benchmarks/

Perez, S. (2020, September 17). *Facebook launches Facebook Business Suite, an app for managing business accounts across Facebook, Instagram, and Messenger*. TechCrunch. https://techcrunch.com/2020/09/17/facebook-launches-facebook-business-suite-an-app-for-managing-business-accounts-across-facebook-instagram-and-messenger/

Sells, I. (2026, June 28). *TikTok Shop Seller Center: A Complete 2026 Guide*. JoinBrands. https://joinbrands.com/blog/tiktok-shop-seller-center/

Sergeev, S. (2026, May 15). *Social Media Benchmarks by Industry in 2026: TikTok, Instagram, YouTube, Facebook & LinkedIn*. Improvado. https://improvado.io/blog/social-media-benchmarking

Srivastava, A. & Paul, D. (2025, July 3). *Social Media Algorithm and How They Work in 2025*. Sprinklr. https://www.sprinklr.com/blog/social-media-algorithm/

TikTok Shop GMV Max Guide 2026 (2026, March 24). Vozai. https://www.vozai.net/en/ads-copy/tiktok-shop-gmv-max-guide/

Ultimate Guide to TikTok Shop Traffic Attribution (2026, January 16). Emplicit. https://emplicit.co/ultimate-guide-tiktok-shop-traffic-attribution/

West, C. (2026, January 13). *21 social media metrics you must track for success in 2026*. Hootsuite. https://blog.hootsuite.com/social-media-metrics/

Wong, L. (2026, March 9). *TikTok analytics 2026: The ultimate guide for marketers*. Hootsuite. https://blog.hootsuite.com/tiktok-analytics/

Chapter 8
Video Analytics

Ask any marketer what the most engaging content format on the internet is, and nearly all of them will tell you the same thing: video.

That answer has been true for the better part of a decade, and every year the data reinforces it. Users consume billions of hours of video content daily across YouTube, Instagram, TikTok, Twitch, Facebook, connected televisions, and a growing list of streaming platforms. Brands have followed that attention, and advertising budgets have followed in the same direction. According to eMarketer, digital video advertising spend in the United States alone surpassed $60 billion in 2024 and continues to grow. Marketers invest in video production, launch campaigns across multiple platforms, watch the view counts climb, and then struggle to answer a deceptively simple question: is it working? The reason that question is hard to answer is not a lack of data — video platforms generate an enormous amount of information. The challenge is knowing which data points actually reflect success, which ones are vanity metrics dressed up as performance indicators, and how to connect video behavior to the business outcomes that leadership actually cares about.

This is one of my favorite marketing channels for a number of reasons: I enjoy the process of creating video content and the power of video in driving real brand awareness can't be ignored. We're going to start this chapter with a brief history of online video and the strategic role video plays in marketing. We'll then dive into the specific metrics available to you across the platforms where video lives today starting with YouTube and extending to the social platforms where short-form video has become the dominant content format. By the end, you will have a practical framework for evaluating video performance that goes well beyond view counts.

The History of Video Online

It is easy to forget how recently online video became a normal part of daily life. For most of the first decade of the web (what we described in

Chapter 1 as Web 1.0) video on the internet was largely a novelty. Dial-up connection speeds made streaming anything longer than a few seconds almost impossible and definitely an exercise in frustration, and most websites were built around text and static images. Video files were large, bandwidth was limited, and the infrastructure simply was not there to support widespread video consumption.

That began to change in the early 2000s as broadband internet adoption accelerated. Adobe Flash-based video players emerged and made it possible to embed short video clips on web pages without requiring users to download a dedicated media player. An agency that I worked with developed a number of animations and video in this format and at the time, it was considered bleeding edge technology (which is funny looking at where we are now). News organizations and entertainment companies began experimenting with streaming clips, and the idea that the web could be a meaningful video distribution channel started to take shape.

The real inflection point came in February 2005, when three former PayPal employees — Chad Hurley, Steve Chen, and Jawed Karim — launched a website called YouTube. The concept was straightforward: a platform where anyone could upload, share, and watch video content. The first video ever uploaded to YouTube, an eighteen-second clip of co-founder Jawed Karim at the San Diego Zoo, was posted on April 23, 2005. It seems almost comically modest by today's standards, but what followed was anything but modest. By mid-2006, YouTube was serving more than 100 million video views per day. In October 2006, less than two years after launch, Google acquired YouTube for $1.65 billion in stock, one of the most consequential acquisitions in the history of the internet.

The timing of YouTube's rise aligned with the broader Web 2.0 shift described in Chapter 1; the movement toward user-generated content and the democratization of media. For the first time, ordinary people had a distribution channel with global reach. You did not need a television network or a production company. You needed a camera, an internet connection, and something worth watching. That combination unlocked a creative explosion that reshaped entertainment, news, education, and eventually marketing.

Insight: Giving Video Production to the Masses

Before YouTube, reaching a mass audience with video required a television deal or a substantial production budget. YouTube eliminated both barriers. For marketers, this meant video was no longer the exclusive domain of large brands with big budgets.

It also meant that consumers, not just brands, could now shape narratives about products and organizations, a shift that still defines the media landscape today.

The years that followed YouTube's acquisition saw video expand across the web rapidly. Facebook introduced native video uploads in 2009 and autoplay video in 2013, which dramatically increased video consumption within the platform. Vine, the short-form video app that predated TikTok, launched in 2013 and introduced the world to the looping six-second video format, a format that proved audiences had an appetite for extremely brief, highly repeatable video content. Twitter, which had acquired Vine in 2012 before the app ever launched, shut it down in early 2017. Many of its most popular creators migrated to YouTube and Instagram, where they built even larger audiences.

Instagram introduced Stories in 2016, borrowing heavily from Snapchat's format and bringing vertical, disappearing short-form video into the mainstream. Instagram Reels followed in 2020, a direct response to the explosive growth of TikTok, which launched outside China in 2017 and merged with Musical.ly in 2018 to become the fastest-growing social platform in history. TikTok's algorithm, which served content based on viewing behavior rather than social connections, proved to be a fundamental shift in how users discovered video content, and every major platform has since rebuilt its recommendation systems in TikTok's image.

Tip: Match Video Content to the Funnel Stage

A brand awareness video optimized for YouTube discovery is a different creative and analytical challenge than a product demo video embedded on a landing page. Before measuring video performance, define which stage of the funnel the video is meant to serve. The metrics you prioritize should follow from that decision. Measuring a brand awareness video by its conversion rate is like measuring a billboard by the number of purchases it generates directly. Many times those not in marketing struggle with understanding the relationship of the marketing funnel and marketing channels. Video is very powerful, but only if you understand the video's purpose and where it fits in your overall marketing strategy / funnel.

Connected television, or CTV, represents the most recent major chapter in the history of online video. As households cut cable subscriptions and shifted to streaming services like Netflix, Hulu, Peacock, and Amazon Prime Video, advertisers followed. CTV advertising, or placing video ads within streaming content viewed on television screens, grew from a niche channel into a multi-billion-dollar industry in the span of a few years. The analytical implications of CTV are significant and somewhat different from those of platform-based video, and we will address them later in this chapter.

Understanding this history matters for analysts because the platform you are measuring was shaped by the era in which it was built. YouTube's analytics reflect the sensibilities of a platform built for long-form, searchable, subscriber-driven content. TikTok's analytics reflect a platform built entirely around algorithmic discovery and short-form engagement. The metrics each platform emphasizes are not arbitrary as they reflect what each platform values and how it was designed to be used.

Leveraging Video for Marketing

Video's effectiveness as a marketing tool is not simply a function of its popularity. It is rooted in how human beings process information. Studies in cognitive psychology consistently show that people retain information more effectively when it is delivered through a combination of audio and visual stimuli compared to text alone. Movement captures attention instinctively. Emotion is conveyed more readily through a human face on screen than through words on a page. These are not marketing theories. They are features of human perception that video exploits particularly well. For marketers, video serves different strategic purposes depending on where it sits in the sales funnel introduced in Chapter 4. At the awareness stage, video is arguably the most powerful tool available. A well-produced brand video or a compelling short-form clip can introduce an organization to thousands of new potential customers in a way that a search ad or a banner simply cannot. At the consideration stage, product demonstration videos, customer testimonials, and educational content help move users from awareness toward intent. At the conversion stage, video used in email campaigns, on landing pages, or as retargeting ads can provide the final persuasive push that turns interest into action.

The challenge with video in marketing, and the reason video analytics is so important, is that video production carries a cost that most other content formats do not. A blog post can be written and published in a matter of hours. A well-produced video requires scripting, filming, editing, and often motion graphics or voice-over work. That investment creates questions and demands accountability. Marketing teams that invest heavily in video need to be able to demonstrate what that investment is returning, and that requires a clear analytical framework before the camera ever rolls.

Platform selection also matters strategically and analytically. The same video will perform differently across different platforms, not just because the audience demographics differ, but because user behavior and platform mechanics differ. A two-minute brand story that performs well on YouTube, where users often seek out content intentionally, may perform poorly on TikTok, where users are passively scrolling and will swipe away from anything that does not capture their attention within the first two seconds. These behavioral differences are reflected in the analytics, which is why platform-specific measurement matters.

One concept worth establishing before we dive into platform-specific metrics is the difference between earned video views and paid video views. Earned views are organic. Users discovered your video through search, recommendations, or shares without any paid promotion. Paid views come from video advertising, where your content is placed in front of users as an ad. Both matter, but they measure different things and should not be conflated in reporting. This can also apply between the goals of organic and paid metrics across platforms as each platform provides different opportunities as well. A campaign that drove 500,000 paid views and 10,000 earned views tells a different story than one that drove 510,000 views with no organic lift at all.

Insight: Video Views Are Not All Created Equal

An autoplay view counted after two seconds of a video playing silently in a feed is fundamentally different from a user actively searching for and watching your content for four minutes on YouTube. Both may count as "views" in platform reporting, but they represent completely different levels of engagement and intent.

Understanding how each platform defines a view is essential before drawing any conclusions from view count data.

YouTube Analytics

YouTube is the second most visited website in the world and often described as the second largest search engine, behind only Google. For marketers, it occupies a unique position in the digital landscape as it's part social platform, part search engine, and part broadcast network. Users search for something specific, whether that is a product review, a how-to tutorial, an entertainment channel they follow, or a music video. That search-driven behavior makes YouTube analytics particularly rich and particularly actionable.

YouTube provides two distinct analytical environments that serve different purposes. YouTube Studio is the platform's built-in analytics dashboard, available to anyone who manages a YouTube channel. It provides detailed data on channel and video performance including views, watch time, audience retention, subscriber behavior, and revenue for monetized channels. In addition, Google Ads (which we covered in Chapter 6) is the platform used for paid advertising on YouTube. It provides the analytics for paid video campaigns running on YouTube. Understanding which tool answers which question is the first practical skill in YouTube analytics.

YouTube Studio: Core Metrics

When you open YouTube Studio and navigate to the Analytics section at the time of writing, the platform organizes its data into four primary categories: Overview, Content, Audience, and Revenue (or Trends if your account isn't set up to generate revenue). For most marketing analysts, the Overview and Content tabs will be where the majority of your time is spent.

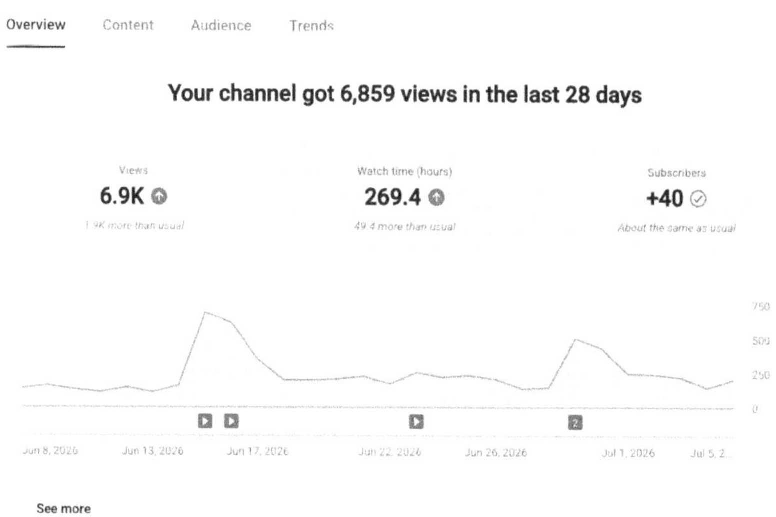

Source: YouTube

YouTube counts a paid view at 30 seconds, or the full ad if shorter. For organic views, YouTube has never published its threshold. It is widely understood to require meaningful watch time rather than a momentary autoplay, which is what distinguishes a YouTube view from platforms that count one after a second or two. That ambiguity is itself worth knowing: you are reporting a number whose definition the platform has not disclosed.

Watch time is the total number of minutes users have spent watching your content, and it is arguably the most important metric in YouTube Studio. YouTube's recommendation algorithm prioritizes watch time heavily. Videos and channels that generate more total watch time are more likely to be suggested to new viewers. This creates a direct connection between your analytics and your organic reach. Growing your channel's total watch time is not just a measure of success; it is the primary mechanism by which YouTube's algorithm amplifies your content to new audiences.

Average view duration and average percentage viewed are the two metrics that tell you how compelling your content is on a per-video basis. Average view duration is simply the average number of minutes viewers watch before leaving.

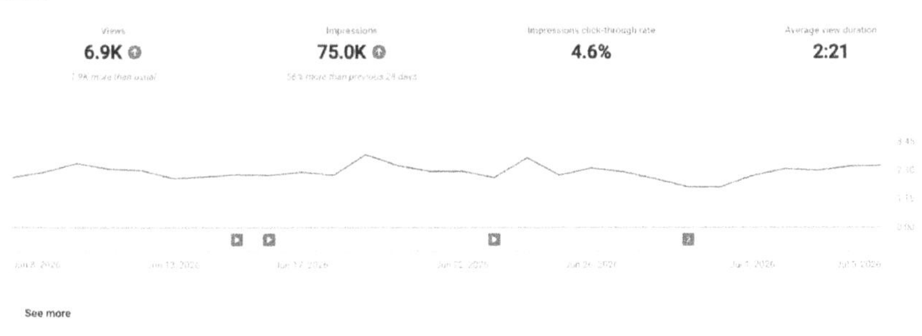

Source: YouTube

Average percentage viewed expresses that as a percentage of the video's total length. In the example above, notice that impressions × CTR (75,000 × 4.6% ≈ 3,450) accounts for only half the 6.9K views. Impressions-and-CTR covers only browse and search surfaces. The rest arrived through suggested video, external embeds, direct links, and playlists which appears in the traffic sources report. For this particular video, the traffic sources report shared that the additional video views were primarily from external embeds.

Tip: Use Average Percentage Viewed to Benchmark Across Videos

Comparing raw watch time between a three-minute video and a fifteen-minute video tells you very little. Average percentage viewed normalizes performance so you can meaningfully compare engagement across your content library regardless of length.

As a general benchmark, an average percentage viewed above 50% is considered strong across most content categories on YouTube.

Audience Retention: The Most Underused YouTube Metric

If there is one report in YouTube Studio that is consistently underutilized by marketing teams, it is the audience retention report. Available for individual videos, this report displays a graph showing exactly what percentage of viewers are still watching at every moment of your video's runtime. The shape of that graph tells you more about your content's effectiveness than any single aggregate metric can.

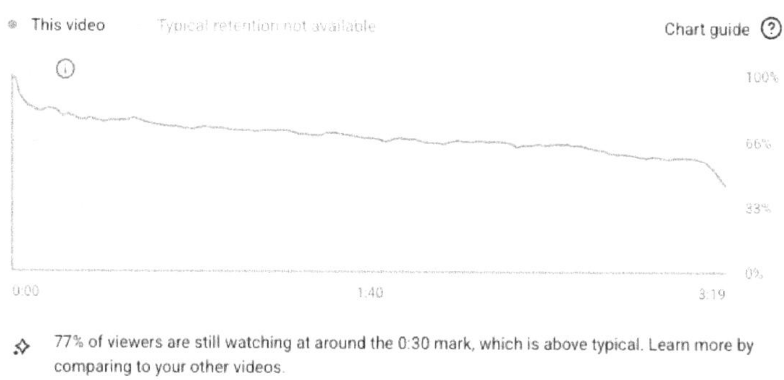

Source: YouTube

Most videos follow a predictable retention curve: a relatively sharp drop in the first few seconds as some viewers immediately decide the content is not for them, followed by a steadier decline through the middle of the video, with another drop at the end. Deviations from this curve are where the insights live. A sudden steep drop at a specific timestamp tells you that something at that moment — a transition, a topic shift, an individual scene, an unexpectedly slow section — is causing viewers to leave. A spike in the retention curve indicates that viewers are rewinding and rewatching a particular moment, which signals content they found especially valuable or entertaining.

For marketers, the audience retention report is a direct feedback mechanism on content quality and structure. If your video drops 40% of its audience in the first fifteen seconds, your opening hook is not working. If there is a consistent drop at the two-minute mark across multiple videos, your editing pacing may need adjustment. This kind of diagnostic information is exactly what separates teams that use analytics to improve their content from those that simply report metrics after the fact.

One client of our agency has found exceptional audience retention by finding the right structure for its content and using that structure consistently. The chart provided on the prior page shows this client's engagement on a recent video, which is typical for their efforts. Their content on YouTube focuses on case studies, technology features, and product announcements to help drive leads and has done so effectively now for over 3 years.

Insight: Does the Number of Views Matter?

Sometimes the most valuable video you produce is one that has the fewest views.

One of our clients let me know that case-study video on YouTube we produced for them had directly closed a sale. How did they know? The buyer told them it was the reason they bought. Better still, the new customer then agreed to be featured in a case-study of their own installation. Three months later, that second video closed another sale the same way. Two videos, two attributable installations, and neither video received more than 1,000 views.

What those videos did well was retain users among a very small and targeted audience: the exact buyers this client needed to reach. A million views from the wrong people would have been worth less than a few hundred views from the right ones. And, success drove more success as the first viewer didn't just convert, they became a second video with another right viewer. That is why audience quality is so important.

This does not mean that view count is meaningless. For an awareness campaign, view volume is the goal. But for a consideration-stage asset like a B2B case study, it's more about who watched the video than how many. Make sure to match the metric to the job of not just the channel, but the actual content.

Click-Through Rate on YouTube

YouTube provides its own click-through rate metric, which measures the percentage of impressions (times your video thumbnail was shown to a user) that resulted in a click to watch the video. This metric applies primarily to organic discovery within YouTube's recommendation system and search results, not to paid ads. YouTube's average CTR across all content sits between 2% and 10%, with significant variation by topic, thumbnail quality, and title effectiveness.

Thumbnail and title optimization is its own discipline within YouTube marketing, and CTR is its primary performance indicator. If your impressions are high but your CTR is low, YouTube is surfacing your content to users who are then choosing not to watch it. This is almost always a thumbnail or title problem as the content looks less compelling than the alternatives next to it. Conversely, a high CTR combined with low average percentage viewed suggests your title or thumbnail is over-promising relative to what the video actually delivers, which YouTube's algorithm will eventually penalize by reducing the content's recommendation frequency. There are a number of different practices to optimize these elements, and, they are all dependent on your brand and what looks or works best for your organization or strategy.

Think: CTR versus Retention as a Trade-Off

A video has a CTR of 12% which is well above average, but an average percentage viewed of 22%. A second video has a CTR of 4% but an average percentage viewed of 68%.

Which video is performing better for your channel's long-term growth, and why?

What does each metric tell you about the relationship between the title or thumbnail and the content itself?

YouTube Traffic Sources

Understanding where your YouTube views are coming from is as important as understanding how viewers behave once they arrive. Similar to Google Analytics data, YouTube Studio's traffic sources report breaks down view volume by source type, including YouTube search (users who found your video by searching within YouTube), suggested videos (users who were recommended your video after watching something else), external (users who came from outside YouTube, such as an embedded video on your website or a link in an email), direct or unknown, and YouTube advertising.

This traffic source data has direct strategic implications. A high percentage of views from YouTube search means your video is ranking for relevant queries and is a signal that your title, description, and tags are well-optimized and that your content aligns with what users are actively looking for. A high percentage from suggested videos means YouTube's algorithm is recommending your content to users who were not specifically searching for it, which typically indicates strong watch time and retention signals. External traffic is particularly valuable for marketers because it often represents the highest-intent viewers. It simply means someone who saw your video shared in a newsletter or embedded in a blog post actively chose to click and watch it. External traffic can also be because your organization has embedded a video in its own website for viewership.

YouTube Paid Video Metrics in Google Ads

When you run paid video campaigns on YouTube through Google Ads, your analytics live in Google Ads rather than YouTube Studio, though the two can be connected for cross-referencing. The metrics available for paid YouTube campaigns introduce several concepts that are specific to video advertising.

Views in paid YouTube campaigns are counted differently depending on the ad format. For skippable in-stream ads (the ads that play before or during a video with a "Skip Ad" button that appears after five seconds) Google counts a view when a user watches 30 seconds of the ad, watches the entire ad if it is shorter than 30 seconds, or interacts with the ad before either of those thresholds. For non-skippable in-stream ads, which run up to fifteen seconds and cannot be skipped (these may run longer in some markets, and up to thirty seconds on connected TV), views are counted for every impression since the user has no choice but to watch.

View rate is the paid video equivalent of click-through rate. It represents the percentage of times your ad was shown that resulted in a counted view. A low view rate on a skippable ad suggests users are choosing to skip it as quickly as possible, which is a creative problem. Your ad is not capturing attention in the first five seconds before the skip button becomes available. Don't take this personally, though as it can also be audience dependent as some audiences skip content more often than others.

Cost per view, or CPV, is the average amount you pay for each counted view of your video ad. Like CPC in paid search, CPV should be evaluated in the context of what that view is worth to your organization, not in isolation. A $0.04 CPV looks like a bargain until you check the reach behind it. If a narrow audience only delivers a few thousand impressions a month, an efficient CPV is buying you almost nothing. YouTube also offers a metric called earned actions, which captures organic behavior that results from a paid ad view. Earned actions include things like additional video views, channel subscriptions, or likes that occurred after someone watched a paid ad but were not directly clicked from within the ad itself. Earned actions are a meaningful indicator of whether paid video is driving genuine interest in your brand and content, beyond the immediate interaction with the ad.

For awareness-focused YouTube campaigns, Google provides brand lift measurement as an additional layer of analytics. Brand lift studies, available to advertisers meeting a minimum spend threshold, survey users who were and were not exposed to your ads and measure the difference in brand awareness, ad recall, consideration, and favorability between the two groups. This approach moves video analytics beyond behavioral metrics and into the perception-based outcomes that brand advertising is actually trying to achieve including outcomes that standard click and view data cannot capture on their own.

Insight: The 5-Second Audition

For skippable YouTube ads, you have exactly five seconds to convince a viewer not to skip your ad. Research from Google's own Creative Lab suggests that the single most effective thing an advertiser can do in those five seconds is create a moment of emotional engagement including curiosity, humor, surprise, or recognition.

Ads that lead with a logo or a product shot consistently underperform compared to ads that lead with a human moment or an unexpected visual. Your analytics will tell you whether it worked: a view rate above 30% on a skippable ad is generally considered a strong creative signal.

Video Analytics for Other Platforms

YouTube may be the most analytically mature video platform, but it is far from the only one that matters for marketers. As discussed in Chapter 7, social media platforms prefer that users stay on the platform rather than be driven off it. (Remember from Chapter 7: organic posts containing links are shown to fewer people.) Facebook, Instagram, TikTok, LinkedIn, and connected television each have their own video metrics, their own definitions, and their own quirks that analysts need to understand. What follows is a practical guide to what matters on each platform and how to think about cross-platform video measurement.

Facebook Video Analytics

Facebook's approach to video has evolved considerably since it introduced native video uploads in 2009. Today, Facebook supports a range of video formats including traditional feed videos, Facebook Reels, Facebook Stories, Facebook Live, and in-stream video ads that run within other videos. Each format has its own reporting nuances, but the core metrics share a common framework.

On Facebook, a view is counted after just three seconds of watch time which is one of the lowest thresholds of any major platform. This makes Facebook's raw view counts among the most inflated in the industry. A video that autoplays on mute as a user scrolls past and is watched for three seconds counts as a view. For this reason, three-second views should be treated as an awareness metric at best, not as a meaningful engagement signal. A far more useful metric is the percentage of video viewed. Facebook reports what percentage of viewers reached the 25%, 50%, 75%, and 100% marks of a video, which gives you a much clearer picture of actual content engagement than raw view counts alone. Note that Meta's 2025 shift to a unified 'views' metric changed the label, not the threshold — a Facebook view is still counted at three seconds, which is why the raw number remains the least informative figure on the dashboard.

One-minute views are also available for videos longer than one minute and represent a considerably stronger engagement signal than three-second views. If your marketing goal is genuine content engagement on Facebook rather than simple awareness, one-minute views and video completion rate are the metrics worth building your reporting around. For maximum reach and virality the current optimal length is 15–30 seconds; if your goal is feed depth and engagement instead, Meta's 2026 guidance points to the 2-to-5-minute range.

Average watch time on Facebook serves a similar purpose to YouTube's average view duration. Average watch time tells you how long, on average, viewers stayed with your content before leaving. Facebook also provides a retention curve similar to YouTube Studio's audience retention report, showing where in a video viewership drops off. The same diagnostic logic applies: sharp drops at specific timestamps point to content or pacing issues worth addressing.

For paid video campaigns on Facebook, the metrics expand to include reach, frequency, cost per thru-play (a thru-play is counted when a user watches at least 15 seconds of a video or the entire video if it is shorter than 15 seconds), and video average play time. Facebook's ad platform also provides estimated ad recall lift, a modeled metric that estimates how many additional people would remember seeing your ad 48 hours later compared to a control group that was not shown the ad. Like YouTube's brand lift measurement, this metric attempts to capture the awareness value of video that behavioral data alone cannot reflect.

Tip: Never Start a Facebook Video Performance Report with Raw Views

Three-second views on Facebook are easy to accumulate and easy to misrepresent. When reporting Facebook video performance to leadership, lead with completion rate and one-minute views alongside reach to give an honest picture of how many people actually engaged with the content versus simply scrolled past it.

Instagram Video Analytics

Instagram's video ecosystem is closely integrated with Facebook's since both are owned by Meta, and much of the reporting infrastructure is shared through Meta Business Suite and Meta Ads Manager. However, Instagram's video formats and the behavior patterns of its users are distinct enough to warrant separate consideration.

Instagram Reels are currently the platform's dominant short-form video format and the primary vehicle for organic video reach on the platform. Reels analytics in Instagram include plays, accounts reached, likes, comments, shares, and saves. Of these, shares and saves are the most meaningful engagement signals. A share means a user found the content compelling enough to send it to someone else or post it to their Story. A save means a user wanted to return to the content later. Both behaviors indicate a level of value that passive likes do not capture.

Reach and plays are distinct on Instagram: reach counts the number of unique accounts that saw the video, while plays counts total views including repeat views from the same account. The ratio between views and reach tells you something about repeatability. Content that people rewatch has a views-to-reach ratio significantly above 1.0, which is a positive signal for the algorithm (and means people watched your video more than once).

Insight: Instagram's Algorithm Rewards Replays

Instagram's recommendation algorithm for Reels places significant weight on replay behavior. Content that users watch more than once either because it is funny, surprising, or dense with information receives a meaningful boost in distribution.

When creating short-form video for Instagram, consider whether your content gives viewers a reason to watch again. This is why rapid cuts, unexpected endings, and text overlays that require a second viewing to fully absorb tend to perform well on the platform.

For paid video on Instagram, the metrics mirror Facebook's ad reporting since campaigns are managed through the same Meta Ads Manager interface. The primary distinction in optimization is format: vertical video formats, particularly those sized for Stories and Reels at a 9:16 aspect ratio, consistently outperform square or horizontal formats for both view rate and cost efficiency on Instagram. This is an easy optimization that many advertisers overlook when repurposing video creative from other channels.

TikTok Video Analytics

TikTok is the most algorithmically powerful video platform in existence for organic content distribution. No other platform gives a brand-new account with zero followers the same potential to reach millions of users with a single piece of content if that content resonates. That potential is also what makes TikTok analytics particularly important to understand. The platform's metrics reflect a fundamentally different user relationship with content than any platform that came before it.

TikTok's primary performance metrics are video views, average watch time, total play time, video completion rate, and shares. Of these, video completion rate is the most algorithmically significant. TikTok's recommendation engine weighs completion rate heavily when deciding whether to push content to the For You Page, which is the discovery feed that drives virtually all organic reach on the platform. A video that is watched to completion, even if it receives few likes or comments, will be distributed more broadly than a video with high like counts but low completion. This inverts the engagement model of older platforms and has important implications for how you create and evaluate TikTok content.

Average watch time on TikTok should be evaluated in the context of the video's length. TikTok allows videos up to sixty minutes long, but the platform's native behavior strongly favors content in the fifteen-to-sixty-second range for organic performance. A thirty-second video with an average watch time of twenty-eight seconds is performing exceptionally well. That same twenty-eight-second average watch time for a five-minute video represents a significant drop-off problem.

TikTok also provides traffic source analytics similar to YouTube's, breaking down views between the For You Page, your follower feed, search, personal profile, and external sources. The distribution between For You Page views and follower feed views is particularly telling. Content that generates the majority of its views from the For You Page is being distributed by TikTok's algorithm to non-followers and is reaching new audiences. Content that receives most of its views from the follower feed is performing well with your existing audience but not breaking through to new users. Growing brands on TikTok need both, but algorithmic reach is what drives channel growth.

Side Quest: TikTok and the Search Opportunity

For years TikTok was thought of purely as a short-form entertainment platform. That characterization has become increasingly outdated! Research from Google as early as 2023 showed that roughly 40% of Gen Z users preferred TikTok or Instagram over Google Maps or Search when looking for lunch. In 2024, TikTok introduccd a full search ads product, allowing advertisers to place video ads within TikTok's search results, bringing search intent targeting to a platform previously associated purely with discovery.

For analysts working with brands targeting younger demographics, TikTok search analytics including search impressions, clicks, and conversion data from search ads represents an emerging and increasingly important data stream worth tracking alongside traditional search analytics from Google and Bing.

LinkedIn Video Analytics

LinkedIn's video analytics occupy a different position than the consumer platforms discussed so far. LinkedIn's audience is defined by professional context, which means video content on the platform is typically more formal, more industry-specific, and more directly oriented toward business outcomes. B2B marketers, professional services firms, and organizations focused on thought leadership and talent acquisition will find LinkedIn video analytics worth paying close attention to.

LinkedIn provides analytics for native video posts including views, unique viewers, watch time, completion rate, and demographic breakdowns of who watched including job title, industry, company size, seniority level, and geography. That last point is the most distinctive feature of LinkedIn video analytics. No other platform gives you the ability to see that your video about supply chain software was watched predominantly by logistics managers at companies with more than 500 employees. For B2B marketers, this demographic overlay on video analytics is genuinely valuable data for understanding whether your content is reaching the right audience.

LinkedIn defines a view as any video play of at least two seconds and requires roughly 50% of the player to be in view, which is similar to Facebook's threshold and means raw view counts should be contextualized with completion rate and average watch time just as they would be on any other platform. For paid video campaigns on LinkedIn, the metrics include cost per view, video completion rate, and the platform's own version of click-through rate measuring how often viewers clicked from the video to a landing page or company page.

Connected Television and Streaming Video

Connected television, or CTV, deserves mention in any comprehensive treatment of video analytics, even though it operates quite differently from the social and search-based video platforms discussed so far. CTV refers to video advertising delivered through internet-connected television screens including smart TVs, streaming sticks like Roku and Amazon Fire, and gaming consoles. The content environment is streaming services including Hulu, Peacock, Paramount+, and ad-supported tiers of platforms like Netflix and Disney+.

The fundamental analytical challenge with CTV is that it is a largely non-clickable environment. Users watching a streaming service on their television cannot click on an ad the way they would in a social feed or a YouTube video. This shifts the entire measurement framework toward awareness and brand lift metrics rather than direct response. The primary metrics in CTV advertising are impressions, completion rate (CTV ads are typically non-skippable and run fifteen to thirty seconds, so completion rates are naturally high), reach and frequency, and cost per completed view.

Attribution in CTV is more complex than in any of the other video environments discussed in this chapter. Because there is no click to follow, connecting a CTV ad exposure to a downstream conversion on a website or in a store requires more sophisticated measurement approaches. These typically include household IP matching (identifying that the household that saw a CTV ad also visited the advertiser's website from a desktop device on the same network) and third-party measurement providers like Comscore, Nielsen, or iSpot.tv that specialize in cross-screen attribution. For analysts working with brands that invest significantly in CTV, understanding the limitations and methodologies of these attribution approaches is important context for how to interpret and present the data.

Insight: CTV Reaches Cord-Cutters You Miss on Other Platforms

One of the most compelling arguments for CTV advertising is audience composition.

The households that have cancelled cable subscriptions, which in the United States now outnumber those that still subscribe, are largely unreachable through traditional television advertising. CTV is the primary mechanism for reaching those audiences through a television screen.

For brands whose target audience skews toward younger demographics, CTV's reach into cord-cutter households represents meaningful incremental coverage that is invisible in traditional broadcast or cable media plans.

Cross-Platform Video Measurement

One of the most practical challenges in video analytics is making sense of data that spans multiple platforms simultaneously. A video campaign might run as a paid ad on YouTube, be posted organically to Instagram Reels and TikTok, and be embedded on the organization's website all at the same time. Each platform reports its own metrics using its own definitions, making aggregate comparison genuinely difficult.

The most important discipline in cross-platform video reporting is definitional consistency. Before building any cross-platform video dashboard, you need to decide how you are going to define a meaningful view across all platforms. Given the wide variation in how platforms count views, from two seconds on LinkedIn to thirty seconds on YouTube, picking a common denominator that reflects genuine engagement is a judgment call that should be made deliberately and documented clearly so that anyone reading your reports understands what they are looking at.

A practical approach many analysts use is to report platform-native view counts alongside a consistent secondary metric (typically video completion rate) that travels across all platforms with a more consistent meaning. Completion rate is not perfectly standardized either, since a 100% completion on a sixty-second video and a 100% completion on a three-minute video represent very different viewer experiences. But as a directional indicator of content quality and audience engagement, completion rate is more meaningful and more comparable across platforms than raw view counts.

As artificial intelligence continues to reshape how users find and consume content, video is not immune to those changes. AI-powered recommendation systems already govern a significant share of video discovery across YouTube, TikTok, and Instagram. Generative AI tools are beginning to change video production itself, reducing the cost and time required to create professional-quality video content. For analysts, this means the volume of video content competing for audience attention will continue to grow, the platforms' algorithms will become increasingly important gatekeepers of reach, and the metrics that reflect genuine audience engagement rather than passive exposure will become even more critical to measure and report accurately.

Tip: Build a Cross-Platform Video Summary with Only Four Metrics

When reporting video performance across multiple platforms to leadership, use a consistent four-metric summary for each platform: total reach (unique people reached), total views (platform-native definition, labeled clearly), average completion rate, and total shares or saves. This framework allows meaningful side-by-side comparison without requiring identical definitions across platforms, because each metric is clearly labeled with its source and definition.

Video analytics is ultimately about answering the same question that animates all of digital marketing analytics: is what we are doing creating value? For video, that question starts with whether people are watching, moves through whether they are engaging, and ends with whether any of that watching and engaging is translating into outcomes that matter to the organization. The job of the analyst is to connect the dots.

Video's reach across platforms — from YouTube's search-driven long-form ecosystem to TikTok's algorithmically distributed short-form content — reflects the breadth of channels available to modern digital marketers. But video is just one component of a broader presence, and the metrics that matter extend well beyond video views. In the next chapter, we turn to email analytics, one of, if not the, web's oldest platforms and how powerful this platform remains as part of any marketing strategy.

References

The ABCDs of effective YouTube creative (2020). Think with Google Creative Lab. https://www.thinkwithgoogle.com/consumer-insights/consumer-trends/YouTube-creative-abcds/

About TrueView video campaigns (n.d.). Google Ads Help. https://support.google.com/google-ads/answer/6340491

About YouTube Analytics metrics. (n.d.). YouTube Help. https://support.google.com/youtube/answer/9314311

Ads Manager video metrics. (n.d.). Meta Business Help Center. https://www.facebook.com/business/help/1714393655377619

Benes, R. (2024, March 14). *US digital video ad spending forecast 2024.* eMarketer. https://www.emarketer.com/content/us-digital-video-ad-spending-forecast-2024

Biddle, S. (2022, July 12). *TikTok's algorithm is one of the most powerful in the world.* The Intercept. https://theintercept.com/2022/07/12/tiktok-algorithm/

Brand lift measurement (n.d.). Google Ads Help. https://support.google.com/google-ads/answer/6354258

Chen, J. (2024, February 22). *How the Instagram Reels algorithm works in 2024.* Sprout Social. https://sproutsocial.com/insights/instagram-reels-algorithm/

Connected TV advertising guide (2024). The Trade Desk. https://www.thetradedesk.com/us/resource-hub/connected-tv-advertising-guide

Frier, S. (2020). *No filter: The inside story of Instagram.* Simon & Schuster.

Herrman, J. (2019, March 10). *How TikTok is rewriting the world.* The New York Times. https://www.nytimes.com/2019/03/10/style/what-is-tik-tok.html

How YouTube's search and discovery system works (2022). Think with Google. https://www.thinkwithgoogle.com/marketing-strategies/video/YouTube-discovery-system/

Hutchinson, A. (2024, April 3). *TikTok launches search ads.* Social Media Today. https://www.socialmediatoday.com/news/tiktok-launches-search-ads/712103/

Me at the zoo [Video] (2005, April 23). YouTube. https://www.youtube.com/watch?v=jNQXAC9IVRw

Molla, R. (2023, September 12). *Gen Z is using TikTok as a search engine.* Vox. https://www.vox.com/technology/23972792/gen-z-tiktok-search-engine-google

Naffis, D. (2025, December 12). *Everything You Need to Know About Is Cord Cutting Slowing Down?.* Adwave. https://adwave.com/resources/cord-cutting-trend-2025

Newberry, C. (2024, January 17). *TikTok analytics: The complete guide for marketers.* Hootsuite. https://blog.hootsuite.com/tiktok-analytics/

Smith, C. (2024, February 6). *YouTube by the numbers: Stats, demographics & fun facts.* DMR Business Statistics. https://expandedramblings.com/index.php/YouTube-statistics/

Video ads on LinkedIn (n.d.). LinkedIn Help. https://www.linkedin.com/help/linkedin/answer/a548369

Wagner, A. (2017, August 23). *Are You Maximizing The Use of Video In Your Content Marketing Strategy?*. Forbes. https://www.forbes.com/sites/forbesagencycouncil/2017/05/15/are-you-maximizing-the-use-of-video-in-your-content-marketing-strategy/

YouTube by the numbers (n.d.). YouTube for Press. https://www.youtube.com/intl/en_GB/about/press/

YouTube Statistics 2024 (2024, January 9). Brandwatch. https://www.brandwatch.com/blog/YouTube-stats/

Chapter 9
Email Analytics

A subscriber list of 40,000 names. A 38% open rate. A click-through rate above industry average. By every traditional measure, this quarterly newsletter campaign from a mid-sized software company was a success. So when the VP of Sales asks, "How many of these opens turned into sales?" the marketing team had no answer. They could tell you who opened the email. They could not tell you who became a lead, who became a Marketing Qualified Lead, or who eventually showed up on an opportunity report with a dollar amount attached to it.

A lot of this language may be new to you, but this is the language of email and marketing automation analytics. This is also the gap that trips up a lot of new marketers and marketing analysts. Email analytics is often taught and practiced as if it ends at the inbox: did the user open the email, did they click on a link, or did they unsubscribe. Those engagement metrics matter, and we will spend the first half of this chapter on them. But email is rarely the finish line in a B2B or high-consideration purchase. It is usually the bridge between a marketing automation platform like HubSpot and a customer relationship management (CRM) system like Salesforce, where a click on a pricing email eventually has to be translated into a term a sales leader cares about: not just a lead, but a qualified lead.

In this chapter, we will cover the core metrics every email marketer should track, why some of those metrics (especially open rate) have become less reliable than they used to be, and how email engagement data feeds into the marketing automation concepts of Marketing Qualified Leads (MQLs) and Sales Qualified Leads (SQLs). We will also look at how three of the most commonly used platforms in the industry (HubSpot, Mailchimp, and Salesforce) divide up this work.

Before the Data: Why Design and Subject Lines are the First Analytical Decisions You Make

There has historically been a dividing line between design and analytics leaving design to the designers and analytics to the analyst. That division produces beautiful emails few people open, and dashboards full of data that mean little. The reality is that every decision made before an email is sent is already an analytics decision. How the subject line is written, how the preview text is used, how the layout guides the reader's eye to important content, and even the text on the call to action button or link all apply to analytics. While the data and analytical measures covered in this chapter are largely the result of the choices made in design and copy, all departments involved have to work together to accomplish results.

Let's start with the subject line. This is the single highest-leverage element of real estate in an email campaign as it is the first to be seen. A subscriber scanning their inbox early on a Wednesday morning is making split-second decisions about what gets opened and what gets archived. Your subject line has roughly two seconds to make the case that opening this email is worth their time. Research across millions of sends consistently points to a few patterns worth noting: subject lines under fifty characters tend to outperform longer ones because they display completely on a mobile screen without being cut off, and somewhere between 60% and 70% of email is now opened on a phone. Using a subscriber's first name, referencing a previous behavior, or acknowledging something specific about their relationship with the brand consistently lifts open rates above generic emails, though that's only true if you know the user's first name or their behavior and the information is accurate. Urgency and specificity outperform vague copy. 'Your cart expires tonight' does far more than 'Don't miss out,' and '3 things we learned from 10,000 customer reviews' tends to beat 'Our latest update,' because the reader knows exactly what they're getting.

The short line of copy that appears beneath the subject line in many email clients is called the preview text. This is an underutilized tool because if it isn't set manually, the email platform will pull the first line of the email body into this space. If the first line of your email is 'View this email in your browser' or 'Having trouble viewing this message?', it doesn't leave a great first impression. Using this text intentionally can be powerful.

Design of the email itself works differently than subject lines but toward the same end goal: reducing the distance between the email open and doing the things the email was sent to accomplish. A well-designed email isn't necessarily visually complicated. Single-column layouts consistently outperform complicated multi-column layouts on mobile devices. White space is functional rather than decorative as it guides the reader's eye to what matters. Buttons consistently outperform hyperlinked text for calls to action because they are easier to see and easier to tap on a touchscreen. Even images should be treated carefully as some corporate email clients block images by default so alternative text (alt text) is critical and image size should be considered so when they do load, you have done the work to minimize load time. Even purposefully designing emails to look as if they came directly from a staff member, especially in B2B, can be a great tactic.

None of this requires a graphic design background or expensive email templates. It requires you as the analyst to ask honest questions before the email goes out: if someone gives this thirty seconds of their attention, is the one thing we want them to do clear and can they easily find it? An email with a clear answer to that question will produce better results than a beautifully designed email that requires the user to play "hide and go seek" to find the information that you want them to find.

Why Email Still Matters

Despite decades of predictions that email marketing would be replaced by social media, push notifications, or messaging apps, email remains one of the most trusted and highest-performing channels marketers have. It is also one of the few channels a brand fully owns: an organization does not need to pay a platform for access to its own email list the way it increasingly has to pay for organic reach on social media. That ownership is precisely why email is treated differently in this book than channels like paid or organic social. Email is a direct, permission-based relationship with a contact, and almost everything we measure in this chapter exists to answer one question: is that relationship getting stronger or weaker?

The numbers back this up emphatically. As of 2026, there are an estimated 4.7 to 4.8 billion email users worldwide, a figure that continues climbing year over year even as newer channels launch and compete for attention. Roughly 88 to 99% of email users check their inbox at least once a day, and most check it several times, which means email reaches an audience with a consistency that algorithm-dependent platforms simply cannot match. That reach translates directly into return on investment: across multiple independent benchmark studies, email marketing continues to generate an average return of roughly $36 to $42 for every $1 spent, a figure that consistently outperforms paid search (closer to $2), social advertising (around $2.80), and display advertising (around $1.35). Email also converts at a meaningfully higher rate than social media with some studies putting average email conversion rates near 3 to 4%, compared to well under 1% for social. Why? Because email reaches people who have already opted in, already know the brand, and are not competing for attention against any algorithm's other priorities. None of this means email is easy; it means email is durable, measurable, and still one of the highest-leverage channels available to a marketer in 2026.

Insight: Owned Reach Versus Borrowed Reach

The reason email's ROI has held up for two decades while newer channels rise and fall is structural, not stylistic. As a reminder, a single social media post on Facebook is shown to, on average, 2-5% of your audience. An email lands in the inbox of every subscriber who hasn't opted out. Marketers sometimes describe this as the difference between owned and borrowed reach: a follower list is borrowed from a platform that can change the rules at any time where a permission-based email list is owned outright. That distinction is why so many experienced marketers treat list building as one of their most valuable long-term assets.

Why CRM and Marketing Automation Are So Powerful

If email's value comes from being an owned channel, a CRM's value comes from being the system that remembers everything that channel produces. In simple terms, customer relationship management platforms centralize every interaction a contact has had with an organization including emails opened, pages visited, deals discussed, and support tickets filed into a single record. On the other hand, marketing automation is what turns that record into action without requiring a human to manually trigger every email, lead score, or handoff across departments. Sometimes these two tools are in the same platform and other times as two separate platforms. Either way, the combination of these two tools is powerful enough that it shows up clearly in results: an older Salesforce study found that businesses that adopt CRM systems report an average increase in sales of around 29%, a roughly 34% improvement in sales productivity, and a sales forecasting accuracy improvement of over 40%. CRM adoption is also strongly tied to company size and maturity. Roughly 91% of businesses with ten or more employees now use a CRM, compared to about half of businesses with fewer than ten, suggesting that as organizations scale past the point where a founder can track every relationship from memory, CRM stops being optional.

Insight: Apple Mail Privacy Protection (MPP) and What It Has Done to Email Analytics

Apple's Mail Privacy Protection (MPP), introduced in September 2021 as part of iOS 15, iPadOS 15, and macOS Monterey, fundamentally disrupted one of email marketing's oldest measurement conventions. MPP works by routing all remote email content through Apple's proxy servers before a recipient ever sees the message. Because Apple's proxy pre-fetches the tracking pixel that detects opens when the email arrives rather than when a human actually opens it, every email delivered to an Apple Mail user with MPP enabled registers as "opened" in an email platform's reporting, regardless of whether the recipient looked at it. The practical consequence is severe:

Apple Mail now accounts for approximately 49% to 52% of all email opens across the industry, meaning that for many senders, close to half of their reported open rate reflects automated proxy activity rather than a human interaction. One practitioner documented a client celebrating a 42% open rate whose audience was 65% Apple Mail users. Actual engagement, once MPP opens were stripped out, was much closer to 18%. The list was effectively inactive, and the open rate had completely hidden that fact. iOS 18, released in 2024, compounded the problem further by adding AI-generated inbox previews, new inbox categorization, and link tracking protection that strips UTM (tracking URL) parameters from links opened in Apple Mail and Safari meaning that even the click-level attribution that replaced open rate as the recommended engagement signal is now subject to its own erosion.

The lasting implication for any analyst working with email data is that open rate, as a standalone metric, can no longer be trusted as an absolute measure of audience engagement, but only as a directional, comparative one. Comparing this week's send to last week's send, using the same list and the same methodology, still surfaces relative trends worth acting on. Treating the raw open rate as an accurate picture of how many people actually read an email is no longer valid. Email platforms have responded inconsistently: some exclude MPP opens by default, some include them, and some have reversed their own defaults in response to user complaints that their numbers looked lower than competitors' reports. This makes cross-tool benchmark comparisons unreliable without first understanding how each tool handles MPP in its specific reporting configuration. The recommended adaptation, endorsed across the industry by Twilio SendGrid, Bloomreach, and most major Email Service Providers (ESPs), is to shift primary engagement measurement from open rate to click-through rate and click-to-open rate, audit any automated workflows that use "email opened" as a trigger for an Apple Mail audience segment, and treat open rate as supporting context rather than evidence of campaign or list health.

Marketing automation specifically, inclusive of workflows, lead scoring, and triggered sends, shows an even sharper before-and-after effect inside email performance. Automated, behavior-triggered emails (welcome series, abandoned cart flows, lifecycle nurture sequences) consistently outperform one-off batch sends by a wide margin; multiple 2025 and 2026 industry reports put automated email revenue per send several times higher than standard campaign sends, and one widely cited e-commerce benchmark found automated emails accounted for only about 2% of total sends but drove roughly 30% of total email-attributed revenue. The mechanism is simple even if the technology behind it is not: an automated email triggered by a specific behavior (someone abandoned a cart, someone hit a lead-scoring threshold, someone went quiet after being active for a certain period of time) arrives at the moment it is most relevant, rather than whenever a marketer happened to hit send. Combined, the relevance of what a CRM and marketing automation platform are ultimately selling is not more emails, but better-timed and more strategic ones.

Insight: Be Skeptical of Decade-Old ROI Numbers

You will frequently see a CRM ROI statistic cited as "$8.71 in return for every $1 spent." This specific figure traces back to a single Nucleus Research study from 2014 and gets recycled across hundreds of marketing blogs more than a decade later, often without that context.

More recent, independent reporting puts CRM ROI in a wide range, commonly cited between roughly $3 and $9 per $1 spent depending on company size, CRM maturity, and how well the data inside the system is maintained. This is a useful reminder: a statistic's age and original source matter just as much as the number itself, and a frequently repeated figure should not be mistaken for a current statistic.

Average Industry Benchmarks for Email and Marketing Automation Metrics

Benchmarks are most useful as a check on your work as a marketer, not a target for your organization's efforts. A marketer whose open rate sits well below the table on the following pages should ask why; a marketer whose open rate sits well above it should ask whether their list has simply gotten smaller and more self-selecting. With that caveat, the figures below represent commonly cited overall and industry averages from major 2025–2026 benchmark studies (Mailchimp, Brevo, Klaviyo, WebFX, and Demand Sage among them). Because no two benchmark providers measure identically (some divide by emails sent, others by emails delivered; some adjust for Apple Mail Privacy Protection, others do not) treat these as directional ranges rather than precise targets, and always prioritize comparing your own performance against your own historical trend first.

Metric	Overall Average (All Industries)	Notes
Open Rate	19% - 22%	Government & non-profit emails run highest (28-35%); retail / e-commerce often lowest (15-16%)
Click-Through Rate (CTR)	~2% - 2.5%	B2B averages tend to be higher (2-6%) than B2C / retail; Technology & electronics is consistently amongst the highest-performing verticals
Click-to-Open Rate (CTOR)	~6.5% - 15%	Generally considered more reliable than open rate; B2B programs often report figures toward the higher end of this range

Metric	Overall Average (All Industries)	Notes
Conversion Rate	~2% - 4%	Varies heavily by email type; automated, behavior-triggered emails convert at multiples of standard campaign sends
Bounce Rate	~2%	Total bounce rate above 2% is widely treated as a deliverability warning sign; hard bounces should be removed from a list immediately
Unsubscribe Rate	~0.1% - 0.5%	B2B programs typically run lower (~0.1-0.2%) than B2C (~0.2-0.3%) reflecting more deliberate opt-ins
Email Marketing ROI	$36 to $42 per $1 spent	Some retail / e-commerce segments and highly segmented programs report figures well above this average
MQL-to-SQL Conversion Rate	~13%	Commonly cited cross-industry benchmark; varies significantly by lead source with referrals and website-originated leads typically converting at a higher rate

Core Email Engagement Metrics

The benchmarks above outline just some of the many analytical metrics that we use to determine success in email marketing. We'll go through the definition of these benchmarks momentarily.

Before an organization can talk about leads, MQLs / SQLs, scoring, or revenue, it needs clarity on whether its emails are reaching people and whether those people care. The following metrics form the foundation of nearly every email analytics report, regardless of which platform produces it. Most email marketing systems automatically calculate many of these metrics, but it's always good to know how these measures are calculated.

Delivery Rate

What It Is: the percentage of sent emails that actually arrive in a recipient's inbox (or at least pass through the receiving server) without bouncing. This calculation speaks to the quality of your email list.

$$\text{Delivery Rate} = \frac{\text{Emails Delivered}}{\text{Emails Sent}}$$

Open Rate

What It Is: the percentage of delivered emails that were opened by a recipient. Historically the headline metric for email performance, open rate is calculated when a recipient's email client downloads a small tracking pixel embedded in the message. This can also be telling of the value of your list and if they are engaged although the value of this metric has changed.

$$\text{Open Rate} = \frac{\text{Emails Opened}}{\text{Emails Delivered}}$$

Click-Through Rate (CTR)

What It Is: the percentage of delivered emails that generated at least one click on a link inside the message. CTR is a cleaner signal of interest than open rate because a click requires intentional action, not just a loaded image.

$$\text{Click-Through Rate} = \frac{\text{Unique Clicks}}{\text{Emails Delivered}}$$

Click-to-Open Rate (CTOR)

What It Is: the percentage of openers who went on to click something. Because CTOR removes deliverability and open-rate noise from the equation, many marketers now treat it as a more trustworthy measure of content quality than open rate alone.

$$\text{Click-to-Open Rate (CTOR)} = \frac{\text{Unique Clicks}}{\text{Unique Opens}}$$

Conversion Rate

What It Is: the percentage of delivered emails that resulted in a recipient completing the email's intended goal — filling out a form, registering for a webinar, or making a purchase. This is the metric that finally connects an email to a business outcome, and it requires the email platform to be integrated with web analytics or e-commerce tracking.

$$\text{Conversion Rate} = \frac{\text{Conversions}}{\text{Emails Delivered}}$$

Bounce Rate (Soft and Hard)

What It Is: the percentage of sent emails that were rejected by the recipient's server. A soft bounce is typically temporary (a full inbox, a server that is briefly down, vacation response), while a hard bounce is permanent (the address does not exist). A healthy list usually keeps overall bounce rate below 1 to 2 percent; a high hard bounce rate signals a list that has not been cleaned or updated in some time.

$$\text{Bounce Rate} = \frac{\text{Bounced Emails}}{\text{Emails Sent}}$$

Unsubscribe Rate

What It Is: the percentage of delivered emails that resulted in a recipient opting out of future communications. A spike in unsubscribes is worth investigating, but so is a steep decline as both can indicate a shift in how content is resonating with a list.

$$\text{Unsubscribe Rate} = \frac{\text{Unsubscribes}}{\text{Emails Delivered}}$$

List Growth Rate

What It Is: the net rate at which a subscriber list is gaining (or losing) contacts once unsubscribes are factored in. This metric tells a marketer whether top-of-funnel acquisition of new emails is keeping pace with natural list decay. Some marketers (and email marketing platforms) also remove hard bounces from the numerator.

$$\text{List Growth Rate} = \frac{(\text{New Subscribers - Unsubscribes})}{\text{Total Subscribers}}$$

Revenue per Email (or per Click)

What It Is: the amount of revenue generated by a campaign divided by the number of opens or clicks it received, providing a sense of how efficiently an email converted attention into dollars.

$$\text{Revenue Per Email (or per click)} = \frac{\text{Total Campaign Revenue}}{\text{Number of Opens (or clicks)}}$$

From Engagement to the Funnel: Introducing MQLs and SQLs

Once an organization can reliably measure whether people are opening, clicking, and converting on email, the natural next question is what to do with that information. This is where email analytics stops being a stand-alone report and starts feeding into marketing automation — the practice of using software to score, segment, and route contacts based on their behavior, often without a human reviewing every single interaction.
Two acronyms come up constantly in this conversation, and new marketers often use them interchangeably even though they describe two very different moments in a contact's journey.

Side Quest: Unique Clicks versus Gross Clicks

Most platforms report click data two ways, and mixing them up is a common mistake for new analysts. Unique clicks count each recipient once, no matter how many times they click. Gross (or total) clicks count every click, including a recipient who clicks the same link five times. If 100 recipients each click a link five times, that's 100 unique clicks and 500 gross clicks. Use unique clicks when you want to know how many people engaged; use gross clicks when you want to understand the intensity of engagement from those who did.

Marketing Qualified Lead (MQL)

What It Is: a contact that marketing has evaluated against a defined set of behavioral and demographic criteria often a lead score built in part from email engagement, content downloads, and website activity and determined to be ready for a conversation with sales. In simple terms, an MQL is simply a lead that has not spoken to sales yet.

How to Calculate It: These are typically just measured in counts of MQLs. So if you have 100 MQLs, that means that you have 100 prospective leads that have been vetted by marketing in some way. Some organizations also score these leads and track MQLs in a points system using a points-based lead score (for example, 100 points), where actions like opening a pricing email, visiting a product page repeatedly, or downloading a case study add points, and inactivity over time subtracts them.

Sales Qualified Lead (SQL)

What It Is: an MQL that a sales representative has personally reviewed, contacted, and confirmed is worth pursuing typically by validating fit against criteria such as Budget, Authority, Need, and Timeline (BANT). An SQL is a lead sales has accepted, not just one marketing has flagged.

How to Calculate It: SQL status is usually a manual or semi-automated judgment call by a sales rep, not a formula, though many organizations track an MQL-to-SQL conversion rate to evaluate how well marketing's qualification criteria match what sales actually wants. A commonly cited industry benchmark for MQL-to-SQL conversion is in the range of 13%, though this varies significantly by industry and lead source.

Email plays a central role in generating both. A contact's email engagement (opens, clicks, and especially clicks on high-intent content like pricing pages or demo invitations) is one of the most common inputs into a lead scoring model. A contact who consistently ignores newsletters but clicks through every product update email is behaving very differently than one who clicks everything indiscriminately, and a well-built scoring model should treat them differently too.

How HubSpot, Mailchimp, and Salesforce Divide the Work

There are a number of different platforms that each have powerful tools to make CRM and marketing automation all work within one platform. From SugarCRM to Zoho, Pipedrive to Monday, each platform has pros and cons. The same is true for email marketing platforms like Mailchimp, Constant Contact, and Emma. To accomplish any of the marketing activities discussed in this chapter, you have to determine what is right for you. I've used HubSpot, Mailchimp, and Salesforce as examples as they are some of the most commonly used platforms in email, CRM, and marketing automation. Marketers can choose to use one of the platforms listed above for a variety of purposes. From my experience alone, I've used Salesforce for email, CRM, and marketing automation. I've had clients ask to use a hybrid of Monday and Mailchimp for the same purposes. I've also seen clients attempt to use Mailchimp as a standalone platform for marketing automation and email. There's no "one right way" to leverage these platforms.

Insight: Lifecycle Stage is Not the Same as Lead Status

It's easy to confuse these two properties, especially in HubSpot, where both live on the contact record. Lifecycle stage (things like Subscriber, Lead, MQL, SQL, Opportunity, Customer that explain where the customer is in your process) is a macro-level milestone that should move in one direction and rarely changes. Lead status (e.g., Attempted to Contact, In Progress, Connected) is a micro-level property that tracks a sales rep's day-to-day activity within the SQL stage. Reporting on lifecycle stage tells you about funnel health. Reporting on lead status tells you about sales activity. Mixing the two into a single report is one of the most common reporting mistakes new marketing analysts make as they are different.

For example, of the three platforms I've discussed throughout this chapter, HubSpot's primary role is marketing automation with some limited capabilities as a CRM system. It's widely loved by marketers because it is a marketing platform first. Mailchimp, on the other hand, is a known email service provider (ESP) and campaign builder across multiple channels and does offer limited marketing automation capabilities and connects to a number of CRM systems for tracking. Salesforce is an incredibly powerful CRM and sales pipeline system that can be customized to meet almost any need. It also can operate as a marketing automation platform while also offering capabilities to connect to other platforms or even its own additional SaaS platforms.

New marketers are often surprised to learn that no single platform owns the entire email-to-revenue story and that not every platform is the same or offers the same services. In practice, many organizations run Mailchimp or HubSpot as the engine that sends and measures the email itself, while Salesforce (or a similar CRM) holds the system of record for whether that engagement ever became real pipeline. HubSpot occupies a slightly different position than Mailchimp because it was built to combine marketing automation and light CRM functionality in one product, which is why HubSpot's reporting can natively show a contact's full journey from first email open to closed-won deal, while Mailchimp's reporting typically stops at the campaign level unless it is integrated with another system.

Tip: Ask Where the Data Lives Before You Build the Report

Before building any report that spans email engagement and lead status, confirm which platform holds the source of truth for each piece of data. A surprising number of reporting disagreements between marketing and sales come down to two teams pulling the same metric, for instance, "MQLs this month," from two different systems that were never properly synced.

Think: Whose Number is Right?

If HubSpot reports 220 new MQLs this month but Salesforce shows only 180 new leads assigned to the sales team, what are some possible explanations?

Is this a data sync issue, a definitional disagreement between marketing and sales, or a process delay?

How would you investigate before reporting either number to leadership?

Being Practical: Emails and Sales

This chapter introduces a lot of email and sales-driven analytics to the mix. So, let's suppose a B2B company sends a quarterly product update email to its full list of 40,000 contacts using HubSpot. The email is delivered to 39,200 contacts (a 98% delivery rate), opened by 14,896 of them (38% open rate), and clicked by 1,568 (a 4% click-through rate, or roughly 10.5% click-to-open rate). Of those clicks, 210 land on a single link: a request for a product demo.

On their own, the open rate and click-through rate would be reported as solid, slightly above-average performance, and a marketer focused only on engagement metrics might stop there. But the demo-request click is the real signal. In this organization's lead scoring model, a demo request is worth far more points than a newsletter open, and it is enough on its own to push many of those 210 contacts over the MQL threshold. HubSpot's workflow automation updates their lifecycle stage to Marketing Qualified Lead and routes them to a sales queue. From there, the journey moves over to Salesforce: a sales rep reviews each contact against budget, authority, need, and timeline, and over the following two weeks, 31 of the 210 are marked Sales Qualified, with 6 eventually appearing as Opportunities with dollar values attached.

This is the difference between reporting on an email and reporting on what an email produced. The newsletter's open rate told the team that the subject line worked. The demo-request click told them who to call. And the SQL and Opportunity data in Salesforce, weeks later, told them whether any of it mattered to the business. A new marketing analyst who only reports the first number is technically correct, but the story is substantially incomplete. The success lies in the details that are presented throughout this customer's journey.

In the next chapter, we will shift from owned channels like email to paid media analytics, where many of the same engagement and conversion principles apply, but the cost of acquiring that attention is a central part of the analysis.

References

40 Real CRM Statistics For 2026: AI, ROI, & Market Data. (2026, June 3). Breakcold. https://www.breakcold.com/blog/crm-statistics

Analyze marketing email performance. (n.d.). HubSpot Knowledge Base. https://knowledge.hubspot.com/marketing-email/analyze-your-marketing-email-campaign-performance

Bernatavičiūtė, M. (2026, January 30). *Email Marketing Statistics 2026: Key Insights*. Omnisend. https://www.omnisend.com/blog/email-marketing-statistics/

Berry, S. (2025, December 29). *2026 Email Marketing Benchmarks by Industry*. WebFX. https://www.webfx.com/blog/marketing/email-marketing-benchmarks/

Best Practices for Email Subject Lines. (n.d.). Mailchimp. https://mailchimp.com/help/best-practices-for-email-subject-lines/

Boychuk, A. (2026, February 2). *Email Marketing Benchmarks for 2026*. Flowium. https://flowium.com/blog/email-marketing-benchmarks/

CRM Statistics 2026: Market, Adoption and ROI Data. (2026, June 12). Digital Applied. https://www.digitalapplied.com/blog/crm-statistics-2026-market-adoption-roi-data-reference

Decima, C (2026, February 23). *Email Marketing in 2026 Is Still the Highest Driver of ROI.* WSI World. https://www.wsiworld.com/blog/why-email-still-delivers-the-highest-roi-in-2026-and-how-to-max-it

Elder, D. (2025, December 3). *Email marketing benchmarks by industry and by region for 2026*. MailerLite. https://www.mailerlite.com/blog/compare-your-email-performance-metrics-industry-benchmarks

Email Marketing Benchmarks: Region & Industry Data. (2026, May 27). Brevo. https://www.brevo.com/blog/email-marketing-benchmarks/

Email Marketing Statistics for 2026: 50+ Data Points. (n.d.). Robly. https://blog.robly.com/email-marketing-statistics-for-2026/

Email Marketing Statistics 2026: the latest data and trends (n.d.). EmailChef. https://emailchef.com/emailchef-academy/all-email-marketing-statistics-updated/

Haan, K. & Watts, R. (2026, July 1). *49 Top Email Marketing Statistics.* Forbes Advisor. https://www.forbes.com/advisor/business/software/email-marketing-statistics-jun-26/

How to Report on Leads, MQLs, and SQLs in HubSpot. (2023, May 12). SmartBug Media. https://www.smartbugmedia.com/blog/how-to-report-on-leads-mqls-and-sqls-in-hubspot

HubSpot Lifecycle Stages Explained: Setup, MQL/SQL & Advanced Setup. (2026, May 6). onthefuze. https://www.onthefuze.com/hubspot-insights-blog/hubspot-lifecycle-stages-explained

Jimenez, A. (2025, November 4). *Email marketing benchmarks by industry (+ email open rate data).* HubSpot. https://blog.hubspot.com/sales/average-email-open-rate-benchmark

Marketing Automation Statistics 2026: 130+ Key Metrics. (2026, April 8). Digital Applied. https://www.digitalapplied.com/blog/marketing-automation-statistics-2026-data-points

MQL vs SQL: A Comprehensive RevOps Guide for Salesforce and HubSpot (2026, January 5). MarTech Do. https://martechdo.com/mql-vs-sql/

Negi, S. (2026, Apr). *50+ CRM Statistics for 2026: ROI, AI, productivity, and market trends*. Salesmate. https://www.salesmate.io/blog/crm-statistics/

Nye, C. (2018, November 18). *Top 10 Email Marketing Metrics for Ecommerce*. Practical Ecommerce. https://www.practicalecommerce.com/11-email-marketing-metrics-ranked-in-order-of-importance

Nye, C. (2022, July 26). *Understanding Email Marketing Metrics in 2022*. Practical Ecommerce. https://www.practicalecommerce.com/understanding-email-marketing-metrics-in-2022

Partal, B. (2026, March 24). *B2B Email Marketing Benchmarks 2026. (Key Metrics & Insights)*. Popupsmart. https://popupsmart.com/blog/b2b-email-marketing-benchmarks

Santiago, E. (2026, February 3). *Email analytics: 13 email marketing metrics you should track*. HubSpot. https://blog.hubspot.com/marketing/metrics-email-marketers-should-be-tracking

The Ultimate Email Best Practices Guide (n.d.). Campaign Monitor. https://www.campaignmonitor.com/resources/guides/the-ultimate-email-best-practices-guide/

The Ultimate Guide to Preview Text in Email (2024, November 8). Litmus. https://www.litmus.com/blog/the-ultimate-guide-to-preview-text-support

Top CRM Statistics You Need To Know In 2026 (2026, April 28). SellersCommerce. https://www.sellerscommerce.com/blog/crm-statistics/

Welch, M. (2025, December 26). *MQL vs. SQL: What they are and how they differ*. HubSpot. https://blog.hubspot.com/sales/sales-qualified-lead

Chapter 10
Paid Media Analytics

A regional furniture retailer once asked a simple question in a budget meeting: "Which of our paid media is actually working?" The honest answer took three weeks to assemble, because the word "paid media" was doing an enormous amount of work in that sentence. The retailer was running banner ads through a psychographically-targeted programmatic exchange, retargeting site visitors who had abandoned a cart, a Connected TV campaign during the local evening news lineup, a handful of digital billboards near their two busiest stores, sponsored product placements on a major retailer's marketplace, and an affiliate relationship with three home-decor bloggers. Each of those channels had its own dashboard, its own definition of a "conversion," and its own idea of what a good result looked like. None of them spoke the same language as any other.

This is the central challenge of paid media analytics. Unlike search or social, which we've treated as single chapters because each lives inside one or two dominant platforms, "paid media" is really an umbrella term for nine or more genuinely different channels, each with its own buying mechanics, its own measurement standards, and its own definition of success. A click means something different on a banner ad than it does on a podcast (where there often is no click at all). A view-through conversion on retargeting display means something different than a view-through conversion on Connected TV. However these ads can be bought on the same or similar platforms. Thus, paid media has become a catch-all term for a select group of advertisements that can be placed on the web. This chapter will walk through the major paid media channels one at a time: what each one is, how it's typically bought, and the specific metrics that determine whether it's working.

Banner and Tile (Display) Advertising

Display advertising are the banners, tiles, and rectangles that appear alongside content on websites and apps. They are the oldest form of digital paid media and, in many ways, the most misunderstood. I consider them the "billboards" and "magazine ads" of the web. The very first banner ad ran on HotWired.com in 1994. Three decades later, display still anchors a huge share of programmatic ad spend, even though its click-through rates have fallen so low that many practitioners forget display was ever meant to be clicked on in the first place.

Click-Through Rate (CTR)

What It Is: the percentage of impressions that result in a click. Display CTR is very low; commonly cited industry averages sit around 0.05% to 0.46% depending on format and measurement methodology. Unlike search, the user wasn't actively looking for what the ad is offering.

$$\text{Click Through Rate (CTR)} = \frac{\text{Clicks}}{\text{Impressions}}$$

Viewability Rate

What It Is: the percentage of served impressions that actually met a recognized visibility standard — under the IAB/Media Rating Council guideline, at least 50% of an ad's pixels visible for a minimum of one second (two seconds for video). An ad that was never actually seen delivers zero value no matter how good the creative is.

$$\text{Viewability Rate} = \frac{\text{Viewable Impressions}}{\text{Total Impressions}}$$

Cost per Mille (CPM)

What It Is: the price paid for every 1,000 impressions delivered, which varies enormously by inventory quality. Open-exchange display ads commonly runs $2 to $6 CPM; curated private marketplace and brand-safe inventory can run $8 to $15 or more.

$$\text{Cost Per Mille (CPM)} = \frac{\text{Total Spend}}{\text{Impressions}} \text{ X } 1{,}000$$

View-Through Conversion Rate

What It Is: the percentage of users who saw (but did not click) a display ad and later completed a conversion within an attribution window (typically measured in 30/60 days dependent on industry), capturing display's real strength: building familiarity that pays off later rather than driving an immediate click.

$$\text{View-Through Conversion Rate} = \frac{\text{View-Through Conversions}}{\text{Viewable Impressions}}$$

Insight: Viewability is the Floor, Not the Ceiling

It's tempting to treat viewability as the finish line: once an impression is viewable, the job is done. These are considered the "billboards" of the web so shouldn't that be the target? Actually, in practice, viewability only confirms an ad had the opportunity to be seen. It says nothing about whether anyone actually looked. A sticky footer ad can achieve near-100% viewability while still suffering from banner blindness severe enough to produce a below-average CTR. Treat viewability as a prerequisite for a good campaign, not proof of one. Page placement, ad creative, and more need to be considered for all ads and as a metric of how the ad is performing, so consider A/B testing to see if different types of creative drive CTR AND viewability.

Retargeting

Retargeting (sometimes called remarketing) serves display, video, or native ads specifically to people who have already interacted with a brand. This means the user has either visited a website, viewed a product, or abandoned a cart and by using a tracking pixel or a list of known customer identifiers, the user or group of users have been followed across the web. Because retargeting reaches an audience that has already shown intent, it consistently and dramatically outperforms cold-prospecting display on nearly every engagement metric. While it is powerful, there are limitations as to what and who can be tracked.

Retargeted CTR

What It Is: the same click-through rate that you already know but focused among a retargeted (warm) audience, which commonly runs three to four times higher than standard prospecting display because the audience already knows the brand.

Cart Recovery Rate

What It Is: the percentage of users who abandoned a cart, were served a retargeting ad, and went on to complete the purchase — a direct measure of retargeting's most common use case in e-commerce.

$$\text{Cart Recovery Rate} = \frac{\text{Recovered Carts}}{\text{Total Abandoned Carts Targeted}}$$

Frequency

What It Is: the average number of times an individual user was served the retargeting ad over a given period. Frequency is one of the few levers a marketer fully controls, and it has a clear ceiling: pushing too many impressions at the same user erodes both performance and brand sentiment because of over-communication.

$$\text{Frequency} = \frac{\text{Impressions}}{\text{Reach}}$$

Tip: Privacy Law has Changed What Retargeting Pixels Can Actually See

A retargeting pixel may be installed and firing correctly and still be missing a substantial share of the audience it's meant to reach not because of a technical failure, but because of a legal one. Under GDPR, a retargeting pixel cannot fire until a visitor has given explicit, specific, informed consent for advertising tracking; a generic cookie banner that bundles retargeting into a broad "analytics" category does not meet that standard, and regulators have made clear they will treat it accordingly. Under CCPA and CPRA privacy laws in California, the pixel may fire by default but must be suppressed the moment a user exercises their opt-out right (including through a Global Privacy Control browser signal) and 2025 enforcement actions cited businesses specifically for displaying an "opt-out honored" message while their tag management system continued firing retargeting pixels in the background. Separate from consent, browser-level restrictions compound the problem: Safari's Intelligent Tracking Prevention and Firefox's Enhanced Tracking Protection already block or severely limit third-party cookie-based retargeting, and ad blockers prevent an estimated 30% to 40% of browser-side pixel requests from ever firing. The practical implication is that a retargeting audience built today is meaningfully smaller than the same strategy would have produced two or three years ago, and an analyst who benchmarks current retargeted CTR or cart recovery rate against historical data without accounting for this structural audience shrinkage is comparing two genuinely different things. The industry response has been server-side tagging and Conversion APIs (Meta CAPI, Google Enhanced Conversions) that route event data through a brand's own server rather than the visitor's browser. This preserves more measurement than browser-side pixels can, but does not eliminate the underlying consent requirement; server-to-server data transmission still constitutes personal data processing under GDPR and sharing under CCPA, regardless of how the signal was sent.

Native Advertising

Native advertising refers to paid content designed to match the form and function of the platform it appears on. For instance, an in-feed sponsored post that looks like an organic post, a sponsored article on a news site styled like editorial content, or a content recommendation widget (the familiar "You May Also Like" boxes from networks like Taboola and Outbrain) at the bottom of an article. Because native ads don't interrupt the reading or scrolling experience the way a banner does, they tend to outperform standard display on nearly every engagement measure.

Native CTR

What It Is: the click-through rate on native units, which commonly clears 0.2% to 0.5% (roughly four to ten times a standard display banner's CTR!) because the ad blends into the surrounding content rather than competing against it for attention.

Engagement Time

What It Is: how long a user spends with sponsored content after clicking through, particularly relevant for sponsored articles or branded video. Just like measuring time on page, this metric measures depth of attention, not just the click itself.

View-Through and Assisted Conversions

What It Is: conversions credited to users who were exposed to a native unit but converted later through another channel, which matters because native frequently performs an upper-funnel role rather than a last-click role.

OTT and CTV (Connected TV) Advertising

Over-the-top (OTT) and Connected TV (CTV) advertising refers to video ads delivered through internet-streamed television content. These are the ads you see on Hulu, Peacock, Tubi, Roku Channel, or YouTube TV.

Tip: Cap Your Frequency Before It Caps Your Results

Empirical sweet spots for 2026 display campaigns commonly fall between five and seven impressions per user per week for cold prospecting, and three to five per week for retargeting. Beyond that range, incremental CTR collapses and brand sentiment measurably erodes. If a retargeting campaign's performance is sliding even as spend increases, frequency, not creative, is often the first thing worth checking.

OTT advertisements are viewed on tablets, phones, gaming devices, and other streaming platforms that are not on a television. CTV ads are viewed on a smart TV or streaming device rather than over cable or satellite. CTV has become one of the fastest-growing paid media categories precisely because it combines the production quality and big-screen impact of traditional television with the targeting and measurement infrastructure of digital advertising. I've included it here as many OTT and CTV advertising placements are ordered or purchased on the same platforms that you purchase banner and tile, retargeting, and other similar ads.

Video Completion Rate (VCR)

What It Is: the percentage of video ad impressions that played through their entire duration. Because most CTV inventory is non-skippable and viewers are in a lean-back, actively chosen viewing context, VCR on CTV is dramatically higher than almost any other digital video environment. VCR is commonly 90% to 97%, compared to roughly 60% for combined mobile and desktop video.

$$\text{Video Completion Rate} = \frac{\text{Completed Views}}{\text{Video Starts}}$$

Household Reach and Frequency

What It Is: the number of unique households exposed to a CTV campaign, and how many times each household saw it on average. Because streaming devices are tied to a household rather than an individual, CTV reach is typically measured and capped at the household level rather than the user level.

Cost per Completed View (CPCV)

What It Is: the price paid for each fully completed video view, which standardizes comparisons across formats with very different completion rates. Why calculate CPCV? A $30 CPM ad with a 95% completion rate is a more efficient buy than a $20 CPM ad that only 50% of viewers finish.

$$\text{Cost per Completed View (CPCV)} = \frac{\text{Total Spend}}{\text{Completed Views}}$$

Side Quest: Why CTV Attribution is Still Really Hard

Even with high completion rates, connecting CTV ad exposure to a later conversion is more difficult than it sounds. A streaming device doesn't generate a click the way a banner ad does, and a single household television is frequently watched by multiple people (marketers refer to this as co-viewing) which means one ad impression may represent several different potential customers, or none of them, depending on who was actually in the room. The industry has responded with automatic content recognition (ACR) data, data clean rooms that match exposure logs to purchase data without exposing raw personal information, and old-fashioned lift studies that compare exposed versus unexposed households. Marketers can also utilize scannable QR codes connected to UTMs for tracking for direct conversion but usage of these by consumers can be limited. None of these solve attribution as cleanly as a tracked click, which is why most CTV reporting leans on directional lift rather than precise, deterministic attribution.

Digital Out-of-Home (DOOH) Advertising

Digital out-of-home advertising refers to paid content shown on digital screens in public, shared spaces like digital billboards, transit shelters, airport displays, mall and gym screens, and digital signage at the point of purchase. Unlike its static predecessor (a printed billboard that runs the same creative for weeks), DOOH content can update dynamically in real time and, increasingly, can be bought programmatically (pDOOH) the same way a marketer would buy display or video inventory online. So, while you can buy DOOH in traditional fashions, since online inventories exist and they can be purchased programmatically, we've included DOOH under the category of paid media.

Impressions and Dwell Time

What It Is: DOOH impressions are estimated rather than directly tracked, calculated from traffic counts, anonymized mobile location data, and dwell time (the average amount of time an audience spends within view of a screen). Dwell time varies enormously by location: a few seconds for a roadside billboard glimpsed by a passing driver, several minutes for a screen near a food court or transit waiting area, and creative length should be matched to that context.

Foot Traffic Attribution

What It Is: a measurement of store visit lift measured by comparing mobile location data for audiences exposed to a DOOH placement against an unexposed control group, used to connect an outdoor impression to a real-world visit days or hours later. In simple terms, it calculates whether foot traffic increases from those exposed to DOOH placement versus those that were not exposed to the DOOH placement.

Programmatic DOOH (pDOOH) Share

What It Is: the percentage of DOOH inventory bought through automated, real-time bidding platforms rather than traditional manual negotiation. This represents your share of messaging relative to all pDOOH inventory available on the platform. Programmatic DOOH has grown rapidly because it lets a single campaign respond to triggers like weather, time of day, or live audience composition rather than running a fixed, pre-negotiated schedule.

Insight: DOOH Measurement Has Moved from Guesswork to Verified Impressions

Out-of-home advertising spent decades being measured on traffic estimates and census data that advertisers more or less took on faith. Modern DOOH has shifted toward sensor- and mobile-data-driven measurement using anonymized device counts, dwell time, and verified proof-of-play logs that function much closer to digital-style reporting. This matters for an analyst because it means DOOH performance claims from five years ago and DOOH performance claims today may not be directly comparable; always confirm which measurement methodology produced any DOOH number before using it to plan a budget.

Audio and Podcast Advertising

Digital audio advertising covers ads served through streaming music (Spotify, Pandora) and podcasts, typically as pre-roll, mid-roll, or post-roll spots, and delivered either as a produced, programmatically inserted ad or as a host-read endorsement recorded by the show's host personally. Podcast advertising in particular has grown into a serious paid media category because it pairs unusually high completion rates with a level of audience trust that's difficult to manufacture in other formats.

Completion Rate / Listen-Through Rate (LTR)

What It Is: the percentage of an audio ad that plays through to the end. Because most podcast and streaming audio ads are non-skippable, completion rates run remarkably high (commonly 70% to 90%+) particularly for mid-roll placements, where the listener is already invested in the episode and would lose their place by skipping.

$$\text{Completion Rate} = \frac{\text{Completed Plays}}{\text{Ad Starts}}$$

Cost per Mille (CPM)

What It Is: podcast and audio CPMs vary widely by genre and placement. They can range from $15 to $25 for pre-roll, $25 to $45 for host-read mid-roll, and well above that for tightly defined, high-value B2B or finance audiences reflecting the fact that advertisers are paying as much for the host's credibility as for the impression itself.

Promo Code / Custom URL Response Rate

What It Is: the percentage of listeners who redeem a show-specific promo code or visit a custom landing page mentioned in the ad, which remains the most common and most reliable way to attribute action to a channel that, unlike most digital media, doesn't generate a click.

Host-Read vs. Programmatic

Host-read ads, in which the podcast host personally voices the endorsement, consistently outperform pre-produced, programmatically inserted spots on response rate and brand recall, often substantially so. The tradeoff is scale and consistency: host-read ads require a direct relationship with each show, while programmatic audio buying allows an advertiser to reach many shows at once with a single produced spot, at a lower CPM but a lower response rate per impression.

Retail Media Networks

Retail media refers to advertising sold by a retailer within its own digital and physical properties including paid search, sponsored product listings, on-site display, and increasingly in-store screens using the retailer's first-party purchase data to target shoppers at or near the moment of purchase. Amazon Ads and Walmart Connect are the two largest retail media networks in the United States, but the category also includes grocery, pharmacy, and big-box networks, along with demand-side platforms like Criteo that help brands buy across dozens of retail media networks through a single connection rather than negotiating with each retailer separately.

Return on Ad Spend (ROAS)

What It Is: revenue generated per dollar of retail media spend, the headline efficiency metric on every retail media platform — though cross-platform comparisons should be made carefully, since each network defines and attributes a "sale" differently.

$$\text{Return on Ad Spend (ROAS)} = \frac{\text{Total Ad Revenue}}{\text{Total Advertising Spend}}$$

Advertising Cost of Sale (ACoS)

What It Is: the inverse of ROAS, expressed as the percentage of sales consumed by advertising spend. A target ACoS should be set against a product's actual gross margin (break-even ACoS = (1 - gross margin) × 100) rather than against a generic platform average.

$$\text{Advertising Cost of Sale (ACoS)} = \frac{\text{Total Ad Spend}}{\text{Total Attributed Sales}}$$

New-to-Brand (NTB) Rate

What It Is: the percentage of attributed sales that came from customers who had not purchased the brand before, used to separate genuine customer acquisition from sales to existing, already-loyal buyers.

Incrementality

What It Is: the share of attributed sales that would not have happened without the ad as opposed to sales the retailer would have captured anyway through organic search or brand loyalty. A growing share of retail media buyers now rank incrementality, not raw ROAS, as their top KPI, precisely because reported ROAS can be inflated by sales the brand would have made regardless.

Think: A High ROAS Can Still Be a Bad Result

Imagine a campaign reports a 6x ROAS on a well-known, frequently searched product. Before celebrating, ask: **how many of those buyers would have found and purchased the product anyway through organic search, simply because it's a popular item with strong reviews?**

If the honest answer is "most of them," the campaign may be capturing credit for sales it didn't actually cause. This is a textbook case of why incrementality testing has become as important to retail media measurement as ROAS itself.

In-Game Advertising and Advergaming

In-game advertising places paid media inside video games and mobile apps — banners along the edge of a game screen, full-screen interstitials between levels, and rewarded video ads that a player opts into in exchange for an in-game benefit like extra lives or currency. Advergaming takes this further by building a playable mini-game or interactive ad unit specifically as the advertisement itself, letting a user experience a brand inside gameplay rather than simply viewing an ad alongside it.

Effective Cost per Mille (eCPM)

What It Is: the effective revenue (or cost) per 1,000 impressions, used because actual pricing in mobile game advertising is often blended across an auction-based waterfall of demand sources rather than a single fixed rate. eCPM varies dramatically by format: commonly under $1 for banners, several dollars for interstitials, and $15 to $40 or more for rewarded video in top-tier markets.

Opt-In Rate (Rewarded Video)

What It Is: the percentage of eligible players who voluntarily choose to watch a rewarded video ad in exchange for an in-game benefit. Because the action is voluntary, opt-in rate functions as a direct signal of how much value players place on the reward being offered.

$$\text{Opt-in Rate} = \frac{\text{Opt-Ins}}{\text{Eligible Impressions Offered}}$$

Completion Rate

What It Is: the percentage of started rewarded or interstitial ads watched to completion. Because rewarded video is opt-in, completion rates commonly clear 85% to 95%+ — among the highest of any digital ad format, for the same structural reason CTV completion rates run high: the viewer chose to be there.

$$\text{Completion Rate} = \frac{\text{Completed Views}}{\text{Ad Starts}}$$

Affiliate Advertising

Affiliate advertising compensates third-party publishers, content creators, influencers, and websites for driving a measurable action like a sale, lead, or signup through a unique tracked link or code, usually on a cost-per-acquisition or revenue-share basis rather than a fixed rate per impression or click. Because affiliates are only paid when the desired action happens, affiliate marketing carries some of the most favorable risk economics of any paid media channel for the advertiser, while shifting much of the channel's success or failure onto the quality of the affiliate's audience and content.

Earnings Per Click (EPC)

What It Is: the average commission an affiliate earns per click sent to an offer, which combines conversion rate and commission rate into a single number affiliates use to judge whether a program is worth their traffic.

$$\text{Earnings Per Click (EPC)} = \frac{\text{Total Commissions Paid}}{\text{Total Clicks}}$$

Affiliate Conversion Rate

What It Is: the percentage of affiliate-referred visitors who complete the desired action. Industry-wide averages commonly run 0.5% to 1%, with 1% to 5% considered strong performance, though high-intent verticals like software or finance can run meaningfully higher.

$$\text{Affiliate Conversion Rate} = \frac{\text{Conversions}}{\text{Affiliate-Referred Clicks}}$$

Side Quest: Commission = Vanity / EPC = Sanity

Experienced affiliates judge a program by EPC, not by the commission rate printed on the page, and the difference matters more than it first appears. A program offering a 30% commission but converting at only 2% can produce a lower EPC than a program offering 6% commission at a 12% conversion rate. Why? Because EPC is a function of both numbers multiplied together, not the commission rate alone. As an analyst, if you're ever asked to recruit or retain high-quality affiliates, recruiting on commission rate alone while ignoring your own site's conversion rate is one of the most common (and most expensive) mistakes a program manager can make.

Commission Rate

What It Is: the percentage of sale value (or flat amount per lead) paid to the affiliate, which varies enormously by category. For retail and e-commerce, the rate is typically 5 to 10% of the sales value and well above 20% for digital products and software where there's no physical cost of goods to protect.

Comparing the Channels at a Glance

No single table can do justice to so many genuinely different channels, but the comparison on the following page is a useful starting orientation particularly for spotting which channels are built for upper-funnel reach versus lower-funnel, attributable performance.

Channel	Funnel Role	Primary Metric
Banner / Tile / Display	Awareness / Retargeting	Viewability / View-Through Conversion
Retargeting	Lower-funnel, warm-audience conversion	Cart Recovery Rate / Retargeted CTR
Native Advertising	Upper-to-Mid-funnel content engagement	Engagement Time / Native CTR
OTT / CTV	Upper-funnel brand awareness and reach	Video Completion Rate (VCR)
Digital Out-of-Home	Upper-funnel reach, local awareness	Verified Impressions / Foot Traffic Attribution
Audio / Podcast	Upper-to-Mid-funnel trust building	Completion Rate / Listen-Through Rate (LTR)
In-Game / Advergaming	Awareness and app monetization	eCPM / Completion Rate
Affiliate Advertising	Lower-funnel, performance-based	EPC / Conversion Rate

Being Practical: Back to the Beginning

Let's go back to the beginning of this chapter and our furniture retailer. Once each channel's data was pulled into its own properly labeled report, a much clearer picture emerged. The CTV campaign, evaluated on household reach and VCR (94% completion across the local news buy), was doing exactly its job: building broad awareness ahead of a seasonal sale, with a measurable lift in branded search the week it aired. The retargeting campaign, evaluated on cart recovery rate, was recovering roughly 9% of abandoned carts which is considered a healthy range and clearly justified its budget on its own terms. The DOOH billboards near the two flagship stores showed a 14% foot traffic lift with attribution among exposed mobile devices compared to a control group, a result that would have been invisible without location-based attribution.

The affiliate program, however, told a more complicated story. Commission payouts looked healthy on paper, but EPC had quietly fallen by a third over two quarters. Digging in, the retailer's top affiliate, a home-decor blogger responsible for the majority of the program's revenue, had shifted her content from blog reviews to short-form video, and her audience was converting at a meaningfully lower rate on the retailer's slow-loading mobile checkout page than it had on desktop. No single channel-level metric flagged this. It took comparing EPC against conversion rate along with Core Web Vitals data to find a problem that had nothing to do with the affiliate relationship itself and everything to do with a checkout experience nobody on the marketing team had tested on a phone.

This is the recurring lesson of paid media analytics: every channel will provide for you metrics that looks reassuring in isolation. The job of an analyst is to know which metric actually answers the question being asked and to recognize, as in the affiliate example above, when the real story is hiding in the relationship between two metrics rather than in either one alone.

Now, we turn from paid media spend to earned media including the coverage, mentions, and word-of-mouth a brand receives without paying directly for placement, and the very different set of metrics required to measure something no one bought.

References

11 metrics for CTV measurement (2026, March 6). Keen. https://keends.com/blog/metrics-for-ctv-measurement/

21 Essential Affiliate Marketing Benchmarks & KPIs for Success in 2026 (n.d.). Partnero. https://www.partnero.com/articles/21-essential-affiliate-marketing-benchmarks

Affiliate Marketing Statistics 2026: 130+ Data Points (2026, April 21). Digital Applied. https://www.digitalapplied.com/blog/affiliate-marketing-statistics-2026-data-points

Bartucz, B. (2026, February 19). *Affiliate Marketing Conversion Rate Benchmarks & Best Practices (2026)*. OptiMonk. https://www.optimonk.com/affiliate-marketing-conversion-rate

Belfiore, F. (2025, November 11). *Rewarded Ads Unpacked: Performance Insights and What's Coming for 2026*. MAF. https://maf.ad/en/blog/rewarded-ads-stats/

Bur, B. (2026, January 13). *Retargeting Done Right: Complying with 2026 Privacy Rules*. The Ad Firm. https://www.theadfirm.net/retargeting-done-right-complying-with-2026-privacy-rules/

Cardoza, K. (2026, March 24). *Podcast Advertising Metrics That Matter More Than Downloads*. MillionPodcasts. https://www.millionpodcasts.com/blog/podcast-advertising-metrics/

Clark, P. et. al. (2026, January 15). *FAQ on native advertising: Formats, AI opportunities, and the best metrics for 2026*. EMARKETER. https://www.emarketer.com/content/faq-on-native-advertising--formats--ai-opportunities--best-metrics-2026

CTV Advertising Benchmarks 2026: $15 - $85 by Industry (Real Data). (n.d.). North American Media Experts. https://www.namediaexperts.com/blog-posts/ctv-advertising-benchmarks-2026-cpm-vcr-roas

Digital Out of Home Advertising: The Complete Guide to DOOH in 2026. (2026, February 18). Refuel Agency. https://www.refuelagency.com/blog/digital-out-of-home/

Display Advertising Benchmarks 2026: 150+ Data Points. (2026, April 20). Digital Applied. https://www.digitalapplied.com/blog/display-advertising-benchmarks-2026-data-points

Display Advertising Benchmarks 2026: CTR, CPM & Viewability (2025). OwlClaw Technologies. https://owlclaw.com/benchmarks/display-ads-benchmarks/

Display Advertising Statistics 2026: 93+ Stats & Insights [Expert Analysis]. (n.d.). Marketing LTB. https://marketingltb.com/blog/statistics/display-advertising-statistics/

Dixon, A. (2019, April 3). *OTT Performance Marketing & Advertising Metrics Guide*. Strategus. https://www.strategus.com/blog/ott-ad-metrics-explained

Esau, D. (2026, June 9). *How Tracking Pixels Work: A 2026 Marketer's Guide.* Click Track Marketing. https://www.clicktrackmarketing.com/blog/how-tracking-pixels-work-a-2026-marketers-guide

Graham, K. (2026, February 20). *The 2026 AdMob & Mobile Monetization Playbook*. MonetizeMore. https://www.monetizemore.com/blog/admob-monetization/

Harutyunyan, M. (2026, May 13). *Must-Know Podcast Statistics in 2026.* Loopex Digital. https://www.loopexdigital.com/blog/podcast-statistics

Hyder, N. (2026, May 28). *Native Ads in Retail Media 2026: Benchmarks & Platforms*. Osmos. https://www.osmos.ai/blog/native-advertising-retail-media-benchmarks-2026

Hyder, N. (2026, July 1). *Retail Media Evolution: The Complete Guide (2026)*. Osmos. https://www.osmos.ai/blog/retail-media-evolution-the-complete-guide

Hyder, N. (2026, May 18). *ROAS Benchmarks by Platform and Ad Format in 2026: The Definitive Guide for Retail Media Networks*. Osmos. https://www.osmos.ai/blog/roas-benchmarks-platform-ad-format-2026

Joles, P. (2026, May 21). *Retargeting Pixels and Privacy Law: What Marketing Teams Need to Get Right*. Lokker. https://lokker.com/blog/retargeting-pixels-consent-privacy-law

Malkhasyan, T. (2026, February 23). *What is CPCV (Cost Per Completed View) - And Why It Matters for Video Advertising*. AI Digital. https://www.aidigital.com/blog/cpcv

McWilliams, M. (2026, June 14). *What is EPC in Affiliate Marketing?*. The Affiliate Guy. https://www.mattmcwilliams.com/what-is-epc-affiliate-marketing/

Mikho, C. (2026, May 8). *DOOH: What It Is, How It Works, and Why It Matters in 2026*. Improvado. https://improvado.io/blog/dooh

Mohtasham, H. (2026, May 18). *What Is Viewability Rate? The Complete 2026 Guide to Measuring Ad Visibility*. CUFinder. https://cufinder.io/blog/wiki/marketing-metrics/viewability-rate/

Moss, S. (2026, January 7). *What is programmatic DOOH (pDOOH) and how does it work*. AI Digital. https://www.aidigital.com/blog/programmatic-dooh

Podcast advertising CPM benchmarks: what brands actually pay in 2026. (n.d.). Pod Partnerships. https://podpartnerships.com/blogs/podcast-advertising-cpm-benchmarks

Podcast Advertising ROI: CPM Rates, Listener Action & Brand Lift from 1,000+ Campaigns & 2026 Industry Reports [2026 Analysis]. (2025, December 30). DollarPocket. https://www.dollarpocket.com/podcast-advertising-roi-report/

Programmatic Advertising Statistics 2026. (2026, March 17). Searchlab. https://searchlab.nl/en/statistics/programmatic-advertising-statistics-2026

Retail Media Benchmarks 2026: Amazon, Walmart Connect, & Instacart ROAS and CPC Compared. (2026). North American Media Experts. https://www.namediaexperts.com/blog-posts/retail-media-benchmarks-2026-amazon-walmart-instacart

Retail Media Market Guide 2025 – How to Start Your Retail Media Ads. (2025, May 19).. RMIQ. https://www.rmiq.net/walmart/retail-media-guide/

Rewarded Video. (n.d.). Coinis. https://coinis.com/glossary/rewarded-video

Stock, D. (n.d.). *Video Completion Rate (VCR): What Is It & How To Calculate*. MNTN. https://mountain.com/blog/video-completion-rate/

The Global Privacy Rules Every Marketing Team Should Understand. (2026). OneTrust. https://www.onetrust.com/blog/the-global-privacy-rules-every-marketing-team-should-understand/

US State Privacy Laws 2026: What Marketing Teams Must Know. (2026, February 10). Secure Privacy. https://secureprivacy.ai/blog/us-state-privacy-laws-2026-marketing

Wi-Fi tracking in DOOH: how to measure the real audience of digital screens in 2026. (n.d.). Advision. https://www.advision.digital/2026/06/04/wi-fi-tracking-in-dooh/

Chapter 11
Earned Media Analytics

One of our agency's clients spent $5,000 on a paid influencer campaign to drive visibility to their products in store at Costco. Doing so drove clear data in terms of views, clicks, and clearly attributable to foot traffic and sales. A month later, an editor on a food blog independently writes a glowing, unsolicited review of one of the brand's products after trying it at a local grocery store just a week earlier. The article gets picked up by two aggregator sites, gets linked from a handful of Reddit threads, and a noticeable bump in branded search appears the following week. No one on the marketing team (or from our agency) asked for any of it, paid for any of it, or controlled a single word of it. And almost nobody on the marketing team knows how to report it.

That is how earned media works. The visibility, mentions, links, reviews, and word-of-mouth a brand can receive without directly paying for the placement. It is, by definition, the channel a brand controls the least and the channel that audiences trust the most which seems like a contradiction that makes it both extremely valuable and notoriously difficult to measure. Over my career, I've worked with reporters to achieve these results but the relationship-building and product-explaining that goes into finding success in earned media really takes one major resource: time.

This chapter focuses specifically on digital earned media: not traditional press clippings or broadcast mentions, but the measurable, trackable earned channels that exist online from digital PR and earned backlinks, online reviews and ratings, social mentions and user-generated content, and the word-of-mouth signals that increasingly determine whether a brand shows up in a synthesized answer from an AI platform.

Owned, Paid, and Earned: Why Earned Is the Hardest to Measure

Marketers commonly sort media into three buckets. Owned media is anything a brand fully controls from its website, its email list, its creative assets, and its social accounts (as much as one can own social media accounts). Paid media, the subject of the previous chapter, is anything a brand pays a platform or publisher to distribute. Earned media is everything else: the coverage, links, reviews, and mentions a brand receives because someone else, either a journalist, a customer, a stranger on Reddit, chose to talk about it, unprompted and unpaid.

The reason earned media analytics deserves its own chapter, rather than being folded into search or social, is that earned media doesn't live on a single platform with a single dashboard. A single piece of earned coverage can simultaneously produce a backlink (an SEO signal), a spike in referral traffic (a web analytics signal), a handful of social shares (a social signal), and a mention an AI search tool might cite months later (a GEO signal). Measuring earned media well means pulling threads from several of the chapters already covered in this book and assembling them into a single, coherent picture of unpaid visibility.

Digital PR and Earned Backlinks

Digital PR is the modern, search-aware evolution of traditional public relations. Instead of (or in addition to) pitching a story for its own sake, digital PR practitioners pitch original research, data, and expert commentary specifically to earn a link and a mention from a high-authority publication. While there are certainly elements of traditional PR efforts (building relationships with reporters, understanding outlets, pitching stories, etc.), digital PR comes with the additional benefit of providing backlinks and pivotal citations / mentions. For years, digital PR has become the dominant link-building tactic in SEO precisely because the links it earns are editorially chosen rather than negotiated or purchased which is exactly the kind of link search engines, and increasingly AI search tools, treat as a genuine signal of authority.

Referring Domains and Domain Rating (DR) / Domain Authority (DA)

What It Is: the number of unique websites linking back to a brand's content, and the relative authority of those linking sites as scored by tools like Ahrefs (Domain Rating) or Moz (Domain Authority). Domains are the unique websites that link to your site where backlinks are the number of actual links. One website (referring domain) can provide multiple backlinks to a site (similar to the idea of users and sessions in web analytics). A handful of links from well-respected, high-authority publications carries more SEO and credibility weight than dozens of links from low-authority sites. The more backlinks and more domains, the more popular your own website becomes thus increasing its Domain Rating (DR) or Domain Authority (DA). Higher authority means higher rankings as your website becomes more of an authority in and of itself.

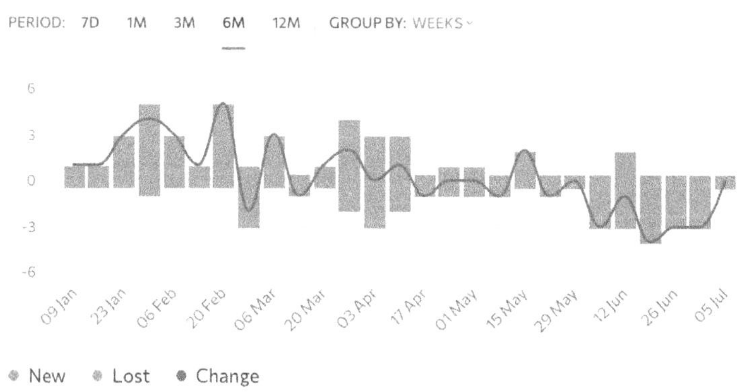

Source: SE Ranking

Referral Traffic from Earned Placements

What It Is: the actual human visits arriving at a brand's website from a specific piece of earned coverage, tracked through web analytics. Unlike a backlink's SEO value, which can take months to show up in rankings, referral traffic from a well-placed article can be measured the same week it publishes.

Brand Mention Volume

What It Is: the total number of times a brand is referenced across the web, with or without an accompanying link, tracked using media monitoring or social listening tools. A successful digital PR campaign should produce a measurable increase in mentions that extends well beyond the handful of direct links it generated. As noted in previous chapters, brand mentions both on social media and beyond can provide as much value, if not more, than backlinks in terms of both SEO and GEO activities.

Side Quest: SparkToro Uses Audience Research as an Earned Media Strategy

Most earned media planning starts from the wrong question. A brand asks "which publications should we pitch?" or "which podcasts should we sponsor?" and then spends weeks guessing based on name recognition and circulation numbers that may have nothing to do with whether a given outlet actually reaches the audience the brand cares about. SparkToro, the audience intelligence platform co-founded by Rand Fishkin (co-founder of popular SEO platform Moz and one of the most widely cited practitioners in the SEO and content marketing world) was built specifically to answer the better question first: where does your target audience actually pay attention?

SparkToro works by drawing on behavioral data from tens of millions of public social and web profiles, aggregated and anonymized, to produce a detailed picture of any describable audience's media consumption. It looks at the websites they visit, the podcasts they listen to, the YouTube channels they watch, the subreddits they participate in, the social accounts they follow, and the keywords they search. As of January 2026, the platform added natural language audience descriptions, meaning a marketer can now describe a specific audience in plain English and receive comprehensive behavioral data about the segment within seconds. Simply ask SparkToro to help you find where "B2B marketing directors at mid-sized SaaS companies" or "women over 40 training for their first marathon" consume content and it provides a response without building complex filter combinations. For earned media specifically, this matters because the platform answers a question that brand mention volume, share of voice, and backlink reports cannot: where should we be earning those mentions in the first place? A digital PR team that uses SparkToro before pitching a campaign knows which publications, podcasts, and creators already hold the attention of the exact audience they want to reach saving time and resources. The same data can surface influencer and creator partnership opportunities (the platform's SparkScore metric evaluates the engagement quality of a social account relative to its follower count, a more honest signal than follower count alone), identify which industry websites are worth earning a backlink, and inform which channels deserve more earned media investment going into the next planning cycle.

One important caveat: the platform's data is strongest for English-speaking, US-centric audiences and thinner for non-English markets, which is worth checking on a free-tier search before committing a subscription budget.

AI Citation Rate

What It Is: how often a brand is referenced or cited when AI platforms like Claude, ChatGPT, Perplexity, or Google's AI Overviews answer a relevant query. This is a metric that did not meaningfully exist as a tracked KPI before 2025 and has rapidly become one of the most closely watched earned-media outcomes in 2026. Of note is that no platform currently does this perfectly as of yet and this metric is still a work in process as it does require an attempt to collect not only the brand's mentions, but those of competitors to provide a measurable rate.

Insight: Mentions May Now Matter More Than Links

I've mentioned this before in this text, but it's worth repeating and from an earned media perspective. For two decades, the backlink was the undisputed currency of earned digital visibility. That is changing. A widely cited 2025–2026 analysis of tens of thousands of brands found that unlinked brand mentions across the web correlate with AI Overviews visibility roughly three times more strongly than traditional backlinks do. In addition, brands in the top quartile for web mentions receive roughly ten times more AI-generated visibility than those in the bottom half. The reason is simple: a generative AI system is synthesizing an answer from patterns across many sources, not crawling a link graph to rank pages. Thus, simply being talked about on a review site, Reddit thread, YouTube video, or a product comparison page carries real weight even when no one links back to the brand's own website.

This new data doesn't make backlinks obsolete as they still drive traditional search rankings and remain a meaningful AI signal in their own right. What it does mean is that an earned media strategy built only around earning links, while ignoring earning mentions, is now optimizing for half of the modern visibility equation.

Online Reviews and Ratings

Online reviews are one of the oldest forms of digital earned media and remain among the most directly tied to revenue. A review left on Google, Yelp, Trustpilot, the App Store, or a B2B platform like G2 is, functionally, unsolicited customer testimony that a brand cannot fully control but can meaningfully influence. These reviews feed not just human purchase decisions but the local search and AI responses covered in previous sections. The real life value of reviews for some businesses can be directly seen in revenue.

Average Star Rating

What It Is: the mean customer rating across a review platform, which functions as both a trust signal to other customers and a ranking input for local search. A rating below roughly 4.0 stars is a widely cited tipping point below which a meaningful share of consumers will not consider a business at all.

$$\text{Average Star Rating} = \frac{\text{Sum of All Star Ratings}}{\text{Total Number of Reviews}}$$

Review Volume and Review Velocity

What It Is: the total number of reviews a business has accumulated, and the rate at which new reviews are arriving. Volume alone serves as a snapshot of both positive and negative sentiment. The velocity at which these reviews are received also tell a story about sentiment. A business with hundreds of reviews but none in the last six months can lose ground to a newer competitor whose reviews are fewer in number but consistently fresh, since most consumers weight recent reviews far more heavily than older ones.

$$\text{Review Velocity} = \frac{\text{New Reviews Received}}{\text{Time Period (typically 30 days)}}$$

Review Response Rate

What It Is: the percentage of received reviews, particularly negative ones, that receive a public response from the business. Consumer expectations for a response are high and most businesses fall well short of meeting them, which makes response rate one of the more achievable, low-cost improvements available in earned media management.

$$\text{Review Response Rate} = \frac{\text{Reviews Responded To}}{\text{Total Reviews Received}}$$

These metrics matter beyond reputation for its own sake. Each additional star of rating has been tied to measurable revenue lift in independent research, and businesses that actively respond to reviews report meaningfully higher revenue than those that don't thus making review management one of the few earned media activities with a fairly direct, demonstrable line to the bottom line.

Social Mentions, User-Generated Content, and Share of Voice

Chapter 7 introduced the concept of social share of voice (SSoV), or the percentage of total industry conversation on social media that belongs to a brand rather than its competitors, as an organic social metric. It belongs equally in this chapter, because an unprompted mention, tag, or piece of user-generated content (a customer's unboxing video, a fan's meme, or an enthusiastic tweet) is earned media in its purest form: content a brand did not create, pay for, or directly request. The tools used to capture this type of data vary but prominent platforms include BrandWatch, Sprout Social, InMoment, Agorapulse, and many more.

Brand Mentions (Tagged and Untagged)

What It Is: the total count of references to a brand across social platforms, distinguishing between direct, tagged mentions ("@brand") and indirect, untagged mentions (a post that names the brand without tagging its account). Untagged mentions are often the more candid and more numerous of the two, and many brands miss the majority of their own earned conversation by monitoring tags alone.

Sentiment

What It Is: the proportion of brand mentions that are positive, negative, or neutral, typically derived through automated natural-language analysis of mention text. Sentiment adds a dimension that raw mention volume cannot: a spike in mentions during a product recall and a spike during a viral product launch will look identical on a volume chart and completely different on a sentiment chart. An example of a sentiment analysis dashboard from Sprout Social is shown below.

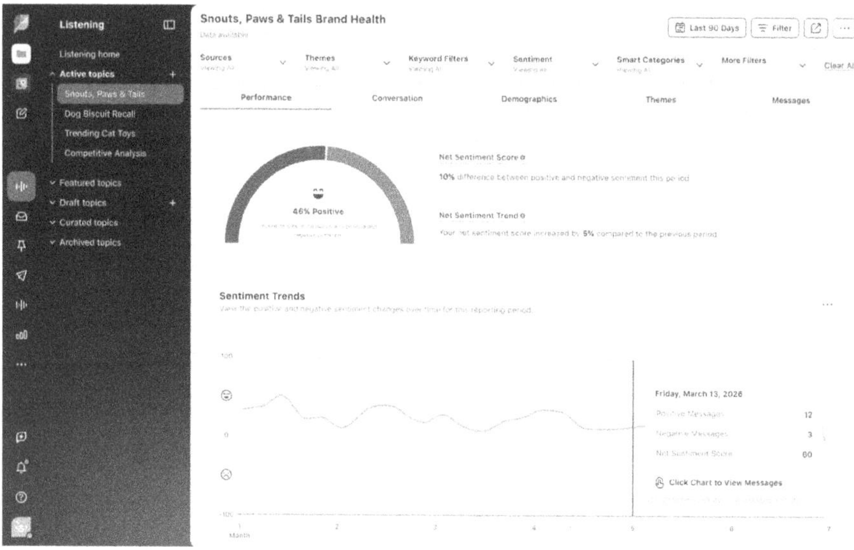

Source: Sprout Social

Virality Rate

What It Is: introduced in Chapter 7 as a paid-and-organic social metric, virality rate, or the ratio of a post's reach among non-followers to its reach among existing followers, is just as relevant here when the content driving that spread is user-generated rather than brand-published. A piece of UGC that travels far beyond its original audience is earned media in motion, and tracking its reach the same way a brand would track its own viral post is the only way to know whether that earned moment is worth amplifying further.

Word of Mouth and Referral

Word of mouth is the oldest form of earned media, and the digital era hasn't replaced it so much as given it new, trackable surfaces. Now, marketers can use a referral link, a promo code shared in a group chat, or even the famous Net Promoter Score survey that quantifies how likely a customer is to become an advocate in the first place.

Net Promoter Score (NPS)

What It Is: a customer loyalty metric derived from a single question — "How likely are you to recommend us to a friend or colleague?" on a 0–10 scale that sorts respondents into Promoters (9–10), Passives (7–8), and Detractors (0–6). NPS functions as a leading indicator of earned media output, since the overwhelming majority of positive word of mouth comes from Promoters and the overwhelming majority of negative word of mouth comes from Detractors.

Net Promoter Score (NPS) = % of Promoters - % of Detractors
(results in a score from -100 to +100)

Think: Is NPS Telling You What Already Happened, or What's About to Happen?

NPS is often discussed as if it predicts growth, and the broader research connecting NPS movement to revenue growth supports that framing at the aggregate, industry level. But for an individual brand asking "why did our score drop ten points this quarter," NPS usually behaves more like a lagging indicator and a summary of customer experiences that already happened, surfaced after the fact through a survey. If a brand wants NPS to function as an early warning system rather than a quarterly postmortem, it has to pair the score with the open-ended follow-up question ("why did you give us that score?") and act on detractor feedback quickly, since research suggests a meaningful share of detractors can still be converted if a business closes the loop within days rather than months.

Referred Customer Performance

What It Is: the lifetime value, retention rate, and acquisition cost of customers who arrived through a referral compared to customers acquired through other channels. Referred customers consistently outperform nonreferred customers on retention and lifetime value, because they arrive with a degree of trust a brand didn't have to build itself.

Earned Media Value (EMV): A Cross-Channel Rollup

Because earned media spans so many channels with so many different native metrics, many organizations roll everything up into a single estimated dollar figure called Earned Media Value (EMV). EMV is an attempt to answer the executive-level question "what would it have cost us to buy the equivalent exposure?" EMV models typically blend estimated reach, engagement, and a paid-media equivalent rate by platform and format to produce a single comparable number across a backlink, a review, a social mention, and a piece of UGC alike.

Side Quest: The Honest Limits of EMV

EMV is useful for one specific job: giving a non-technical stakeholder a directionally meaningful number to compare against a paid media budget, especially for brand-awareness work where no direct sale is being tracked. It is not a precise measurement, and treating it as one is a common analytical mistake. There is no single universal formula for EMV. Literally every platform and agency model's paid-media equivalent rate is slightly different, which means an EMV figure from one tool is not directly comparable to an EMV figure from another. While I have seen it used effectively (for instance a friend who once oversaw social media at Arby's used EMV to calculate the value of a major viral moment during the Grammys), it was, again, meant for non-technical stakeholders to understand the value created from the viral moment.

The best way to use EMV is as a relative, internal trend line (showing your estimated earned value growing quarter over quarter, using the same methodology each time) rather than as an absolute number to defend in a budget meeting against a precisely tracked paid media result. This use makes more sense, allows for historical benchmarking and doesn't provide opportunities for manipulation to benefit the marketing or PR teams when necessary.

Comparing the Earned Media Signals at a Glance

With earned media being available in so many channels, I thought it might be helpful to once again share a chart to share the earned signal, where it is used, and the primary metric used for tracking. This is not an exhaustive list but a tool that can be used when trying to determine what to measure and where to make the next best decision in your earned media marketing efforts.

Earned Signal	Where It's Used	Primary Metric
Digital PR / Earned Links	Search rankings, AI citations, referral traffic	Referring Domains / AI Citation Rate
Online Reviews	Local search, purchase decisions, AI summary responses	Average Star Rating / Review Velocity
Social Mentions / UGC	Social platforms, brand conversation share	Brand Mentions / Sentiment / Virality Rate
Word of Mouth / Referrals	Customer acquisition, Retention	NPS / Referred Customer LTV

Being Practical: Understanding Signals

Let's return to the brand from the opening of this chapter. The unsolicited editor review, tracked properly, turns out to be measurable on nearly every axis covered in this chapter. The article itself produced two earned backlinks from a moderately authoritative domain and a noticeable bump in referral traffic the week it published. The aggregator pickups and Reddit threads added roughly a dozen additional, mostly untagged brand mentions, with sentiment running overwhelmingly positive. Branded search volume rose 9% the following week, suggesting some of that traffic arrived through search rather than direct links. And three months later, when a customer asked an AI shopping assistant for product recommendations in that category, the brand was cited, not because of the backlinks alone, but because the volume of mentions the article triggered across multiple independent sites had, in aggregate, made the brand more visible to a system that weighs mentions as heavily as links.

None of this shows up in a single dashboard, and none of it was something the marketing team could have bought directly. What they could do, and what this chapter has been building toward, is recognize each piece of the signal for what it was. Whether it's a backlink, a referral spike, a mention, a citation, it doesn't necessarily matter. What does matter is reporting on it using the right vocabulary for each, rather than either ignoring an earned win because it doesn't fit neatly into a paid media report, or rolling it all into a single EMV number and calling the analysis done. Earned media rewards attention precisely because it can't be commanded. An analyst's job is to notice it, measure it honestly across the channels it actually touches, and feed what's working back into the strategy that earned it in the first place. This way, no matter the next campaign, you can learn what works, what doesn't, and be prepared for the next round.

In the next chapter, we'll wrap up our discussions around channel metrics as we turn to mobile app analytics. Mobile apps are a channel where many of the engagement and retention concepts introduced across this text take on a distinct set of platform-specific metrics of their own.

References

Boonzaaijer, R. (2026, June 3). *50 net promoter score statistics you need to know in 2026*. Ringly. https://www.ringly.io/blog/nps-statistics-2026

Dubey, E. (2026, May 25). *What Is Net Promoter Score (NPS)? A Complete Guide [2026]*. Kayako. https://kayako.com/blog/net-promoter-score-nps/

Get Instant Audience Research Do Better Marketing. (n.d.). SparkToro. https://sparktoro.com/product

Google Review Response Statistics: 30+ Data Points for 2026. (2026, February 12). ReplyOnTheFly. https://www.replyonthefly.com/blog/google-review-response-statistics

Ghimire, S. (2026, March 25). *The Ultimate Digital PR And Link Building Guide*. Outpace SEO. https://outpaceseo.com/article/link-building/

Hass, M. (2026, April 15). *Google Review Benchmarks by Industry (2026): How Do You Compare?*. Feedback Guru. https://www.feedback-guru.com/blog/google-review-benchmarks-by-industry

Henshaw, J. (2026, June 14). *Audience research platform SparkToro, gets a new look and significant new features*. Coywolf. https://coywolf.com/news/content-marketing/audience-research-platform-sparktoro-gets-a-new-look-and-significant-new-features/

Link Building Statistics 2026: 70+ Data Points (Including AI Search). (2026, May 13). QuickSEO. https://quickseo.ai/blog/link-building-statistics-2026-70-data-points-including-ai-search

Medina, T. & Do, D. (2026, May 4). *What is a good domain authority score? (and how do you actually improve it?)*. Launchcodex. https://launchcodex.com/blog/seo-geo-ai/what-is-a-good-domain-authority-score/

Net Promoter Score Benchmarks by Industry 2026: Average NPS Data. (2026, June 14). StealthAgents. https://stealthagents.com/research/net-promoter-score-benchmarks-2026

Online Reviews Statistics 2026: Trust, Local SEO & Reputation Data. (n.d.). BizIQ. https://biziq.com/blog/online-reviews-statistics/

Raileanu, G. (2026, April 15). *What is a Good Net Promoter Score? (2026 NPS Benchmark).* Retently. https://www.retently.com/blog/good-net-promoter-score/

Schroth, B. (2026, June). *Digital PR Link Building: The Data-Backed Guide.* Reporter Outreach. https://www.reporteroutreach.com/blog/digital-pr-link-building

Singh, S. (2026, May 26). *56+ Digital PR Statistics 2026: Cost, ROI & AI Trends.* LinkBuild Agency. https://linkbuild.agency/digital-pr-statistics/

SparkToro Review 2026: Features, Pricing & Top Alternatives. (2026, June 3). MaxAEO. https://maxaeo.ai/ai-tools/tool/sparktoro/

The Complete Roadmap to Using SparkToro in 2026. (2026, May 1). Marketing Agent Blog. https://marketingagent.blog/2026/05/01/the-complete-roadmap-to-using-sparktoro-in-2026/

Vaghasiya, K. (2026, May 22). *53 Google Review Statistics Every Business Must Know (2026).* WiserReview. https://wiserreview.com/blog/google-review-statistics/

Chapter 12
Mobile App Analytics

With the power of Google Analytics 4 (GA4), many marketers rely on data from GA4 to track events across any of their apps. This is a reasonable strategy as the platform allows for this and using data streams wisely can allow you to track all of your owned sites and apps in one location. But, it is important to note that apps and websites do differ in a number of different ways.

For instance, let's say a meditation app spends six months and a meaningful chunk of its marketing budget driving downloads. The campaign is, by every paid acquisition metric covered in earlier chapters, a clear success: installs are up, cost per install is comfortably below a set target, and the app briefly cracks the top 50 in its category. Three months later, a board member asks a much simpler question: "How many of those people are still using it?" The honest answer that you have to provide is fewer than one in twenty. The download, it seems, was never the difficult part. Getting someone to open the app a second time, and a thirtieth time, was near impossible.

Mobile app analytics exists to answer these sorts of hard questions. Unlike a website, where a visit is often a single, self-contained event, an app is something a user installs once and (ideally) returns to repeatedly over weeks, months, or years. That means our most important metrics aren't about a single key event. Our most important metrics track user behavior over time. This chapter covers that relationship in three stages: how users discover and install an app, how they engage with it (or don't) over time, and how that engagement eventually converts into revenue.

Discovery and Acquisition

Before an app can be measured for engagement, it has to be found and installed, and that discovery happens through two distinct paths that will sound quite familiar: organic, through an app store's own search and browse algorithms, and paid, through install advertising on networks like Meta, Google, TikTok, and even other games or apps.

App Store / Google Play Store Conversion Rate

What It Is: the percentage of people who view an app's store listing (its icon, screenshots, description, and reviews) and go on to install it. A well-optimized listing commonly converts in the 3% to 5% range, and because this number compounds across every paid campaign sent to that listing, app store optimization (ASO) is one of the few growth levers that improves both organic and paid performance simultaneously.

$$\text{App Store Conversion Rate} = \frac{\text{Installs}}{\text{Store Page Views}}$$

Cost per Install (CPI)

What It Is: the average paid media cost to acquire a single install, which varies enormously by platform, category, and geography. CPI is commonly higher on iOS than Android, and meaningfully higher for finance and subscription apps than for casual games, reflecting the higher lifetime value those users represent.

$$\text{Cost per Install (CPI)} = \frac{\text{Total Ad Spend}}{\text{Attributed Installs}}$$

Organic vs. Paid Install Ratio

What It Is: the share of total installs coming from unpaid app store discovery versus paid advertising. A healthy organic share suggests an app's ASO and word-of-mouth are going well; a campaign that drives only paid installs with no organic lift is paying for every single user with no compounding benefit.

Download-to-Registration Conversion Rate

What It Is: the percentage of users who download an app and go on to complete account creation, onboarding, or whatever initial step formally activates them as a user inside the product. Croll and Yoskovitz, authors of *Lean Analytics*, treat this as a distinct and critical early-funnel metric because a large gap between downloads and registrations signals an onboarding problem that no amount of acquisition spend can solve. Without registration, you are simply filling a funnel faster at the top while losing the same proportion at the first meaningful step inside the app.

$$\text{Download-to-Registration Conversion Rate} = \frac{\text{Completed Registrations}}{\text{Total Downloads}}$$

Remember that downloads all have a cost: either in resources from organic optimization or directly through paid media. A user who downloads an app and never completes registration represents the worst possible return on your investment as you paid some resource to acquire them but they never become customers. Thus, tracking the gap between installation and engagement is critical. If a gap does exist it can be for a variety of reasons: the app is requesting too much information too early, permissions requests to access the camera, location, or more before the users trusts the app, or you've yet to show the user the core value of your application and are asking them to commit to an account they aren't ready to commit to.

One additional discipline that Croll and Yoskovitz specifically call out for mobile is that customer acquisition cost (CAC) should never be calculated as a single blended cost across all sources. The lifetime value of users acquired from the app store may be highly valuable whereas customers who convert from paid social media efforts may download the app but never convert and complete registration. So, it may be that your blended CAC is acceptable, but when reviewed channel by channel one channel's leads may be more valuable than another. Thus, if an organization's goal is to acquire the highest-value lifetime value customers possible, then focusing on the channels that drive those types of customers would never be discovered if you only are calculating a blended CAC.

Insight: CPI Tells You What an Install Cost, Not What It Was Worth

It seems obvious to treat a low CPI as an unambiguous win, but CPI is a volume metric, not a quality metric. CPI says nothing about whether the people who have installed are likely to stick around or ever pay. A campaign that drives installs at half the CPI of another channel can still be the worse investment if those users leave (or churn as they say in the mobile app industry) within a day. Most experienced user acquisition teams treat CPI as a diagnostic to compare channels and creative, while bidding and budgeting decisions are made against a deeper metric like cost per trial, cost per purchase, or projected lifetime value, that accounts for what happens after the install.

Engagement and Retention

Once a user has installed an app, the central question shifts from "did they download it" to "did it become part of their routine." This is where mobile app analytics diverges most sharply from website analytics. Rather than measuring a single visit, an analyst must track an install cohort over time and watch how quickly, and how completely, that cohort disappears.

N-Day Retention (D1 / D7 / D30)

What It Is: the percentage of users from an install cohort who return to the app exactly N days after installing. Day 1 (D1) retention reflects whether onboarding delivered enough value to bring someone back the next day; D7 reflects whether a habit is forming and they have come back within 7 days; D30 reflects whether the app has become a genuine part of someone's routine as they have come back within 30 days. Retention drops fastest between D1 and D7 for nearly every app category, and benchmarks vary widely. For instance, messaging and habit-forming finance apps often see D1 above 50%, while categories like education commonly see D30 fall below 3%.

$$\text{N-Day Retention Rate} = \frac{\text{Users Active on Exactly Day N}}{\text{Original Cohort Size}}$$

DAU, MAU, and Stickiness

What It Is: Daily Active Users and Monthly Active Users measure the size of an app's active user base at two different time windows; stickiness (DAU ÷ MAU) measures what share of an app's monthly users are showing up on any given day. A stickiness ratio around 20% is generally considered healthy, and above 25% to 30% is considered strong. Similar to retention, the right benchmark depends heavily on whether an app is meant to be used daily (a habit tracker) or only occasionally (a tax-filing app).

$$\text{Stickiness} = \frac{\text{DAU}}{\text{MAU}}$$

Session Length and Session Frequency

What It Is: how long a typical session lasts and how many sessions a user opens per day or week. These two numbers should be read together: a high session count paired with very short sessions often signals a quick, transactional use case (checking a balance), while long sessions paired with low frequency may signal a content- or task-driven use case (completing a workout). These may be app-dependent or may speak to issues within how the users are actively using the application.

Viral Coefficient (K-Factor)

What It Is: a measure of organic, user-driven growth. Specifically, viral coefficient measures how many new users each existing user generates through referrals, sharing, or social features built into the product. Croll and Yoskovitz, authors of *Lean Analytics*, are among the clearest writers on K-factor for mobile: a K-factor above 1.0 means the app is growing on its own without paid acquisition (each user brings in more than one new user on average); a K-factor below 1.0 means every cohort is smaller than the last without ongoing acquisition spend to replenish it. Most apps operate below 1.0; even a K-factor of 0.5 meaningfully reduces the paid acquisition budget required to hit a growth target.

$$K = (\text{average invitations sent per user}) \times (\text{average conversion rate of those invitations as a decimal})$$

This metric is only meaningful if the consumer has become attached to the app and has cleared the so-called "stickiness" threshold as previously discussed. An app with poor retention and a K-factor of 0.8 is losing users faster than it can refer new ones. Measuring this calculation before fixing retention is like measuring how quickly a bucket fills while ignoring the hole in the bucket. This measure is only helpful once the app has demonstrated it can keep the users it already has.

Think: Is Your App Sticky or Compulsive?

Croll and Yoskovitz draw a distinction in *Lean Analytics* that rarely appears in a standard mobile analytics dashboard but matters enormously for building a product worth growing. The distinction is simply the difference between an app people use frequently because it genuinely improves their life (sticky) and an app people feel compelled to open out of anxiety, habit, or engineered variable reward with little to no value from the interaction (compulsive).

DAU/MAU stickiness ratios can look nearly identical for both types of product. A meditation app that genuinely reduces its users' stress and a social app engineered to trigger FOMO can both post a 25% stickiness ratio, because the metric only measures frequency, not the quality of the experience driving it. The difference only surfaces in qualitative feedback, long-term retention curves that eventually diverge (genuinely sticky products tend to retain at higher rates past D90; compulsive products often see a cliff), and in regulatory attention as governments look more closely at engagement-maximizing design patterns. As an analyst, when DAU looks strong but NPS is flat or negative and long-term retention is quietly eroding, it is worth asking whether the engagement being measured is the kind the product should be proud of.

Crash-Free Rate

What It Is: the percentage of sessions that complete without a technical crash, tracked because technical health is itself a retention driver. Platforms increasingly factor crash and "application not responding" (ANR) rates into app store visibility, meaning a buggy release can quietly suppress reviews, organic discovery and the retention numbers above it.

$$\text{Crash-Free Rate} = \frac{\text{Crash-Free Sessions}}{\text{Total Sessions}}$$

Tip: Read DAU and Retention Together, Not Apart

A stable or growing DAU can mask a serious underlying problem if reviewed on its own. An app can hold steady daily active user counts for months while actual retention quietly worsens as new user acquisition is replacing churned users in equal measure. Always pair a top-line metric like DAU with cohort retention curves so you can see activity at both the top and bottom of the funnel.

Monetization

Engagement is critical to long-term success of any app. However, if the app is never monetized success cannot last. Mobile monetization runs through three broad revenue mechanisms: in-app purchases, subscriptions, and advertising. These mechanisms work across multiple business models. The metrics below apply to all, with the underlying revenue events differing by model.

ARPU and ARPDAU

What It Is: Average Revenue Per User (ARPU) measures revenue generated per user over a defined period, typically monthly; Average Revenue Per Daily Active User (ARPDAU) measures the same idea on a daily basis and is the standard efficiency metric in mobile gaming. Healthy ARPDAU benchmarks vary by monetization model — ad-supported casual games often run in the few cents per day, while in-app-purchase-driven titles can run well above that — making cross-app comparisons only meaningful within the same monetization model and category.

$$\text{ARPDAU} = \frac{\text{Total Daily Revenue}}{\text{DAU}}$$

ARPDAU's value as a metric depends on how you monetize the app. Reading this metric without that context can produce misleading conclusions. According to Croll and Yoskovitz in *Lean Analytics*, there are five primary business models and the component of ARPDAU that matters most differs across each. The following table below lists these different models, which components of ARPDAU matter most, and what a decline in each could signal. I would also make note that if the app is free with physical goods (like a retail app, subscription app, or direct-to-consumer native app), you'll need to also bridge the learnings from this chapter on mobile app analytics with e-commerce analytics as the conversion occurs partially inside the app and partially inside the e-commerce system. This dual measurement connects back to Chapter 4 on cross-channel attribution.

Monetization Model	ARPDAU Component that Matters Most	What a Decline Usually Signals
Paid Download	Revenue per new install and refund rate	Slowing install velocity, increasing refund requests from users whose expectations weren't set correctly by the store listing, or a competitor releasing a comparable app at a lower price point
Free with Advertising	eCPM and ad fill rate	Inventory quality decline, audience targeting drift, ad format fatigue, or seasonality in advertiser demand particularly visible in Q1 when ad budgets reset after the holiday spend surge

Monetization Model	ARPDAU Component that Matters Most	What a Decline Usually Signals
Free with In-App Purchase (IAP)	Average transaction value and purchase frequency per active user	Paywall placement friction, offer fatigue from overexposure to the same purchase prompts, or a shift in the active user mix toward lower-intent users who were acquired cheaply but were never likely to spend
Freemium / Subscription	Trial-to-paid conversion rate and monthly logo churn	Onboarding value delivery failure (the free tier is not demonstrating enough of the product's value to motivate upgrade) or a competitive alternative entering the market at a lower price point
Free with Physical Goods	Conversion rate from app engagement to physical purchase, average order value, and repeat purchase rate	Disconnect between in-app browsing behavior and checkout completion, shipping or fulfillment friction surfacing in reviews, or a seasonal demand pattern not being anticipated in inventory planning

Lifetime Value (LTV)

What It Is: the total revenue (or gross profit) a single user is projected to generate over their entire relationship with the app, which functions as the denominator for nearly every user acquisition decision. A channel's CPI is only sustainable if it's comfortably below the projected LTV of the users it brings in.

Purchase / Trial Conversion Rate

What It Is: the percentage of active users who convert into a paying customer, whether through a one-time in-app purchase or a subscription trial. Industry figures commonly cited put this conversion in the single digits for many consumer apps, which is exactly why pairing a cheap CPI with a weak purchase conversion rate can still produce an unprofitable acquisition channel.

$$\text{Purchase / Trial Conversion Rate} = \frac{\text{Paying Users}}{\text{Active Users}}$$

Once you've generated the conversion, much like that of reviews in earned media, maintaining a quality App Store / Google Play Store rating and review velocity can drive future growth and organic discovery. Waiting until you've generated a number of negative reviews is too late as the damage is done and will likely hurt visibility.

App Store Rating and Review Velocity

What It Is: average star rating across the App Store and Google Play, and the rate at which new reviews are arriving. *Lean Analytics*' authors Croll and Yoskovitz treat ratings as a growth metric rather than simply a reputation metric, because both major app stores use rating as a factor in algorithmic search visibility. A drop below approximately 4.0 stars suppresses an app's appearance in relevant App Store Search results, which directly reduces organic install volume making a declining rating simultaneously a product quality signal and a user acquisition problem.

$$\text{Average Rating} = \frac{\text{Sum of All Star Ratings}}{\text{Total Reviews Received}}$$

Measuring the velocity of new reviews can also be important as reviews improve visibility on mobile platforms.

$$\text{Review Velocity} = \frac{\text{New Reviews Received}}{\text{Time Period (typically 30 days)}}$$

A Quick Reference by Stage

Because of the similarities mobile apps have with website metrics even in use, I'm not going to belabor this topic. The outline below helps provide some direct correlation between the stages of app usage, their core questions, and headlining metrics. It's important to note that ALL of the metrics discussed throughout the text, from paid media metrics to NPS, all can apply at various stages.

Stage	Core Question	Headline Metrics
Discovery & Acquisition	Are people finding and installing the app efficiently?	Store Conversion Rate / CPI / Organic/Paid Ratio
Engagement & Retention	Is the app becoming part of someone's routine?	D1/D7/D30 Retention / DAU/MAU Stickiness
Monetization	Is engagement converting into sustainable revenue?	ARPDAU / LTV / Purchase Conversion Rate

Being Practical: Analytics and Experience

Return to the meditation app from the opening of this chapter. A closer look at the cohort behind that successful-looking acquisition campaign reveals the real story: D1 retention came in around 22%, roughly in line with the health-and-fitness category average, but D7 fell to under 5% which is well below what similar apps in the category typically see. What does that mean? Well, acquiring new customers isn't the problem. Onboarding them is a problem. New users were never shown enough of the app's core value in their first session to form a habit, so the campaign was filling a leaky bucket and not building a retained user base. Armed with that distinction, the team's next move was to leave acquisition spend flat, redirect product effort toward a shorter, more personalized first-session experience, and re-measure D7 retention on the next install cohort before spending another dollar on growth. Mobile app analytics is about understanding the app experience in a way that allows for the tracking of retention and long-term monetization.

This concludes the channel-specific chapters of this book. In the chapters that follow, we shift from measuring individual channels to the harder work of avoiding analysis paralysis and bringing these channels together into a single, coherent measurement strategy.

References

Alt, S. (2026, April 21). *Mobile App Retention Benchmarks by Industry (2026)*. UXCam. https://uxcam.com/blog/mobile-app-retention-benchmarks/

Cost per Install (CPI). (n.d.). Coinis. https://coinis.com/glossary/cost-per-install

Croll, A., & Yoskovitz, B. (2013). *Lean analytics: Use data to build a better startup faster*. O'Reilly Media.

DAU (Daily Active Users) (n.d.). MWM. https://mwm.ai/glossary/dau

Delioglu, O. (2026, March 13). *The Complete Guide to App Store Optimization in 2026*. Appalize. https://www.appalize.com/blog/app-marketing/the-complete-guide-to-app-store-optimization-in-2026

Doboaca, O. (2026, June 19). *App Store Optimization Metrics: The Complete 2026 Guide to ASO Tracking*. AppFollow. https://appfollow.io/blog/app-store-optimization-metrics

Gil, J. (2025, November 4). *Mobile app retention benchmarks for creators: course & coaching apps*. Passion.io. https://passion.io/blog/mobile-app-retention-benchmarks-for-creators-course-coaching-apps

Guilleminot, C. (2026, March 17). *Mobile Game KPIs 2026: 20 Make-or-Break Benchmarks by Genre*. Game Growth Advisor. https://gamegrowthadvisor.com/blog/2026-03-17-mobile-game-kpis-benchmarks-2026/

Kamran (2026, July). *How to Boost Your Mobile App Conversions: A Step-by-Step Guide*. ConversionXperts. https://conversionxperts.com/app-conversion-rate-optimization-guide/

Kvasnevska, A. (2025, November 20). *Increase app retention 2026: Benchmarks, strategies & examples*. Pushwoosh. https://www.pushwoosh.com/blog/increase-user-retention-rate/

Mohtasham, H. (2026, June 26). *What Is Cost Per Install (CPI)? Mobile Acquisition Metrics 2026*. CUFinder. https://cufinder.io/blog/wiki/marketing-metrics/cost-per-install/

Retention (D1 / D7 / D30). (n.d.). MWM. https://mwm.ai/glossary/retention

What Is a Good Retention Rate for an Application. (2026, March 13). Lovable. https://lovable.dev/guides/what-is-a-good-retention-rate-for-an-app

Chapter 13
Avoiding Analysis Paralysis

Based on what you've learned thus far, have you stopped to think about all of the platforms that you would need to review to collect data on every single media placement, website, social media network, etc.? It feels like a lot because it is. Every one of the platforms a digital analyst uses contains a lot of information and spreadsheets that can be downloaded and analyzed for days. And then when you do figure out what you need to look at (thanks to this book!) the data feels as if it is scattered across not just platforms, but star systems. It can be overwhelming to the point of absolute analysis paralysis. There is so much to look at you can't figure out where to look!

Insight: More Data Does Not Automatically Produce Better Decisions

Leadership may assume that an organization with more analytics tools, more dashboards, and more historical data is better positioned to make good decisions than one with less. In practice, the relationship between data volume and good decisions breaks down past a certain point. Beyond a handful of well-chosen metrics tied directly to a decision, additional data tends to add noise, conflicting signals, and analysis time without adding proportional clarity. The goal of measurement, as this book has emphasized since Chapter 3, is to determine the next best step. A shorter report that clearly answers "what should we do" beats a longer report every single time.

This chapter is about that feeling of overwhelming anxiety, and it has nothing to do with a lack of data. As you have seen, every channel covered in this book (website, search, social, video, email, paid media, earned media, and mobile) produces a genuine flood of measurable numbers. What we're building toward is about judgment: knowing which of those numbers actually deserves your attention because you know what each of the metrics help you figure out. You just need the discipline to stop collecting more of them once you have the answer you're seeking. I'd attribute to any collectible trading card game: you don't have to catch all of the metrics. You only need to collect the ones that move you forward. In analytics, that skill has a name when it goes wrong, and learning to recognize it is the first step toward avoiding it.

What Analysis Paralysis Actually Is

Analysis paralysis is the state of having access to so much data, across so many tools, that an organization becomes unable to make a timely decision. The answer is there. But because there are too many competing numbers, too many details, and too much fear of choosing the wrong metric to act on any of them with confidence, as they say in the South, it's 'hard to see the forest for the trees.' It's sort of like when you are scrolling through your favorite streaming network looking at all of the options of things you could watch then, two hours later, you've yet to select a movie or show. And yes, I've done that too.

It rarely looks like what the name suggests. Nobody sits at a desk literally paralyzed. It looks, most often, like the analyst from this chapter's opening: capable, diligent, and surrounded by so much measurable activity that she cannot tell leadership where to point the next dollar.

The irony is that analysis paralysis is almost always a symptom of abundance, not scarcity. A small organization with one channel and one dashboard rarely experiences it. There's only so much data to disagree about. It shows up precisely where this book has been encouraging you to look: at organizations sophisticated enough to be tracking website analytics, search, social (organic and paid), video, email, paid media across nine or more sub-channels, earned media, and mobile, often with a different tool measuring each one. Every chapter in this book has handed you another set of metrics. This chapter exists because that's a genuine risk, and the responsible use of everything you've learned requires knowing when to stop adding metrics and start choosing among them.

The Vanity Metric Trap

One of the most common roads into analysis paralysis runs through what's commonly called a vanity metric: a number that looks impressive in a slide deck, is easy to measure, and tends to only ever go up but doesn't actually tell anyone whether the business is healthier or not. Total social media impressions, total email list size, total app downloads, and total website page views: each of these has appeared somewhere in this book as a legitimate data point, and each one can also become a vanity metric the moment it's treated as evidence of success on its own, disconnected from what it actually predicts.

The term was popularized by entrepreneur Eric Ries in a widely cited 2010 piece on metrics that makes the team feel good, but mean nothing. And, the underlying idea has only become more relevant as the number of channels (and the number of dashboards reporting on them) has multiplied. A vanity metric isn't inherently useless; "website page views by marketing channel," to borrow an example from product analytics literature, can be a genuinely useful diagnostic. The trouble starts when a vanity metric is reported in isolation, presented as if it answers a strategic question it was never built to answer.

Side Quest: A Short History of "Vanity Metrics"

I was personally introduced to the term "vanity metrics" in a book I've already leaned on as a resource *Lean Analytics*. However, the phrase has been around for some time.

The phrase entered common usage through Eric Ries's 2010 Harvard Business Review piece "Entrepreneurs: Beware of Vanity Metrics," written in the context of lean startup methodology, where founders eager to show progress to investors would highlight numbers like total registered users while ignoring whether those users ever did anything of value. The lean startup movement's broader contribution was a simple test: does this metric change the next action you take? If a number going up or down wouldn't actually change a single decision, it's a vanity metric, no matter how good it looks in a report. Fifteen years later, the same test applies just as cleanly to a brand's follower count, or a raw count of app downloads. While the channels have multiplied, marketers will still use vanity metrics to mask real problems.

The "So What" Test

Every metric can pass or fail a simple, single test before it earns a place in a report: if this number changes, what would we actually do differently? A metric that survives that question, whether a falling D7 retention rate that would trigger a redesign of your onboarding process or a rising MQL-to-SQL conversion rate that would justify increasing a specific campaign's budget, is always worth reporting. A metric that doesn't survive it belongs, at best, in an appendix, not the headline of a report.

Tip: Ask the Question Before You Pull Apart a Report

It's far easier to apply the "so what" test before building a report than after. Before opening a single dashboard, write down the specific decision the report needs to inform: "should we increase next quarter's paid social budget," not "how did social media do last quarter." Every metric you then pull should trace a direct line back to that decision. If a metric is interesting but doesn't inform the decision at hand, save it for a different report or section in your dashboard rather than including it out of habit. Starting from the decision rather than what you think you should report on prevents analysis paralysis.

Testing Your Way to Better Answers: A/B and Multivariate Testing

Too many metrics is one of the obvious ways to fall into analysis paralysis. The other is from having too many opinions. A marketing team will frequently find itself in a meeting where one person believes a green button converts better than a blue one, another is convinced the problem is the headline, and the CEO is ready to overhaul the entire landing page. Without a structured way to test those competing beliefs against real user behavior, the conversation stays in the room with more data requested, more caveats raised, and absolutely no decision reached. I've seen this happen frequently when opinions outweigh data. A/B testing and multivariate testing exist precisely to resolve that deadlock by replacing opinion with evidence, one controlled experiment at a time.

What A/B Testing Is

An A/B test, also referred to as a split test, is a controlled experiment in which two versions of a single variable are shown to randomly divided audiences at the same time, and the results are compared against a pre-defined success metric. Version A is the control: whatever currently exists. Version B is the challenger: the one change being tested. Because the two groups are randomized and run simultaneously, any difference in outcome between them can reasonably be attributed to the one variable that changed rather than to external factors like day of week, seasonality, or a news cycle that happened to favor one version.

The discipline in A/B testing isn't in the technology. At one point in the history of the web, this was a difficult task and full textbooks were written on methodology to accomplish this sort of testing on a website. Now, nearly every major platform covered in this book now offers some form of testing natively, as detailed below. The challenge now is ensuring it is setup correctly.

A good A/B test starts with a specific hypothesis with three parts: what is being changed, what outcome is expected to change as a result, and why, based on what is already known about the audience. For example, changing the CTA button copy from 'Learn More' to 'Get My Free Quote' will increase click-through rate because visitors to this page have shown high intent but low conversion, suggesting the current language "undersells the offer" is a testable hypothesis. "Let's try a different button" is not. A/B tests must be specific so that the outcome of the test is clear.

As mentioned, a number of the platforms discussed across these chapters offer native A/B testing. I would note that while these platforms offer these tools, they do require a certain amount of data to collect enough information to make a decision. Sometimes that may require significant budget so be aware that A/B testing typically comes with a budgetary requirement. Multivariate testing requires an even higher budget.

What Multivariate Testing Is

Multivariate testing (MVT) takes the same controlled-experiment logic and applies it to multiple variables simultaneously, testing every combination of the variables being changed rather than each in isolation. If a team wants to test two different headlines (A and B) and two different hero images (X and Y), a multivariate test would run all four combinations (AX, AY, BX, BY) at once revealing not just which headline and which image individually perform best, but whether certain combinations of the two outperform what either variable's individual test result would have predicted. This is the key advantage of multivariate testing: it surfaces interaction effects that sequential A/B tests would miss entirely.

The tradeoff is traffic. Every additional variable in a multivariate test splits the audience further, and each combination needs enough observations to produce a statistically meaningful result. As a practical matter, most websites and campaigns do not have sufficient volume to run rigorous multivariate tests beyond two or three variables (unless you're Amazon who's known for running multivariate tests on its homepage). For most organizations most of the time, a disciplined program of sequential A/B tests, each building on the validated winner of the last, produces cleaner, more actionable results than a multivariate testing strategy. The industry guidance is fairly consistent on this: single-variable A/B testing is typically the right answer, and multivariate testing is a tool for organizations whose volume can support it.

Tip: One Primary Metric Per Test, Decided on Before the Test

Before launching any A/B or multivariate test, write down the one metric that determines the winner...and only one. A common mistake is launching a test with conversion rate as the primary metric, then switching to click-through rate mid-way when conversion rate doesn't move the way the team hoped. Changing the success metric after results start coming in is sometimes called "p-hacking" and consistently produces false conclusions that feel like insights. The metric that determines the winning variant should be chosen when the hypothesis is written, not when the results are reviewed. Everything else observed during the test is secondary adding interesting context rather than evidence of success or failure.

Statistical Significance and Why Patience Is Part of the Method

Two concepts from statistics come up in nearly every testing discussion, and a new analyst should be comfortable with both. Statistical significance refers to the probability that the difference observed between Version A and Version B is real rather than the result of random chance. By convention, most practitioners require 95% confidence before declaring a winner, meaning there is only a 5% chance the observed difference is noise rather than a genuine effect of the change. Statistical power, the companion concept, refers to the probability that a test is large enough to detect a real difference if one exists. 80% power is the commonly recommended minimum, meaning a test that comes back inconclusive should not automatically be read as proof that no difference exists. It may simply mean the test didn't run long enough or reach enough users to be able to see a statistical difference.

Both of these concepts point toward the same practical discipline: run tests long enough and with enough volume before calling a winner. Ending a test early because Version B looks like it's winning after three days is one of the most common and most costly testing mistakes a team can make. Early results can be noisy and inaccurate for a variety of reasons and acting on them produces conclusions that don't replicate when moved on as the final decision. Most platform guidance recommends a minimum of seven to fourteen days for any A/B test, and at least one hundred conversions per variant before drawing conclusions, with more complex tests requiring proportionally more.

How the Platforms You Already Use Support Testing

The most practical aspect of A/B and multivariate testing for a new marketing analyst is that the tools required are usually already part of your marketing technology stack. You fortunately don't need a specialized testing platform to start although those do exist. Many of the major platforms covered throughout this book have built testing infrastructure directly into their native interfaces. Most are simple to use and easy to implement.

Google Ads: Experiment Center

Google launched the unified Experiment Center in January 2026, consolidating what had previously been scattered testing functionality across multiple tools into a single dashboard. From Experiment Center, an advertiser can run traditional A/B experiments on campaign settings from bidding strategy, ad copy, landing pages, audience targeting, and budget allocation alongside Brand Lift and Conversion Lift studies that measure the incremental impact of a campaign against a matched holdout group. Needless to say, it's a powerful tool.

Setting up a campaign experiment in Google Ads is a straightforward process. Simply select a running campaign as the base, define what is being changed in the experimental variant, set a traffic split (50/50 is the standard recommendation for clean comparisons), set an end date of at least fourteen days out, and define the primary metric the experiment will be judged on. For bidding strategy tests specifically, Google recommends extending the window to twenty-eight days to allow the algorithm enough time to optimize each variant before results are compared. Google Ads experiments also integrate directly with Google Analytics 4, so that on-site behavior metrics like time on page, pages per session, and conversion paths can be reviewed by experiment arm rather than only in aggregate. This provides a much fuller picture of what happened after a click than the ad platform's own reporting captures.

Meta Ads Manager: Experiments

Meta's Experiments tool, accessible from the main Ads Manager menu for advertising on Meta social media platforms, supports A/B testing at the ad set or campaign level, comparing variables including creative, audience targeting, placement, and budget optimization approach. Meta requires a minimum run time of seven days and recommends fourteen. Once complete, the platform provides both a winning variant and a confidence percentage at the test's conclusion with the explicit guidance that only results at or above 95% confidence should be acted on. Meta also provides an estimated statistical power figure, and results from tests where power was below 80% should be treated with significant skepticism even if a "winner" is displayed as low-power tests frequently produce false positives that don't scale. A useful practical note specific to Meta: just because Meta's algorithm continuously optimizes delivery toward the best-performing creative within a campaign, traditional A/B testing within a single campaign (rather than through the dedicated Experiments tool) can be contaminated by the algorithm's own preference-learning, which will progressively show the variant it believes is winning to a larger share of users before a test has reached significance. We've seen this happen when we will run multiple sets of creative for a client in a given ad group thus not evenly splitting the ad run. The Experiments tool routes traffic through a controlled split that prevents this contamination, which is why using the dedicated tool rather than simply duplicating ad sets within a live campaign produces more reliable results.

Google Analytics 4: The Analysis Layer

GA4 does not have a native A/B testing tool built into the platform. Google Optimize, which previously served that function, was discontinued permanently in September 2023. What GA4 now provides is the analysis layer that makes testing data meaningful: when a third-party testing tool (Optimizely, VWO, Convert, AB Tasty, and similar platforms are commonly used) sends experiment data to GA4 through Google Tag Manager, the experiment variant each user saw is captured as a custom event parameter. That parameter can then be used in GA4's Explore reports to segment every downstream behavior including pages visited, events triggered, and conversions completed by which variant a user was exposed to, giving an analyst a far richer view of an experiment's impact. A visitor who saw Variant B might have converted at the same rate as Variant A but stayed on the site twice as long, visited more pages, and ultimately purchased a higher-value product. In a traditional format, this would not have been clear. However, this is fully visible when the experiment data is analyzed inside GA4.

A/B Testing Across Other Channels

The same testing logic that applies to ads and landing pages applies across the channels covered in this book, even where the platform infrastructure looks different. Email platforms including Mailchimp, HubSpot, and Klaviyo all offer native A/B testing for subject lines, preview text, send time, and content, with winners typically determined by open rate or click rate over a defined test window before the winning version is sent to the remainder of the list. Social platforms including TikTok Ads Manager and LinkedIn Campaign Manager offer comparable split-testing infrastructure for creative and audience variables. The underlying method is identical across all of them: one variable, two versions, simultaneous exposure to randomized audiences, and patience to wait for significance before drawing a conclusion.

Testing and Analysis Paralysis

Going back to the chapter's central theme: A/B and multivariate testing are, when used well, one of the most powerful antidotes to analysis paralysis available to a marketing team. They replace the room full of competing opinions with a structured process that produces a clear answer to a specific question, and do it without requiring more data. The discipline of writing a hypothesis before launching a test, committing to a single success metric before seeing results, and running the test long enough to reach significance before acting is critical. It's also the same discipline required to prevent analysis paralysis: starting from the question rather than the dashboard, choosing one metric that actually answers it, and resisting the pull to act on noise before the signal is clear.

Modern Research Modalities: Seeing What the Data Can't Tell You Alone

Every metric covered tells you what happened: how many people clicked, how many converted, how many churned, or how much something cost. What almost none of those numbers tell you on their own is why. A landing page conversion rate drops by 2% over three weeks. The number is right there in GA4. But is it because visitors are confused by the headline, because the page loads too slowly on mobile, or because a form field is broken in a specific browser? Did a competitor launch a new campaign? Or, maybe the reCaptcha on the form is broken and we can't see it without testing? The metric surfaces the problem. Finding the cause requires a different set of tools and knowledge. There are additional research modalities that sit alongside quantitative analytics and add behavioral, visual, and qualitative context to the numbers a dashboard reports. From heatmaps and session recordings that let analysts observe user behavior directly, to AI-driven intelligence platforms that are beginning to close the gap between having data and knowing what to do with it, it's not only about the platforms we've discussed thus far. Fortunately, there's more.

Heatmaps: Seeing a Page the Way Your Users See It

A heatmap is a visual overlay on a web page, email, or app screen that uses color gradients, typically red for high concentration, blue for low, to show where users click, where they scroll, and where their cursor lingers. Rather than reading a table of numbers, an analyst looking at a heatmap can see, in a single glance, that nobody is scrolling past the first screen of a landing page or that the call-to-action button at the bottom of the page is effectively invisible because most visitors never reach it. Each of those findings is, in isolation, invisible in a standard analytics report. GA4 will tell you the page had a 1.8% conversion rate, but it won't tell you that 65% of visitors never saw the button that was meant to drive that conversion.

The three most common heatmap types each reveal a different dimension of user behavior.

Click heatmaps show where users click or tap, revealing which elements attract attention and, which non-interactive elements users click on under the mistaken impression that they should do something. We call this behavior a "dead click" that reliably signals a UX problem worth fixing. Users may also even "rage click" when they can't click on or find what they are looking for and rapidly click the mouse in anger. That is a measure of negative sentiment and user experience!

Scroll heatmaps show how far down a page visitors typically scroll before abandoning it, which is particularly revealing for long-form landing pages and email campaigns where the key message or call-to-action is placed lower than the average scroll depth.

Move maps track cursor movement across a desktop session and have been shown to correlate with visual attention at a rate in the low-to-mid 80% range meaning a well-analyzed move map can function as a rough proxy for eye-tracking research without the expense and laboratory setup that traditional eye tracking requires.

The Two Tools Most Teams Are Already Using: Microsoft Clarity and Hotjar

Two platforms dominate heatmap and session-recording usage among marketing and analytics teams. They are worth knowing by name because they occupy different positions in the toolset rather than being true alternatives to each other.

Microsoft Clarity is completely free, with no session or recording limits, and it offers something no comparable free tool currently matches: AI-powered session summaries. Powered by Microsoft Copilot, these summaries automatically generate natural language descriptions of what a user struggled with during a recorded session, surfacing patterns across large volumes of recordings without requiring an analyst to watch each one manually. Clarity also uniquely offers error-click heatmaps making it an unusually effective diagnostic tool for finding technical bugs that are suppressing conversion rates. The only challenges with Microsoft Clarity is that data is retained for only thirty days, it has no survey or user feedback capabilities, and its terms of service grant Microsoft rights to use the aggregated behavioral data it collects. While none of these may seem like barriers to entry, the usage rights on the data can trigger compliance consideration for organizations subject to strict data governance requirements.

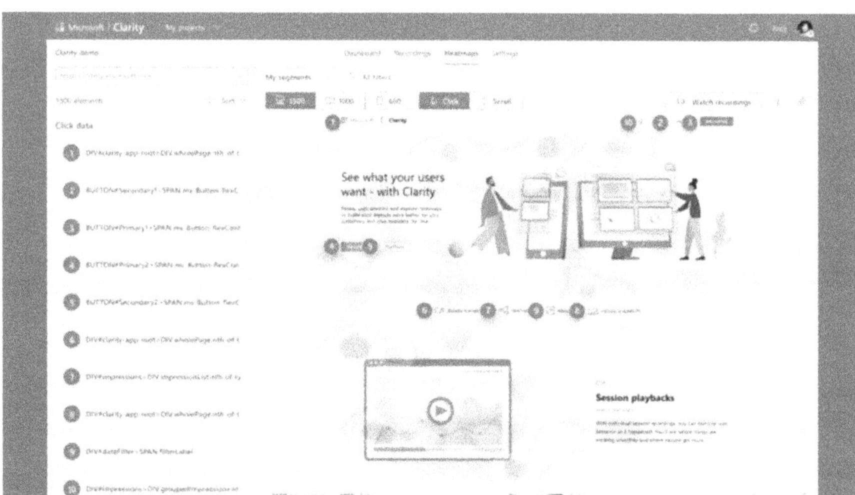

Source: Search Engine Land

Hotjar occupies a broader position: it combines heatmaps and session recordings with user surveys, feedback widgets, funnel analysis, and 365 days of data retention, making it a more complete qualitative research platform. Its free tier is limited to thirty-five sessions per day which is meaningful for a small site but not for serious ongoing analysis. Paid plans also exist for sites that need more meaningful volume for analysis. Move maps, available in Hotjar but not in Clarity, are its behavioral differentiator: by tracking cursor movement rather than only clicks, Hotjar can surface where attention is going even when a user isn't clicking anything. This can assist in diagnosing above-the-fold layout and content prioritization issues.

The practical recommendation for most teams is to run both simultaneously: Clarity for high-volume, automated, zero-cost behavioral observation (and those AI-generated session summaries), and Hotjar for targeted qualitative research when a specific hypothesis needs to be tested with surveys, feedback, or funnel analysis.

Session Recordings: Watching What Analytics Can't Show

A session recording is exactly what it sounds like: a replay of a real user's interaction with a website, email preview, or app, captured anonymously and played back so an analyst can observe scrolling, clicking, hesitation, rage-clicking, and abandonment behavior in context. Where a heatmap can collect behavior across thousands of sessions into a single visual summary, a session recording captures the full texture of one user's experience from the moment they arrive until they leave. That single session might represent a technical bug that may not have otherwise been found without observing the session. Both Clarity and Hotjar offer session recordings as core functionality, with Clarity's Copilot AI now capable of summarizing what happened in a session in plain language without requiring the analyst to watch the full playback.

AI-Driven Intelligence Platforms and the Rise of Conversational Analytics

Beyond heatmaps and session recordings, a new category of AI-driven analytical tools has emerged that does something fundamentally different. Rather than showing you the data and leaving interpretation to a human analyst, these platforms interpret the data and surface the insights directly, often through natural language interfaces that allow a marketer to ask a question of their data the same way they would ask a colleague. These dashboards can be built with a number of different platforms including Claude, Grok, or otherwise, and prominent dashboarding platforms are also introducing tools that can provide this analysis as well.

Google Data Studio and the Agentic BI Shift

Data Studio, Google's free, widely used reporting and dashboard platform, has been undergoing a significant AI-driven transformation that is worth some detail here, because it affects a tool that many new marketing analysts will use before they use anything else. At Google Cloud Next 2026, Google announced what it describes as "Agentic BI." Google described this functionality as a fundamental shift from a reporting tool that displays data passively to a system that actively analyzes it, surfaces insights unprompted, and is beginning to trigger downstream actions based on what it finds.

Several of these features are now in public preview or general availability inside Data Studio and are relevant for a practicing analyst today. The Gemini-powered Insight Assistant, currently in preview, automatically generates summaries and highlights key trends within Data Studio reports answering, in plain language, the "so what" question that this chapter has identified as the central discipline of avoiding analysis paralysis. A campaign report that previously required an analyst to interpret and narrate can now surface its own key findings as text alongside the charts, which changes the role of the analyst from report-builder to insight-validator. Conversational Analytics, now in public preview across Data Studio, allows users to type natural language questions directly into a report. For instance, "What were our top-performing campaigns last quarter?" or "Which traffic source had the highest conversion rate in April?" now receive relevant charts or data tables in response, without writing a single query or building a custom dimension. For a new marketing analyst or a marketing intern who has not yet built comfort with GA4's Explore interface, this feature alone dramatically reduces the barrier to self-service data analysis. The Formula Assistant uses the same natural language interface to write calculated fields. While current analysts have had to learn and write in Data Studio's expression syntax, a user may now describe the metric they want in plain English and the platform generates the formula. Automated slide generation, now generally available for Data Studio Pro users, converts a finished report into a presentation with AI-written text summaries of each visualization.

As of mid-2026, several of the most powerful capabilities (the Insight Assistant, the full Conversational Analytics API, certain Dashboard Agent features) are in preview status rather than stable general availability, which means they may behave inconsistently or change before they reach full release. However, the general availability of these tools is coming soon and may redefine how we think about dashboards and reporting. A practitioner building a production reporting workflow in 2026 should verify the current release status of any specific feature rather than assuming preview features are fully stable.

What AI-Driven Analytics Tools Still Cannot Do

A note about capabilities is appropriate before closing this section, because the gap between what these tools promise and what they currently deliver is still real. An AI that summarizes a session recording can tell you that a user struggled with the checkout form and clicked the submit button three times, but it cannot tell you whether the struggle was caused by a broken script, an unclear field label, or a cognitive mismatch between what the user expected and what the form asked for. An Insight Assistant that surfaces "conversion rate declined 18% week over week" has done useful work, but it has not told you why. These features are likely coming with the acceleration of AI, but even when they are, an analyst must know if the insights provided are real. The tools presented in this section are research accelerators, not meant to be research replacements. They compress the time between having data and finding a starting point for investigation, but the judgment about what is actually worth investigating, and what to do about it once found, remains a human analytical skill.

Building a Metric Hierarchy: North Star, Inputs, and Guardrails

Discarding bad metrics, or those that don't matter, is only part of the job. Analysts also must organize the good metrics so a team always knows which number matters most at any given moment. A widely used framework for this, popularized in product and growth circles and increasingly common in marketing organizations, is the North Star Metric. The North Star Metric is a single number that best represents the value an audience or customer is actually getting, sitting at the top of a small hierarchy of supporting metrics beneath it.

Two well-known examples illustrate the distinction between a North Star Metric and a vanity metric chasing the same general idea. Airbnb could have chosen "number of app downloads" as a headline metric. It's easy to measure, always trending upward, and almost meaningless on its own. Instead, the company is widely cited as having anchored around nights booked, a number that only increases when a real transaction of value has occurred between a host and a guest. Spotify, similarly, could have leaned on registered users or even daily active users (DAU), a metric that rewards a thirty-second app open as much as a genuine listening session. Rather, the company is commonly cited as tracking total time spent listening, a number that only grows when the product is delivering the experience it actually promises.

Beneath a North Star Metric sit input metrics that are the handful of levers a team can directly influence that, taken together, drive that top-line number. The team can also review guardrail metrics which exist not to be optimized upward but to make sure a team isn't accidentally damaging something important (deliverability, churn, brand sentiment) while chasing the North Star. A small, well-chosen hierarchy like this turns an overwhelming volume of available numbers into an ordered, navigable set, where everyone knows what to look at first.

Think: What Is Your North Star and Who Would Disagree With You?

Pick any channel covered in this book and ask: if leadership could only see one number from this channel every week, what should it be, and why? Then ask a harder question: would the team running that channel (paid search, email, etc.) agree with the team running another department that the same number should sit at the top for the whole organization, or would each team defend a different one?

Disagreement here isn't a failure. Remember: we're working toward avoiding analysis paralysis. Departments can easily be working toward the wrong goal if communication across the organization is not clear.

A Practical Framework for Staying Focused

I'm aware that a lot of the ideas in this chapter are easier said than done. If you're currently in marketing or an analyst, your CEO may be asking you to measure things that you know don't matter, and they don't care. They still want the results and are going to measure you against something that you might consider vanity. Or, you may be locked into analysis paralysis because your Chief Marketing Officer (CMO) won't make a decision. At any rate, if you want to move your organization forward, there are four habits that consistently separate organizations that avoid analysis paralysis from those that don't.

Start every report from the decision, not the dashboard. Write the specific question a report needs to answer before opening a single tool, and let that question determine which metrics make the cut.

Limit headline reporting to a small, deliberately chosen set of metrics per objective. Commonly cited guidance suggests somewhere in the range of three to ten core metrics total, not per channel, with everything else available on request rather than included by default.

Establish one North Star Metric per major objective. Your North Star Metric can be supported by a short list of input metrics a team can actually influence, and at least one guardrail metric to catch unintended damage.

Periodically kill dashboards and reports nobody has acted on. If a recurring report hasn't changed a decision in the last two reporting cycles, that's a strong signal it has drifted from a value metric into vanity regardless of how it started.

Comparing Vanity and Value at a Glance

So what is vanity and what provides value? This can be different for every organization, thus one of the difficult parts of any analytical strategy. Sometimes total social impressions tell a major story and other times, they are pure vanity because quantity makes leadership feel good about the effort. Rather than belabor this point, on the next page is a quick chart containing some of the metrics we've discussed in this chapter as prospective vanity and the metrics that may provide more value.

Getting to a Decision

In today's analytical environment, it's easy to get overwhelmed. There are so many decisions that could be made that trying to determine which decision should be made can be trying. Many blame that anxiety-ridden weight that comes with the volume of data. But, the volume isn't really the problem. The lack of focus is the more dangerous opponent. As with any decision, narrowing down the focus to the goal is where you begin. Rather than building the 52nd dashboard as requested by leadership, why not narrow down your North Star, determine how to measure it, and then the inputs and guardrails required to move the organization forward.

Vanity Metric	Value Metric	Why the Shift?
Total Social Impressions	Social Share of Voice / Engagement Rate by Tier	Impressions reward reach alone while share of voice and engagement reveal whether content actually is resonating
Total Email List Size	Email Engagement Rate / Revenue Per Send	List size grows even as engagement may be eroding; revenue per send reflects whether the list is still working
Total App Downloads	D7/D30 Retention / ARPDAU	Downloads measure acquisition only; retention and revenue reveal whether the product delivers actual value
Total Website Page views	Conversion Rate / Engaged Sessions by Source	Page views can rise from low-quality, irrelevant and even spam traffic; conversion and engagement reflect real intent

References

Alt, S. (2026, April 23). *What is a North Star Metric? The Complete Framework Guide.* UXCam. https://uxcam.com/blog/north-star-metric-framework/

Cintra, J. (2025, August 20). *A/B Testing for Paid Ads: Step-by-Step with Google Ads and Meta (2026 Guide)*. Dataslayer. https://www.dataslayer.ai/blog/how-to-use-a-b-testing

Cintra, J. (2025, June 25). *Looker Studio AI: How to Use AI to Supercharge Your Reports (Even for Free)*. Dataslayer. https://www.dataslayer.ai/blog/looker-studio-ai-how-to-supercharge-your-reports

Dwivedi, A. (2025, August 21). *What Are Metrics vs. Analytics?*. HelloPM. https://hellopm.co/metrics-vs-analytics-the-ultimate-guide-to-data-driven-decisions/

Google Ads Experiment Center: Complete Guide to Testing Strategies and Measuring Campaign Impact in 2026. (2026, January 29). ALM Corp. https://almcorp.com/blog/google-ads-experiment-center-guide/

Gupta, D. (2025, October 11). *Deep Dive: Metric Trees*. Optiblack. https://optiblack.com/insights/deep-dive-metric-trees

Hotjar vs Clarity (2026): Free vs $32/Month — Honest Comparison. (2026, February 5). UXHeat. https://www.uxheat.com/blog/hotjar-vs-clarity

Hotjar vs Microsoft Clarity (2026, June 26): Heatmaps Compared — and the Customer "Why" Both Miss. Koji. https://www.koji.so/blog/hotjar-vs-microsoft-clarity-2026

How to Set Up & Analyze A/B Tests in GA4. (2025, November 6). Brillmark. https://www.brillmark.com/how-to-set-up-analyze-a-b-test-in-ga4/

Kumar, D. (2026, June 7). *Hotjar vs Microsoft Clarity (2026): What the Feature Lists Don't Tell You*. Spike. https://getspike.ai/blog/hotjar-vs-microsoft-clarity/

Morcillo, A. (2026, March 4). *Your North Star Metric Is Wrong: How Spotify, Airbnb and Slack Got It Right*. Alex Morcillo. https://alexmorcillo.com/blog/strategy/what-is-a-north-star-and-what-is-not/

Kazinik, B. (2026, January 26). *Marketing metrics explained: how to track performance in 2026*. monday.com. https://monday.com/blog/project-management/marketing-metrics/

Melchor, L. (2025, September 23). *Microsoft Clarity vs Hotjar: Each Tool's True Strengths*. Crazy Egg. https://www.crazyegg.com/blog/microsoft-clarity-vs-hotjar/

Meta Ads A/B Testing: Complete Guide to Split Testing in 2026. (2026, March 24). Benly. https://benly.ai/learn/meta-ads/ab-testing-guide

Microsoft Clarity vs Hotjar in 2026: Honest Comparison. (2026, April 6). Clarity Insights. https://www.clarity-insights.com/blog/microsoft-clarity-vs-hotjar.html

Nguyen, G. (2020, October 28). *Microsoft Clarity, the company's tool for visualizing user experience, is out of beta*. Search Engine Land. https://searchengineland.com/microsoft-clarity-the-companys-tool-for-visualizing-user-experience-is-out-of-beta-342959

North Star Metric Framework. (n.d.). Umbrex. https://umbrex.com/resources/frameworks/strategy-frameworks/north-star-metric-framework/

Ramakrishnan, K. (2026, June 16).*Introducing new Explores and Merge Queries in Looker*. Google Cloud Blog. https://cloud.google.com/blog/products/business-intelligence/looker-explore-ai-and-interface-updates

Ries, E. (2010, February 8). *Entrepreneurs: Beware of Vanity Metrics*. Harvard Business Review. (Cited via secondary sourcing in multiple 2026 marketing analytics guides.)

Rittman, M. (2026, April 26). *Google Next 2026: What's New for Looker, BigQuery, Data Platforms and Agentic Analytics*. Rittman Analytics. https://rittmananalytics.com/blog/2026/04/26/google-next-2026-whats-new-for-looker-bigquery-data-platforms-and-agentic-analytics

Sholtz, J. (2024, August 15). *What Makes a Good vs Bad North Star Metric*. Amplitude. https://amplitude.com/blog/good-bad-north-star-metric

Straube, S. (2022, April 7). *Measuring the right North Star metric*. Mind the Product. https://www.mindtheproduct.com/measuring-the-right-north-star-metric/

Tegan (2026, February 2). *Google Ads A/B: The 2026 Step-by-Step Playbook of Higher Conversions*. Causal Funnel. https://www.causalfunnel.com/blog/google-ads-a-b-testing-the-2026-step-by-step-playbook-to-higher-conversions/

Usa, U. (2026, February 4). *13 Best A/B Testing Tools That Integrate with Google Analytics 4*. Convert. https://www.convert.com/blog/a-b-testing/ab-testing-tools-that-integrate-with-ga4/

Zinsmeister, S., & Ramakrishnan, K. (2026, July 1). *Google named a Leader in 2026 Gartner ® Magic Quadrant™ or Analytics and Business Intelligence Platforms for third year in a row*. Google Cloud Blog. https://cloud.google.com/blog/products/business-intelligence/looker-in-2026-gartner-analytics-and-bi-platforms-mq

Zinsmeister, S., & Ramakrishnan, K. (2026, April 22). *Welcome to the agentic BI era with Looker*. Google Cloud Blog. https://cloud.google.com/blog/products/business-intelligence/looker-updates-for-agentic-bi-at-next26

[GA4] A/B Test. (n.d.). Google. https://support.google.com/analytics/answer/13468470

[GA4] Multivariate Test. (n.d.). Google. https://support.google.com/analytics/answer/13470478

Chapter 14
Building Marketing Dashboards

A marketing team at a growing company spent three months building what their VP called the "perfect dashboard." It pulled data from Google Ads, Meta, LinkedIn, HubSpot, GA4, and Salesforce into a single Data Studio view. It had forty-two metrics, six chart types, color-coded performance indicators, and a filter panel that could slice every number by date range, geography, and campaign objective simultaneously. It was, by every technical measure, a remarkable piece of work. No one on the team used it. The CMO asked for a five-number summary in her weekly email instead. The paid media manager kept his own spreadsheet to keep track of his efforts. The sales team continued to pull pipeline numbers directly from Salesforce because they didn't trust that the dashboard's attribution matched what they were seeing. After six months, the dashboard was quietly retired and replaced with three simpler views that each answered one specific question for one specific audience.

This chapter is about the gap that exists between what people say they want and what is actually used. At some point last year, we built this same sort of dashboard for a client. It was awesome. And then a few weeks before publishing this book I was told they no longer looked at those dashboards. I don't want this to happen to you (although it will at some point in your career), so this chapter is built to give you direction on what you actually need to track in a dashboard. The previous chapter established a discipline for choosing the right metrics: start from the decision, test every analytical candidate against "so what," and organize survivors into a hierarchy with a North Star at the top. Now, let's discuss what a well-designed marketing dashboard actually looks like, who it's built for, how to choose which tool builds it, and how to keep it useful for the long haul.

The First Question Is Never "What Should We Track"

The most common mistake in dashboard design is treating it as a metrics-selection exercise. A team sits down, lists every metric it cares about, and then tries to arrange them on a screen. The result is almost always the kind of dashboard described in the opening of this chapter: technically comprehensive, practically useless, and destined for the graveyard of well-intentioned reporting tools.

Dashboard design starts with two simple questions: who is going to use this, and what decision does it need to help them make? Those two questions determine everything that follows: which metrics belong, how frequently the data needs to refresh, how much detail is appropriate, and what happens when a number moves outside its expected range. A dashboard should be described like this: "This dashboard helps [specific audience] decide [specific thing] by showing them [specific metrics]." If it's not, then we have work to do.

Insight: The Three-Tier Hierarchy That Prevents a Dashboard from Serving No One

Marketing decisions in most organizations happen at three levels, each with a different audience, a different time horizon, and a different definition of "good." There are three tiers of dashboards all based on the audiences they serve.

Strategic dashboards tend to serve C-suite executives who need to answer whether the marketing program is producing the right business outcomes at a sustainable cost. They update daily or weekly and show five to seven metrics maximum, each connected to revenue, pipeline, or brand health. Channel dashboards serve the managers running specific programs like SEO or paid media who need to know whether their specific channel is performing efficiently this week. They show eight to twelve metrics per major channel and update at least daily for active campaigns. Operational dashboards serve the people making daily execution decisions who need to know which specific ad, keyword, or piece of content requires attention right now.

The most important design principle for each tier is the same: every metric on a given tier's dashboard must answer a question that audience is actually asking. Mixing tiers on a single dashboard is the most common reason dashboards become unreadable. If a single dashboard does need to cover all, it should be done on separate pages of the dashboard.

Building Dashboards for Your Audience

Different audiences need different things from the same underlying data, and designing a single dashboard that tries to serve all of them produces a screen that serves none of them well. Consider a B2B SaaS company that replaces one company-wide dashboard with three role-specific views; a CMO view showing monthly MRR impact from marketing, a paid media manager view showing daily budget pacing and cost per lead, and a content team view showing organic traffic and engagement metrics. The data behind all three views was identical; just the way the data was used incorporated separate design elements and metrics.

For a student or intern reading this chapter, you will almost certainly be asked to build or contribute to a dashboard early in your career. When you are asked, the most important thing you can do before opening any tool is have a conversation with the person who will actually use it. Ask them what question they are trying to answer. Ask them how often they look at the data and in what context. Ask them what would make them change a decision. The answers to those questions are the specifications for the dashboard.

This is something we also have to do at our agency. For instance, many small- to medium-sized businesses may not have a goal in their marketing efforts. They just know they need marketing! So, helping them — or an organization's leadership — define not only their dashboard, but their goals can ensure that your dashboard matches to the organization's target.

Audience	Primary Question	Typical Metrics	Refresh Cadence
CMO/ Executive	Is marketing driving revenue at a sustainable cost?	Pipeline Influenced / CAC / Marketing ROI / Budget VS Actual / Revenue Attributed to Marketing	Daily to Weekly
Channel Manager	Is this channel performing efficiently this period	CPL / CTR / Conversion Rate / Spend Pacing / ROAS by Channel	Daily
Campaign Manager / Analyst	Which specific asset or tactic needs attention today?	Ad-Level CTR / Keyword Quality Score / Landing Page Conversion Rate / Frequency	Real-Time to Daily

Design Principles For High Quality Dashboards

Once the audience and decision are clear, the design of the dashboard itself follows a small set of principles that most practitioners converge on regardless of which tool they're using.

The most important metric goes first. Users scan dashboards the same way they scan a page of text using a Z-pattern: top left first, then across, then down. Eye-tracking research consistently also confirms an F-shaped reading pattern, meaning the top row of any dashboard receives far more attention than anything below it. The metric that most directly answers the audience's primary question belongs in the top-left position, in the largest text size, before anything else. Considering both the Z-pattern and F-pattern, dashboards tend to be scanned in a hybrid of these two patterns where the top-left and top row carry the most weight. If the most important number is buried at the bottom of a scrollable view, the dashboard has failed its primary design objective regardless of how good its secondary metrics are.

Tip: Color can be a Powerful Signal

Color is one of the most powerful tools available in dashboard design. It can be used to signal status (green for at or above target, red for below target, gray or black for neutral) and to create visually interesting headers but be careful not to accidentally signal ups or down if it's not meant to be present (green headers, etc.). A dashboard that uses color exclusively as a status signal can be read accurately in under sixty seconds by someone who has never seen it before. That is a standard worth building toward.

Next, work to show trends, not snapshots. A single number in isolation is almost always misleading. "CAC is $1,240" tells a CMO nothing without knowing whether last quarter's CAC was $980 or $1,600, and whether the current number is moving in the right direction. Every headline metric should show at minimum a current value, a prior period comparison (with clarity on the period measured), and a directional indicator like a trend line, a sparkline, or an arrow. This allows the viewer to easily see if things are getting better or worse over time.

From there, context is needed. A metric only means something in relation to something else. You should always be comparing to a goal, a prior period, or an industry benchmark. "1,247 leads this month" is an observation. "1,247 leads this month versus a target of 1,000 and 892 last month" is information that can be acted upon. The best dashboards build that context into the visualization itself rather than leaving the reader to remember what the number is supposed to be.

Last, limit each dashboard to five to seven headline metrics. Research from ThoughtSpot confirms that dashboards tracking five to seven focused KPIs outperform dashboards tracking twenty or more. More metrics simply produce more visual noise and a higher probability that the reader focuses on the wrong metric or the metric that matters the least.

Chart Types and When to Use Them

Chart selection is a design decision that most new analysts make instinctively rather than deliberately. The underlying principle is simple: the chart type should make the comparison the reader needs to make as easy as possible. Here are a few guidelines on what are the best charts based on the data being displayed.

Line charts for trends over time. If the question is "how has this metric changed over time," a line chart is almost always the right answer. Avoid using line charts to compare multiple metrics that operate on different scales without a secondary axis, which can make coincidental movements appear causally related.

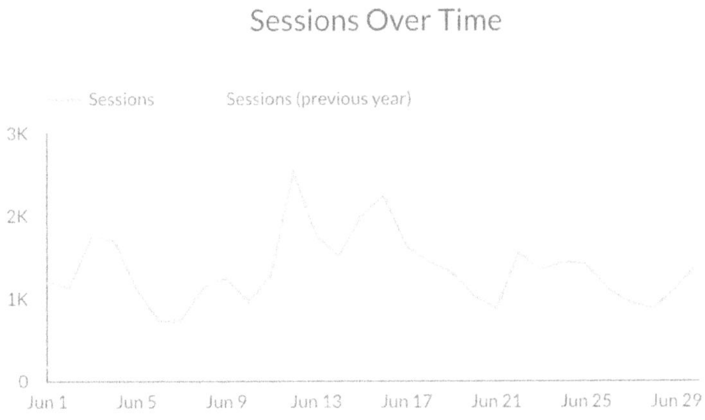

Source: Google Data Studio / Forum Communications

Bar charts for comparisons between categories. If the question is "which channel, campaign, or segment performed best," a bar chart sorted from highest to lowest makes the ranking immediately visible. Horizontal bar charts work better than vertical when category labels arc long.

Scorecards for single headline metrics. A large number with a trend indicator and a comparison to target is more readable than a chart for a metric that only needs to be checked rather than analyzed.

Source: Google Data Studio / Forum Communications

Tables for multiple dimensions. When a reader needs to see performance across several metrics simultaneously for several items whether metrics or channels, a table with conditional formatting is more useful than five separate charts.

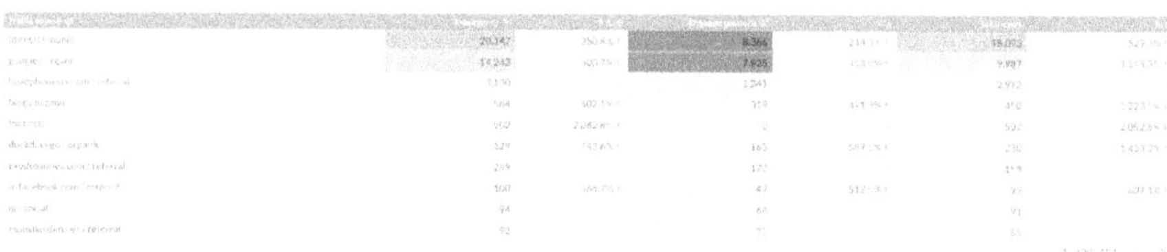

Source: Google Data Studio / Forum Communications

Avoid pie charts for most use cases. Pie charts are only clear when showing a two-part, maybe three-part split. For three or more segments, a bar chart communicates the same information more accurately with less visual processing effort.

The Tool Landscape: Matching Platform to Need

The right dashboard tool is determined by three practical factors: where the data lives, who needs to see the output, and how much technical infrastructure the team has available to maintain it. There is no universally correct answer, but a few clear patterns emerge. On the following page are just some of the dashboarding tools available on the market today including what they are best used for and just some of their limitations. This is not an exhaustive list, but gives you some idea of what's available on the open market.

Tool / Platform	Best For	Limitations
Native Platform Dashboards (GA4, HubSpot, Meta Ads Manager)	Single-channel reporting; teams that primarily work with one platform	Cannot combine data across platforms; limited customizations; visualizations built for the platform's own metrics
Data Studio (free)	Cross-channel reporting for teams with a Google-centric stack; shareable, collaborative views without a software license	Data drift from platform changes and API updates can break reports; limited statistical functionality
Supermetrics / Funnel.io / Improvado	Automated data consolidation from multiple marketing platforms into a single source before visualization	Add-on cost on top of a visualization tool; best treated as a data pipeline rather than a dashboard tool itself
Google Sheets (with connected data)	Small teams, early-stage programs, or situations where flexibility matter more than automation	Manual maintenance; breaks at scale; not suitable as a primary reporting tool for programs running across many channels

For most students and new analysts working with small to mid-sized organizations, Data Studio is the most practical starting point: it is free, it connects natively to GA4 and Google Ads, it has a growing library of community connectors for other platforms. The platform easily produces shareable, professionally presented output without requiring a design background or a business intelligence (BI) software license. Its limitations become meaningful when an organization runs more than eight to ten data sources simultaneously, at which point a dedicated data pipeline tool like Supermetrics or Funnel.io is worth the investment to handle data consolidation before Data Studio handles visualization.

Other platforms also exist that are more popular in other disciplines but have found their way into marketing dashboards including Microsoft Power BI, Tableau, and more. Our agency uses Data Studio and recommends it for a variety of reasons. For transparency, we also use Power My Analytics as our data pipeline / community connector for platforms that are not natively supported by Data Studio.

Side Quest: The Hidden Cost of Manual Dashboards

A dashboard that requires a human to manually export data from multiple platforms, paste it into a spreadsheet, and upload it to a reporting tool is not a dashboard. This takes an immense amount of time and adds an additional resource for every report: time. One practitioner documented a case in which a campaign overspent by $12,000 over a weekend because the dashboard was showing Thursday's data on Monday morning; by the time the team saw the overage, the budget was already gone. Why did this occur? The dashboard was being updated manually. It also speaks to the importance of oversight on projects as well. Before investing significant time in designing any dashboard, confirm that the underlying data can be refreshed automatically at the cadence the audience actually needs. A beautifully designed dashboard running on stale data is more dangerous than no dashboard at all as it creates false confidence in numbers that may no longer be true.

Naming, Governance, and the Maintenance Question

A dashboard is only as trustworthy as the data feeding it, and data trust is almost always a governance question before it is a technical one. One of the most persistent sources of dashboard confusion in multi-platform marketing programs is inconsistent metric naming: Meta calls it "Campaign Name," Google Ads calls it "Campaign," LinkedIn calls it "Campaign Group," and when all three are pulled into a single view, three different labels for the same conceptual field make cross-channel comparison unnecessarily complicated. Even Google Data Studio, the dashboarding tool mentioned in the prior section, was originally named Data Studio, then Looker Studio, and now renamed to Data Studio. Establishing a naming convention for campaigns, channels, and metrics before a program launches, and enforcing it consistently across every platform, is unglamorous work, but it does prevent confusion after the fact and with your dashboard audience.

Dashboard titles deserve the same deliberateness. A dashboard titled "Marketing Overview" tells a reader nothing about what they are looking at or why. A dashboard titled "Weekly Paid Media Pacing: Budget vs. Actuals by Channel" tells a reader exactly what they will find, who it is for, and at what cadence it should be reviewed. Specificity in naming seems a bit silly to need to discuss. However, it is critically important. Ensure that each dashboard (or dashboard page) has a clear title as to its purpose.

Think: Always, ALWAYS, Start With a Reason

Before building anything, write down the single reason your dashboard needs to exist in one sentence, in plain language, addressed to a specific person. "This dashboard helps the paid media manager decide whether to reallocate budget between channels before the end of the week." If you cannot write that sentence, the dashboard is not ready to be designed yet. If you can write it, every subsequent decision includes how to answer that question. The best dashboards tend to look almost boring. They show five or six numbers, they update automatically, and the people they were built for check them every morning because the numbers tell them exactly what to do next.

Finally, dashboards require maintenance, and the expectation of maintenance should be built into the decision to build one. A campaign ends and the dashboard still shows its metrics. A platform changes its field names and the connector breaks. A stakeholder leaves and their successor doesn't understand what the dashboard was built to answer. Every recurring dashboard should be evaluated every quarter against the question of whether it has changed a decision in the last reporting cycle. If the honest answer is no, the dashboard should either be redesigned around a decision it can actually inform or retired. A dashboard nobody acts on is actively contributing to the analysis paralysis described in the previous chapter, adding to the count of reports that demand attention without producing clarity.

In the next chapter, we turn to the governance and legal frameworks that determine what data a marketing team can legitimately collect and display in any dashboard at all. Privacy law, consent infrastructure, and accessibility requirements now sit directly between a user's behavior and the numbers that eventually appear on the screens covered throughout this book.

References

25+ Marketing Dashboard Examples by Channel (2026). (2026, February 17). 1ClickReport. https://www.1clickreport.com/blog/marketing-dashboard-examples-2026

Batchelor, G. (2026, May 22). *CMO Dashboard Examples, Metrics & Templates (2026 Guide)*. Improvado. https://improvado.io/blog/cmo-dashboard-examples-metrics-templates

Bose, S. (2026, May 12). *Best 11 Marketing Analytics Dashboards to Use in 2026*. Saras Analytics. https://www.sarasanalytics.com/blog/marketing-analytics-dashboard

Cintra, J. (2026, May 6). *The Marketing dashboard KPIs Playbook for 2026 (and Anti-Patterns to Cut)*. Dataslayer. https://www.dataslayer.ai/blog/marketing-dashboard-kpis-2026-playbook

Esau, D. (2026, June 14). *What Is a Marketing Dashboard? A 2026 Guide*. Click Track Marketing. https://www.clicktrackmarketing.com/blog/what-is-a-marketing-dashboard-a-2026-guide

Friedman, H. (2026, July 8). *Marketing Dashboard Examples, KPIs & Software for 2026*. Improvado. https://improvado.io/blog/12-best-marketing-dashboard-examples-and-templates

Kazinik, B. (2025, December 31). *Marketing dashboard: how to build and scale reporting in 2026*. monday.com. https://monday.com/blog/marketing/marketing-dashboard/

Kloefkorn, S. (2026, January 5). *Marketing Dashboard Design Guide*. KEO Marketing. https://keomarketing.com/marketing-analytics-attribution-guide-150191-2

Moreno, J. (2025, October 6). *Marketing Dashboard: 15 Best Practices with Free Templates (2026)*. Dataslayer. https://www.dataslayer.ai/blog/marketing-dashboard-best-practices-2025

Van Mossevelde, C. (2026, July 16). *A comprehensive guide to marketing dashboards*. Funnel.io. https://funnel.io/blog/marketing-dashboard-guide

Chapter 15
The Intersection of Governance and Analytics

Privacy law and web accessibility requirements are two of the most consequential forces reshaping digital marketing analytics, and neither of them is optional or negotiable. Privacy law limits what can be collected and when, protecting a user's right to control their own data. Accessibility law requires that the experience across the digital spectrum is usable by everyone, including the roughly 1.3 billion people worldwide who live with a disability. This chapter addresses both.

The first half covers the major privacy frameworks that determine what an analyst can legally track and how. The second half introduces web accessibility compliance, specifically the Americans with Disabilities Act and the Web Content Accessibility Guidelines it references, and explains why accessibility is increasingly an analytics concern, not just a legal or design issue.

GDPR: The Law That Started the Modern Privacy Era

The General Data Protection Regulation (GDPR) is the European Union's comprehensive data protection law, which took effect on May 25, 2018, and remains the single most influential privacy regulation in the world. GDPR governs how organizations collect, store, process, and share the personal data of individuals located in the EU, and it applies extraterritorially. That means a company headquartered anywhere in the world is subject to GDPR the moment it processes the personal data of someone physically in the EU, regardless of where that company's servers or offices sit. If someone from the EU visits your website, your organization now falls under GDPR.

Two features of GDPR matter enormously for analytics specifically. First, GDPR requires an opt-in consent model for non-essential cookies and tracking. A website cannot fire an analytics or advertising tag until a visitor has affirmatively agreed to it, not just ignore the request. Second, GDPR's penalties are substantial enough to function as a genuine deterrent rather than a cost of doing business. Fines can reach up to €20 million or 4% of a company's global annual revenue, whichever is higher, and cumulative GDPR fines have run into the billions of euros since the law took effect.

CCPA and CPRA: California's Opt-Out Model

The California Consumer Privacy Act (CCPA) became the first comprehensive consumer privacy law in the United States when it took effect on January 1, 2020, giving California residents the right to know what personal information a business collects about them and the right to opt out of having that information sold. In November 2020, California voters expanded the law significantly through the California Privacy Rights Act (CPRA), which took full effect in 2023 and created the California Privacy Protection Agency (CPPA), a dedicated regulator with enforcement authority that did not previously exist.

The single most important distinction is that CCPA/CPRA operates on an opt-out model rather than GDPR's opt-in model: under California law, a business may generally begin tracking a visitor by default, and that visitor must take an action (often clicking "Do Not Sell or Share My Personal Information," or activating a Global Privacy Control browser signal) to stop it. This single difference in default state has an enormous practical effect on how much data an organization retains, and it's the reason a consent banner built correctly for GDPR can be entirely the wrong configuration for a CCPA-compliant site, and vice versa.

The Growing US State Patchwork

Unlike the European Union, the United States has no single federal privacy law. In the years following CCPA, more than twenty other states have passed their own comprehensive consumer privacy laws, each broadly similar in the rights they grant, but meaningfully different in scope, thresholds, and specific obligations. Virginia's Consumer Data Protection Act (VCDPA), Colorado's Privacy Act (ColoPA), Connecticut's Data Privacy Act (CTDPA), and Utah's Consumer Privacy Act (UCPA) were among the earliest beyond California, and Indiana, Kentucky, and Rhode Island each brought their own comprehensive laws into effect at the start of

2026, with several existing states' laws gaining significant amendments the same year.

The practical effect of this patchwork is less about memorizing every state's specific threshold and more about recognizing a pattern: an organization operating a US-facing website is very likely subject to multiple overlapping state laws simultaneously, each potentially requiring slightly different consent behavior, and the safest operational posture, much like the GDPR/CCPA reconciliation above, is usually to build toward the most restrictive applicable requirement rather than maintaining a separate configuration per state.

Insight: Opt-In Versus Opt-Out Is the Single Most Consequential Design Decision in Privacy Compliance

GDPR and CCPA are not two versions of the same basic idea. Under an opt-in regime, every percentage point of consent banner friction directly reduces the size of your trackable audience before a single session is ever recorded. Under an opt-out regime, the default is full visibility, and the analyst's job shifts toward correctly identifying and excluding the smaller population that has exercised its rights. Many global organizations resolve this by adopting what privacy professionals sometimes call a "privacy floor," applying the stricter opt-in standard everywhere, regardless of where a visitor is physically located to avoid maintaining two different consent architectures.

How Privacy Governance Reshapes the Practice of Analytics

While these abstract legal concepts may seem unrelated, consumer privacy is actually directly related to everything discussed thus far. These new consumer privacy laws directly determine how much data described throughout this book an analyst can actually see. If a consumer opts-out of tracking on a website, we can no longer track their behavior on the site. These laws can also limit marketer's abilities to complete retargeting ads and even track across any platform dependent on the severity of the law and how the site or third parties activate on these new regulations. However, even with these new restrictions, there are a few mechanisms that are working to still help marketers utilize, or even simulate data, to maintain some method of tracking.

Consent Mode and Modeled Data. Google Analytics 4's Consent Mode adjusts what a site sends to Google based on a visitor's consent status. Thus, a visitor who declines cookies still generates a limited, cookieless signal, and Google uses statistical modeling to estimate what the non-consenting population likely did. This means a meaningful share of the numbers in a modern GA4 report are not directly observed, but are modeled estimates filling a gap that consent declines created. An analyst who doesn't know this is happening will, sooner or later, misread a swing in the data as a real behavioral change rather than a shift in consent rates.

Server-Side Tracking and Data Minimization. Increasingly, organizations route tracking through a server they control rather than firing tags directly from a visitor's browser, which allows personally identifiable information (PII) to be scrubbed or hashed before it ever reaches an analytics or advertising platform. This connects to data minimization, a principle running through nearly every privacy law. Conceptually, the marketer collects only what's necessary for a stated purpose, and retains it only as long as that purpose requires. An analytics team holding years of unused raw event data "just in case" is, in a growing number of jurisdictions, holding a compliance liability rather than a digital asset.

Data Subject Access Requests (DSARs). Most of the laws in this chapter grant individuals the right to ask an organization what data it holds about them and to request its correction or deletion. When that request arrives, an analytics team needs to be able to locate a specific individual's data across every tool in its marketing technology stack inclusive of web analytics, email platform, CRM, and ad platforms. Once located, the analyst should be able to act on the request within a legally defined window. This is far harder to do after the fact than it may be to design a system that is manageable from the start. That's why privacy governance and analytics architecture increasingly need to be planned together rather than as two separate disciplines.

Side Quest: Global Privacy Control

Global Privacy Control (GPC) is a browser- or extension-level signal that automatically communicates an opt-out preference to every website a user visits without requiring them to find and click an individual "Do Not Sell" link on each site. Several US states, including California, now require businesses to honor GPC signals as a valid opt-out request, and regulators have shown a clear willingness to enforce this request. 2025 enforcement actions cited businesses for continuing to fire retargeting and tracking pixels even after detecting an active GPC signal. For analytics teams, this means a consent management platform has to do more than just display a banner. The platform has to actively detect GPC and suppress tracking accordingly, automatically and before any tag fires.

Operationalizing Privacy: Where I've Seen This Work

Understanding these laws conceptually is one thing; operationalizing them inside a real organization is another. In our work at Forum, we've seen the results of these new privacy laws in real time. We've also been fortunate enough to work with some of the best in the industry in implementing privacy tools for our clients to meet these requirements. One of our clients, Red Clover Advisors, is a leading privacy consultancy that helps organizations build and operationalize privacy programs including GDPR, CCPA, and the broader US state law compliance covered in this chapter. We've also had experience working with OneTrust, the consent and privacy management platform that a meaningful share of the organizations Red Clover Advisors supports rely on to actually enforce the consent rules described above.

The lesson from those experiences, more than any single regulation, is that privacy compliance and clean analytics are not competing priorities. While privacy laws do limit marketing's capabilities in terms of analysis, an analyst who treats the privacy team as an obstacle to work around will consistently produce worse analysis than one who treats the privacy team as a partner in deciding what data is even worth collecting.

Tip: Loop In Privacy Before You Loop In a New Tool

Every chapter in this book has introduced a new platform, tag, or pixel that collects data somewhere in a user's journey. Before adding any new tracking technology to a website or app, involve whoever owns privacy compliance at the same stage you'd involve IT. A consent management platform like OneTrust can only block what it knows exists. If you begin adding tags faster than its privacy program can inventory them, often unintentionally, you can build a compliance gap that takes far more effort to find and fix later than it would have taken to prevent.

Comparing the Major Frameworks at a Glance

Framework	Jurisdiction / Scope	Why the Shift?
GDPR	EU residents, applies globally to any business processing their data	Opt-In (consent required before tracking)
CCPA / CPRA	California residents; enforced by the CPPA	Opt-Out (tracking permitted until a consumer objects)
VCDPA, ColoPA, CTDPA, UCPA, and similar state laws	Residents of the respective state	Opt-Out, broadly similar rights to CCPA with state-specific thresholds
Global Privacy Control (GPC)	Browser-level signal, recognized as a valid opt-outin several states	Automatic opt-out signal a site must detect and honor

ADA Compliance and Web Accessibility: The Governance Layer Analysts Often Miss

The Americans with Disabilities Act, signed into law in 1990, was built around physical spaces: accessible parking, ramps, elevator requirements, accommodations in the workplace. It did not anticipate the creation of the internet. For the better part of two decades, whether a business's website was covered by the ADA was a question courts answered differently depending on jurisdiction. That ambiguity has largely been resolved. Courts across the United States now treat websites as places of public accommodation under ADA Title III. The Department of Justice's 2024 final rule under Title II established WCAG 2.1 Level AA as the explicit, binding technical standard for public-sector websites, with a compliance deadline of April 24, 2026 for entities serving 50,000 or more people. For private businesses under Title III, no equivalent federal rule with a specific deadline has been published, but over 5,100 ADA web accessibility lawsuits were filed in US federal courts in 2025 alone, a 37% increase year over year, making the litigation risk effectively continuous rather than deadline-driven. First-time civil penalties under the ADA run as high as $75,000 and repeat violations can reach $150,000, separate from the legal fees, remediation costs, and reputational damage that accompany a public lawsuit.

What WCAG Is and What It Requires

The Web Content Accessibility Guidelines (WCAG), published and maintained by the World Wide Web Consortium (W3C), are the technical standard courts, regulators, and the DOJ consistently reference when evaluating whether a website meets its ADA obligations. WCAG 2.1 Level AA requires, among other things, that all images have descriptive alternative text for screen readers, that all website functionality is operable by keyboard alone without requiring a mouse, that color contrast between text and background meets a minimum ratio for users with low vision, that video content carries captions for users who are deaf or hard of hearing, and that forms are clearly labeled and usable by assistive technology. WCAG 2.2, released in 2023, adds nine additional criteria around modern interaction patterns including minimum tap target sizes, focus visibility, and alternatives to dragging interactions and is also now considered best practice even where 2.1 remains the legal floor. Despite this clarity, the WebAIM Million Project's 2026 analysis of the top one million websites found that 94.8% still had at least one detectable WCAG failure, with low-contrast text (affecting 79.1% of homepages) and missing alternative text on images (affecting 55.5% of homepages) ranking as the most persistent and widespread violations.

Insight: Accessibility Overlays Are Not a Compliance Strategy

One of the most common and most legally dangerous responses to ADA compliance pressure is the installation of an accessibility overlay. These overlays are simple JavaScript widgets that sit on top of a website and claim to make it compliant without changing the underlying code. Overlay widgets do not make a website ADA compliant, a position that the FTC reinforced with a $1 million penalty against an overlay provider in April 2025 for making unsupported compliance claims. In 2025, approximately 32% of all ADA web accessibility lawsuits involved websites that had an overlay installed. Plaintiff attorneys specifically target overlay-using sites because the widget signals a compliance attempt while the underlying code remains inaccessible. Authentic compliance requires code-level remediation: fixing the actual HTML, CSS, and JavaScript so that the site works with screen readers, keyboard navigation, and other assistive technology at the source, rather than papering over broken code with a script that catches some surface-level issues while leaving the majority untouched. That's not to say that all overlay providers don't help meet the requirement, but practice would be to work with a design firm that can meet the requirements of ADA compliance while also utilizing a quality overlay provider to accommodate any prospective site updates that may not have been captured until such time they can be addressed.

Why Accessibility Is an Analytics Problem

Web accessibility barriers don't just create legal exposure. These issues quietly corrupt the data an analyst is trying to work with. A user who cannot navigate a form because it isn't keyboard-accessible will not complete the form. That non-completion appears in an analyst's data as an abandonment, a bounce, or a failed conversion and is indistinguishable in a standard analytics report from a user who simply wasn't interested. A checkout flow that is inaccessible to a screen reader user will produce cart abandonments that look exactly like abandoned carts caused by price concerns, shipping costs, or checkout friction because the analytics platform has no way of knowing the abandonment was caused by an accessibility failure. The scale of the audience this affects is larger than most realize. Approximately 2.2 billion people worldwide have vision impairments of some kind. Around 430 million experience disabling hearing loss. Motor and cognitive disabilities affect hundreds of millions of people who rely on keyboard navigation, voice control, or extended time-on-task to complete digital interactions. This group of individuals is a segment whose behavior may be systematically misread by any analytics setup that doesn't account for the accessibility barriers they may be encountering.

Connecting Accessibility to the Analytics Stack

The practical intersection of ADA compliance and analytics work runs through two activities. The first is audit and remediation tracking. Most web teams will at some point undertake an accessibility remediation project. It's the analyst's job to establish a performance baseline for the affected pages before remediation begins and to monitor those same metrics after remediation is complete. A well-executed accessibility fix should produce measurable improvements in engagement and conversion metrics for the general population, not just for users relying on assistive technology. Accessibility best practices (clear labels, logical structure, keyboard-navigable forms, and adequate contrast) improve usability for everyone. This is sometimes called the curb-cut effect when a design accommodation built for a specific accessibility need consistently turns out to benefit the broader population as well.

The second activity is ongoing monitoring. Accessibility requires ongoing content updates, new features, third-party plugin and updates. Unfortunately, template changes or simple website updates can introduce new violations at any time, and many organizations that achieve compliance in one quarter regress in the next without a monitoring process in place. Automated accessibility scanning tools (Axe, WAVE, Deque, and Siteimprove among the most widely used) can be configured to run on a schedule and flag new failures before they become legal issues, functioning in much the same way an SEO technical audit tool monitors for crawl errors or broken links. For the compliance team, these tools produce structured reports that can be tracked over time: total WCAG failures by page, failure type, and severity giving a compliance metric that belongs alongside the engagement and conversion metrics in any web analytics reporting stack.

Privacy compliance and web accessibility compliance are not separate governance obligations that happen to share a chapter. They are two expressions of the same underlying responsibility: building and maintaining a digital presence that respects the rights of every person who encounters it. Whether it's the right to control how their data is used, or the right to access the platform, every user should be able to navigate a free and democratized web as they see fit. Analysts have responsibilities to make sure this happens. A consent configuration that suppresses a meaningful share of trackable sessions, and an inaccessible checkout flow that produces abandonment data nobody can correctly interpret, are both governance problems that directly corrupt the analytical picture an organization is working from. Neither problem shows up in a dashboard labeled as what it is. Both require an analyst who understands the governance layer well enough to know when a metric that looks like a performance issue is actually a compliance issue in disguise.

Side Quest: Three Places Accessibility Failures Hide in Analytics Data

Web accessibility barriers tend to surface in analytics data in three specific places. First, form abandonment rates that remain stubbornly high despite multiple rounds of copy particularly if the abandonment is concentrated among users on certain browsers or assistive technology combinations. Second, unusually high bounce rates on pages that should hold attention can reflect screen reader users landing on a page where the content is embedded in images without alternative text, rendering it effectively blank from their perspective. Third, disproportionately low conversion rates from certain traffic sources can sometimes be traced to an accessibility barrier in the conversion path that affects the behavior pattern typical of that source's audience. None of these patterns is diagnostic on its own as they have plausible explanations, but a consistently inexplicable underperformance in a specific part of the funnel is worth reviewing for accessibility issues.

References

2025 ADA Website Compliance Lawsuit Annual Report (2026). EcomBack. https://www.ecomback.com/annual-2025-ada-website-accessibility-lawsuit-report

2026 ADA Website Compliance Predictions: More Lawsuits, AI Has Big Impact. (2025, November 28). Accessible.org. https://accessible.org/2026-ada-website-compliance-lawsuits-ai/

2026 Data Security and Privacy Compliance Checklist: Key US State Law Updates, AI Rules, COPPA Changes, and Global Data Protection Risks. (2026, April 13). O'Melveny. https://www.omm.com/insights/alerts-publications/2026-data-security-and-privacy-compliance-checklist-key-us-state-law-updates-ai-rules-coppa-changes-and-global-data-protectio-n-risks/

ADA Website Compliance Deadline 2025–2026: What You Need to Know. (2026, February 23). RatedWithAI. https://ratedwithai.com/blog/ada-website-compliance-deadline-2025-2026

Adela (2025, October 22). *Marketing Data Privacy Compliance Guide: GDPR, CCPA & US State Laws*. Dataslayer. https://www.dataslayer.ai/blog/marketing-data-privacy-compliance-guide-gdpr-ccpa-us-state-laws

Barry, C. (2026, January 23). *2026 U.S. State Privacy Laws: what you need to know*. Ketch. https://www.ketch.com/blog/posts/us-privacy-laws-2026

The Complete Guide to ADA Website Compliance Lawsuits. (2026). AccessiBe. https://accessibe.com/blog/knowledgebase/ada-website-lawsuits

Consent Management Platform. (n.d.). OneTrust. https://www.onetrust.com/products/consent-management/

Consequences of Accessibility Non-Compliance. (2026, March 18). Government Information Center. https://gic.delaware.gov/consequences-of-accessibility-non-compliance/

Data Privacy Consulting Services. (n.d.). Red Clover Advisors. https://redcloveradvisors.com/

Duball, J. (2026, January 5). *New year, new rules: US state privacy requirements coming online as 2026 begins.* IAPP. https://iapp.org/news/a/new-year-new-rules-us-state-privacy-requirements-coming-online-as-2026-begins

Getting the Most From Your OneTrust Deployment with Red Clover. (n.d.). Red Clover Advisors. https://redcloveradvisors.com/onetrust/

Gevorkian, D. (2026, March 12). *The 2026 Web Accessibility Statistics Report.* Be Accessible. https://beaccessible.com/post/web-accessibility-statistics/

Gibson, D. (2026, June 25). *2026 ADA Web Accessibility Standards & Requirements.* Accessibility.Works. https://www.accessibility.works/blog/wcag-ada-website-compliance-standards-requirements/

Goldstick, S. (2026, April 1). *The Compliance Tightrope: Balancing Uniformity and Precision Across U.S. State Consumer Privacy Laws.* Foley & Lardner. https://www.foley.com/insights/publications/2026/04/the-compliance-tightrope-balancing-uniformity-and-precision-across-u-s-state-consumer-privacy-laws/

Nayyar, S. (2026, June 5). *ADA Compliance for Websites: The Complete 2026 Guide.* WebAbility. https://www.webability.io/blog/ada-compliance-for-websites

Ohta, K. (2026, July 8). *Data Privacy Laws by Country and U.S. State (2026).* CDP.com. https://cdp.com/basics/international-u-s-data-privacy-laws-and-regulations-you-need-to-know/

Richt, H. (2026, January 1). *Seven Critical CCPA Compliance Changes Taking Effect January 1, 2026*. Richt Law Firm. https://richtfirm.com/seven-critical-ccpa-compliance-changes-taking-effect-january-1-2026/

US State Privacy Laws 2026: What Marketing Teams Must Know. (2026, February 20). Secure Privacy. https://secureprivacy.ai/blog/us-state-privacy-laws-2026-marketing

Chapter 16
Digital Marketing and Marketing Strategy

Every organization that does digital marketing has a strategy whether they know it or not. Most of them have it written down somewhere and others may have it in their mind's eye with little more than some good ideas. The question here is not whether you have a strategy, but whether the data you've been collecting across the last fourteen chapters is actually connected to it. I'm not asking whether a report is produced after the fact to grade what happened, but as a discipline woven through how the strategy gets built, how it gets adjusted while it's running, and how this cycle's results become next cycle's starting point. Those are three different jobs, and most organizations are only doing one of them consistently well.

Three Jobs Analytics Does for a Strategy

It helps to separate analytics' role into three distinct jobs as each one happens at a different point in a strategy's life and each one fails in a different way when neglected.

Informing the strategy before it's built. Before a single campaign launches, analytics from the prior period should shape what the strategy assumes about the market and the audience, rather than the strategy being built on assumption alone and measurement only arriving afterward to grade it.

Measuring and adjusting the strategy while it's running. Once a strategy is live, analytics should be answering a continuous, narrower question: is this working well enough, right now, to keep doing it as planned, or does something need to change before the next reporting cycle even arrives?

Feeding the next strategy. The results of this cycle should become the starting evidence for the next planning cycle, rather than each new strategy starting from a blank page as if the previous one never happened.

Frameworks exist precisely to keep an organization honest about doing all three jobs, in order, rather than skipping straight to the part that feels most like "being a marketer." As an academic lecturer and long-time marketer, I still use frameworks to both teach students and build plans. Two of the most widely used frameworks in digital marketing planning, SOSTAC® and the RACE Framework, map directly onto this three-job structure.

SOSTAC®: A Planning Framework Built Around a Feedback Loop

SOSTAC®, developed by marketing strategist PR Smith in the 1990s and still consistently ranked among the most widely taught marketing planning models, breaks a strategy into six stages: Situation, Objectives, Strategy, Tactics, Action, and Control. It predates digital marketing, but its structure has aged well. Even modern frameworks use similar structures because it all comes back to analytics favorite topic: control. Control is about measurement. The control stage of any plan is explicitly built to feedback into the Situation Analysis for the next planning cycle. This turns what would otherwise be a one-way, linear process into a continuous loop.

Situation: Where are we now? This stage is built almost entirely from analytics already covered in this book used to honestly assess current position before deciding where to go next. If you're new to marketing, I like to include internal information as well as information about competition as well as environmental analysis, customer analysis, and so on so, as a marketer, you're aware of everything that's around you to help in decision making.

Objectives: Where do we want to be? Objectives set here should be specific and measurable enough that the control stage can later judge them. It's important to build obtainable objectives that can be met using the resources available to you.

Strategy: How do we get there, in broad terms? This is the stage most often rushed, according to practitioners who use the framework heavily, because moving straight to visible activity feels more productive than sitting with the harder strategic choices first. However, those hard strategic choices make the difference in your ability to meet the objectives.

Tactics: What specific channels and activities will we use? This is where the channel-by-channel knowledge from earlier chapters in this book gets selected and sequenced.

Action: Who does what, and by when? This is the operational detail that turns all of the tactics into an executable plan.

Control: How will we know if it's working? This is where the bulk of this book's content has focused: the KPIs, dashboards, and reporting cadences that monitor execution. This stage also lays out what findings become the next cycle's situation analysis.

Insight: Most Strategic Failures Happen Before Tactical Execution

Practitioners who use SOSTAC® extensively report a consistent pattern. Organizations that struggle with a strategy's execution usually rushed through Situation and Strategy to get to the visible, productive work of Tactics and Action. This is not unusual as marketers want to get to the "work" that feels action-oriented. If a strategy is consistently missing its goals despite competent execution, the more useful diagnostic question is often not "what should we change about the tactics" but "was the situation analysis underneath this strategy actually rigorous, or did we treat it as a formality on the way to the parts that felt like real marketing work?"

Tip: Write the Control Stage As You Write Objectives

A useful discipline when building a strategy using SOSTAC is to draft the Objective stage and Control stage at the same time. Being able to align your KPIs, dashboards, and review strategy for your plan allows you to stay aligned from beginning to end. If you can't yet describe how you'll know whether the tactic is working, that's a signal the objective either isn't specific enough or the tactic is wrong for the effort. This habit helps to ensure a streamlined strategic plan from beginning to end and that you don't start sorting out what metrics to use until you're halfway through the plan.

RACE: Mapping Analytics to the Customer Lifecycle

SOSTAC® provides a formal planning skeleton that works for most organizations. The RACE Framework developed by Dr. Dave Chaffey and the Smart Insights team specifically for digital marketing provides a complementary lens focused on the customer's actual journey: Reach, Act, Convert, and Engage (sometimes extended to PRACE with an added Plan stage at the front). Rather than asking "what stage of planning are we in," RACE asks "where is the customer right now, and which of this book's channels and metrics apply at that exact point." It is an action-oriented, practical approach to ensure that your marketing stays in the moment and maintains momentum.

RACE Stage	Customer Question	Channels and Metrics
Reach	Have they heard of us?	SEO, paid search, paid social, display, DOOH, earned media, reach, impressions, share of voice
Act	Are they interested enough to engage?	Social engagement, content engagement, email opens and clicks, on-site behavior
Convert	Have they taken the action we want?	Conversion rate, CPA/CPL, e-Commerce and lead-gen metrics, attribution
Engage	Will they come back and advocate for us?	Retention, email and app engagement over time, NPS, earned media and referral metrics

The practical value of RACE for an analyst is that it prevents a common reporting mistake that I've already outlined: judging a Reach-stage channel (a CTV awareness buy or an earned media placement) by a Convert-stage metric (last-click conversion rate), or vice versa. A metric is only meaningful in the context of which part of the customer journey it's meant to describe, and RACE gives a shared vocabulary for making sure a report's metrics and its stated objective actually belong to the same stage.

A practical execution of using the RACE framework is creating a customer journey map. **Customer journey maps** are simply a visual representation of the steps a consumer takes to get to and purchase your product. These maps can be built in all sorts of different formats using traditional sales funnels, the Awareness - Consideration - Conversion - Loyalty - Advocacy sales funnel provided earlier or really any structure that fits your organization's methodology. If you understand tactically what you are working to accomplish at each stage, then metrics become much simpler. As an example, a sample customer journey map from Smart Insights is provided on the following page.

Ideally, you would know and capture the actions, touchpoints, thoughts, and emotions of the consumer at every point as well as understand the pain point you are working to solve and the resolution you provide to meet their need and provide value. Because of the volume of noise in today's marketplace, research indicates that it takes as many as 50 touchpoints to drive the user to purchase depending on the sales cycle: 1-3 touchpoints for inactive customers; 5-12 touchpoints for warm inbound leads; and, 20-50 touchpoints for cold prospects. On the following page is an example of how this can play out from a practical perspective.

Source: Smart Insights

Side Quest: Why SOSTAC® and RACE Are Usually Used Together

One of the common questions asked is whether to start with SOSTAC® or RACE first. Dave Chaffey, the creator of RACE, has been explicit on this point: the two frameworks were built for different jobs and work best layered rather than chosen between. SOSTAC® is a general strategy development process that applies to any kind of plan, marketing or otherwise. Similar platforms are used across strategic and marketing management academic programs. On the other hand, RACE is a customer-lifecycle model built specifically for digital channels. The practical approach favored by both frameworks' creators is to use SOSTAC® to build the overall strategic plan, then use RACE within the Tactics, Action, and Control stages to organize specifically digital activities and metrics around the customer's actual journey. Neither framework replaces the judgment this book has tried to build chapter by chapter. What the frameworks do provide is a shared structure that's easier to communicate to a team or a client than reinventing the wheel each planning cycle.

The Value Ladder: Designing the Path Before You Measure It

In writing this book, a friend asked how much of Russell Brunson's works I had included as resources. The answer at that point was none, but in discussion, he made a great point about how his personal businesses had grown significantly using Russell's work as a framework and it provides a great deal of value when adding to the overall discussion here around frameworks (plus, it's incredibly practical!).

Russell Brunson is the co-founder of ClickFunnels and author of *DotCom Secrets*, *Expert Secrets*, and *Traffic Secrets*. While Brunson's work is rooted in funnel building and the customer journey rather than analytics specifically, one concept from *DotCom Secrets* belongs in any serious discussion of digital marketing strategy because it explains something SOSTAC® and RACE both assume but neither makes clear: what are you actually asking the customer to do at each stage, and in what order? Brunson calls this the value ladder.

The value ladder proposes that a customer's relationship with a brand should be designed as a sequence of ascending commitments, each delivering more value and asking more in return than the one before it. At the bottom of the ladder sits the lowest-commitment entry point — a free piece of content, a low-cost introductory product, or a trial offer — designed not to maximize immediate revenue but to earn the right to the next conversation. Each rung above it represents a higher level of trust, a higher price point, and a deeper relationship, culminating at the top of the ladder in the highest-value offer the organization has to make. The customer climbs the ladder willingly because each previous rung delivered enough value to make the next one feel worth reaching for. His belief is that few will buy outright. The value ladder is how you get them to the point of the larger purchase.

The aforementioned friend let me take a screenshot of GrowHQ dashboard (minus actual page names and products) as an example.

Each row in this dashboard that contains a page view count is a landing page and below represents the landing page variations of an active A/B test that is running to determine which version drive higher returns. Each page is built along the value ladder.

Page Views		Opt-Ins		Sales					Earnings/Page View	
All	Uniques	All	Rate	Orders	Rate	Quantity	Amount	Avg. cart value	All	Uniques
10864	6813	801	9.09%	489	5.55%	566	$14016.70	$28.66	$3.09	$4.47
5880	4714	427	9.06%	252	5.35%	297	$7337.15	$29.12	$1.25	$1.56
-	-	-	-	252	5.35%	252	$6287.40		-	-
-	-	-	-	19	7.54%	19	$531.05	-	-	-
-	-			26	10.32%	26	$518.70	-	-	
4389	3579	343	9.56%	215	6.01%	244	$6046.80	$28.12	$1.38	$1.69
-	-	-	-	215	6.01%	215	$5364.25	-	-	-
-	-	-	-	16	7.44%	16	$319.20	-	-	-
-	-	-	-	13	6.05%	13	$363.35	-	-	-
595	520	31	5.96%	22	4.23%	25	$632.75	$28.76	$1.06	$1.22
543	492	-	-	121	24.59%	121	$7068.95	$58.42	$24.49	$27.05
216	190	-	-	14	7.37%	14	$139.30	$9.95	$0.84	$0.73

Source: GrowHQ

In a separate example my friend shared with me, the initial product sold from a Facebook ad generated a significant negative loss of $53 per sale. However, if the user continued through the value ladder and was offered additional offerings (what we refer to in marketing as **cross-sales**), and the user adds the second item to their cart the profit margin increased to $0. As additional products are added, the value eventually reached $5-$6 per order. While this seems at odds with logic (as it may not seem like a larger margin) not only does he collect the order, he also collects an email address and contact information for future remarketing. To ensure the highest possible margins, his team constantly tries different combinations of offers to determine (every week - 2 weeks) what drove the highest possible profit margin per day and consistently improves margin and ensure losses are used as learning opportunities and not consistent losses. In another example, through the structured funnel approach of the value ladder, he drove profit margins as high as $200 per sale!

Tying the idea of funnels back to Brunson's works, the value ladder gives you a way to diagnose why your RACE-stage metrics look the way they do. A brand with strong Reach metrics and weak Act metrics has a top-of-ladder problem — it is bringing strangers in but offering them nothing at a low enough commitment level to take the first step. A brand with strong Act metrics and weak Convert metrics has a mid-ladder problem — people are engaged with the introductory offer but the bridge to the next level of commitment is either missing or unclear. A brand with strong Convert metrics but low customer lifetime value may have a ladder that ends too early, with no higher-value rung for a willing customer to move toward. In each case the analytical data is pointing to a structural problem in the customer's journey, not simply a campaign execution problem that more spend or better creative will fix.

The practical implication is that RACE tells you which stage of the customer journey your analytics should be measuring, and the value ladder tells you what that customer journey should be designed to accomplish at each stage. Used together, they give a marketer both the map and a sense of whether the road itself has been built correctly. A campaign that performs poorly against its RACE-stage metrics is one question. A campaign that performs well against its RACE-stage metrics but fails to move customers toward the next rung of the ladder is a different and more fundamental one. It is the kind of question that only gets asked once the value ladder has been defined in the first place.

From Objectives to Metrics, Without Losing the Plot

A strategy's Objectives stage is also where the lessons on analysis paralysis become operational rather than theoretical. Objectives written as SMART goals (the acronym stands for specific, measurable, achievable, relevant, and time-bound) or organized as OKRs (Objectives and Key Results) give a strategy's later Control stage something precise to grade itself against. Just as importantly, the North Star Metric concept introduced in Chapter 13 belongs here as well. When a plan carries too many objectives, no one can tell whether it's working; when the goals are few and pointed, every team can see progress at a glance.

The Optimization Loop: Adjusting Mid-Flight

Between the moment a strategy launches and the moment its results get reviewed at the next full planning cycle, analytics has a narrower, faster job: deciding whether something needs to change now. This is the territory of test-and-learn marketing, agile marketing, and the closely related Plan-Do-Check-Act (PDCA) cycle borrowed from quality management. Where SOSTAC®'s Control stage operates on a planning-cycle timescale (often quarterly or annually), this inner loop operates on a campaign timescale, sometimes adjusting weekly or even daily.

Every channel chapter in this book has been, in its own way, preparing you for this inner loop. Understanding the basics of all of these analytical elements helps you know when something needs to change mid-plan. The instinct to wait for the full strategy review before adjusting anything is, more often than not, the analysis-paralysis instinct rearing its ugly head. Don't fall into the fear of action, but trust your instincts and follow the data to make that mid-flight correction.

Think: How Much Mid-Flight Adjustment Is Too Much?

There's always been a real tension between the discipline of sticking to a strategy long enough to know if it's actually working, and the discipline of adjusting quickly when early data suggests trouble. Agile marketers would say to plan fast, run a bunch of test campaigns, and then lean into the ones that are most successful. Traditional marketers would say to stick it out until the end of the plan. If a team changes tactics every time a weekly number dips, it may never run anything long enough to know if it would have worked. If a team waits for the full quarterly review every time, it may burn an entire budget cycle on something the data flagged as struggling in week two. Typically the answer is "it depends," but consider this: where would you draw that line for a campaign in a channel you know well from earlier in this book, and, what specific metric, watched over what specific time window, would have to move before you'd act on it mid-flight rather than waiting?

Closing the Loop: Letting Results Build the Next Strategy

SOSTAC® and RACE do not make strategic decisions for an organization. These frameworks provide a shared structure from which those decisions can be made, communicated, and evaluated. That distinction matters because the most common failure mode for both frameworks is treating them as a planning ritual rather than a discipline. SOSTAC® is not meant to be a form that is completed because it is required. And, mapping activities to RACE stages is not meant to serve as a constraint that an organization has to operate within.

The discipline that actually enforces the frameworks is not the frameworks themselves. It is the operational rhythm a team builds around. The idea is to work to make sure that data is reviewed, the right people are in the room, and what metrics are needed to change a strategy mid-flight. It's about planning, knowing what's in front of you, and how to leverage every tool in your marketing tool box to meet your objective. That rhythm is what the final chapter of this book is about. Lean analytics and agile marketing frameworks are not alternatives to SOSTAC® and RACE. They are what makes those frameworks work in practice rather than only on paper. Think about it like writing a song. A song without rhythm isn't a song. It's noise. A song without structure but rhythm is still noise. However, structure and rhythm together produce something amazing.

Before we get to the final chapter, I thought it would be good to provide you a number of benchmarks that you can use for reference. Note that this book is being released in 2026 so of all the chapters, this is likely the chapter to become dated the fastest. However, if you're one of those marketers just now starting with a platform like GA4 and you don't have historical data to lean on, at least this can give you a head start.

References

Broadhurst, M. (2022, November 9). *How to Use the RACE Planning Framework for Marketing*. Broadhurst Digital. https://broadhurst.digital/blog/how-to-use-the-race-planning-framework-for-marketing

Brunson, R. (2015). *DotCom Secrets: The underground playbook for growing your company online*. Morgan James Publishing.

Brunson, R. (2017). *Expert Secrets: The underground playbook for creating a mass movement of people who will pay for your advice*. Morgan James Publishing.

Brunson, R. (2020). *Traffic Secrets: The underground playbook for filling your websites and funnels with your dream customers*. Hay House Business.

Buntin, D. (2026, January 18). *Integrating RACE with SOSTAC® for Smarter Marketing Plans*. Boderia. https://www.boderia.io/insights/integrating-race-with-sostac

Chaffey, D. (2020, March 31). *How do I integrate the SOSTAC® and RACE frameworks?*. Dave Chaffey Digital Marketing. https://www.davechaffey.com/digital-marketing-strategy/how-do-i-integrate-sostac-and-race-frameworks/

Chaffey, D. (2022, October 11). *SOSTAC® marketing plan model definition*. Dave Chaffey Digital Marketing Glossary. https://www.davechaffey.com/digital-marketing-glossary/sostac-marketing-plan-model/

Chaffey, D. (2023, October 20). *SOSTAC marketing planning model guide*. Smart Insights. https://www.smartinsights.com/digital-marketing-strategy/sostac-model/

Chaffey, D. (2012, July 17). *SOSTAC® marketing plans [infographic]*. Smart Insights. https://www.smartinsights.com/managing-digital-marketing/capability-performance-review/sostac-marketing-plan-infographic/

Cooper, A. (2025, June 18). *How to create an actionable customer journey map using RACE.* Smart Insights. https://www.smartinsights.com/marketplace-analysis/consumer-buying-behaviour/create-an-actionable-customer-journey-map-using-race/

GrowHQ Screenshot (2026, July 10). GrowHQ

Nilson, D. (2025, March 27). *SOSTAC® Marketing Model – Top Ranked Planning System*. Up Strategy Lab. https://www.daniel-one.com/blog/sostac-marketing-model-planning-system

Rastegar-Panah, M. (2026, May 18). *Customer Journey maps: How to create one (templates + examples)*. zendesk. https://www.zendesk.com/blog/customer-service/customer-journey-map/

SOSTAC Marketing Model Explained: A Complete Guide with Examples. (n.d.). Taya Agency. https://tayaagency.com/sostac-marketing-model/

Swan, S. (2022, January 28). *How to use the SOSTAC® planning model and the RACE Framework.* Smart Insights. https://www.smartinsights.com/digital-marketing-strategy/sostac-plan-example/

Chapter 17
By Industry

A 2% conversion rate would get a luxury jewelry brand's marketing director promoted. The same 2% would get a B2B e-commerce site's marketing director fired. This isn't because one team is better at their job than the other, but because a 2% conversion rate sits well above benchmark in one category and well below it in the other. Now, I'm very aware that historical benchmarks (testing against your own data) are likely the best way to check your results, but knowing where you are in the mix of your industry can be very helpful.

Nearly every metric this book has covered, whether conversion rate, cost per lead, click-through rate, or churn, only means something in relation to what's typical for the specific kind of business generating it. This chapter exists to give you some context, industry by industry, and to make explicit something that could only have been implied earlier.

The sectors below were chosen because each one changes which metrics matter and why, not just what the numbers happen to be. Within each, you'll find a short explanation of what makes that industry's analytics priorities distinct, followed by sourced 2026 benchmarks for the metrics that matter most there.

Global Benchmarks at a Glance

Before diving into the industry-specific sections below, it's worth stepping back and looking across the entirety of the last 300+ pages at once. The data presented here is sourced from a number of websites you can all find in the references section of this chapter. These measurements are not perfect, but certainly serve as a headstart into your data benchmarking. I'd also be remiss to note that when platforms are modified (Google Search Console adding or deleting features, a new version of a platform, or new privacy rules come online), the data can swing in one direction or another. Either way, here are a few benchmarks to hold onto (at least for now).

Email Marketing: Open Rate and Click-Through Rate by Industry

Industry	Open Rate	Click-Through Rate
Government / Public Administration	28% - 35%	3.5% - 4%
Nonprofit	25% - 28%	2.5% - 3%
B2B Technology / Software	15% - 17%	2% - 6%
Retail / e-Commerce	15% - 16%	2.1% - 2.5%
Overall Cross-Industry Average	19% - 22%	2% - 2.5%

Sources: Brevo 2026 Marketing Orchestration Benchmark; WebFX, 2026 Email Marketing Benchmarks by Industry; Demand Sage / Popupsmart B2B Email Marketing Benchmarks 2026 (referenced in Chapter 9)

Tip: Use This Section as a Map, Not a Scorecard

The tables are deliberately placed before any single industry's deep-dive section because the temptation when looking at a benchmark table is to find your row and stop. You need to resist that temptation. The real value here of seeing email, social, display, and NPS metrics side by side is to notice how differently each of these metrics behaves. It's even important to see how they can vary across industries. For instance, NPS compresses within B2B regardless of the vertical, while email open rate can have a swing of twenty points depending on whether the sender is a government entity or a retailer. Savvy analysts know which of their metrics are industry-driven and which are channel-driven.

Social Media: Average Engagement Rate by Platform

Platform	Average Engagement Rate	Context
TikTok	4.25% - 5.53%	Highest of any major platform; algorithmic discovery decouples reach from follower count
Instagram	0.48% - 1.2%	Reels run 3x - 5x higher than static posts; Format choice now matters more than account size
Facebook	0.07% - 0.23%	Organic reach has declined to its lowest level in the platform's history
X (Twitter)	0.04% - 0.10%	Lowest engagement of major platforms; valued more for real-time reach than sustained engagement

Sources: Emplifi Social Media Benchmarks 2026; Socialinsider 2026 Social Media Benchmarks; Apaya, Social Media Benchmarks 2026: Engagement Rates by Industry (referenced in Chapter 7).

Display Advertising: CTR by Format

Format	Average CTR	Context
Standard Banner	0.46%	The historical baseline; suppressed by banner blindness and low-engagement placements
Native Advertising	1.16% - 2.5x standard display	Outperforms because the ad blends into surrounding content rather than competing with it
Rich Media / Animated Ads	1.84%	Roughly 4x a static banner's CTR
Video Display	73% higher CTR than static banners	Completion rate and attention matter more than CTR alone for this format

Sources: Digital Applied, Display Advertising Benchmarks 2026: 150+ Data Points; eMarketer, FAQ on native advertising 2026 (referenced in Chapter 10).

Net Promoter Score (NPS) by Industry

Industry	Typical NPS	Context
Insurance	71 - 80	Among the highest of any tracked industry, driven by post-pandemic trust rebuilding
Professional Services	~68	High-trust, relationship-driven engagements support strong loyalty scores
B2B Software / SaaS	38 - 41	B2B consistently scores 8 - 14 points lower than B2C across nearly every comparable category
Retail / e-Commerce	~45	Close to the cross-industry median 32 - 44
Telecom / Internet & Cable	2 - 27	Among the lowest scores of any tracked industry

Sources: Retently 2026 NPS Benchmark Report; StealthAgents, Net Promoter Score Benchmarks by Industry 2026; Bain & Company NPS threshold research (referenced in Chapter 13).

The following sections on the next few pages break out select industries and provide examples of just some of the metrics (and benchmarks) in each industry. A thorough review of all benchmarks in each industry could be a book in and of itself. If you need industry benchmarks for select key metrics, I'd recommend reviewing data from platforms like eMarketer or doing research online to find reputable sources with quality benchmark data.

Retail

Retail, or brands selling physical goods through a mix of online and brick-and-mortar channels, is unique in this chapter because its digital analytics almost never tell the whole story on their own. Sometimes a click that doesn't convert online may still convert in a store days later, a gap most attribution models still struggle to close. Within paid search specifically, Shopping & Retail sits close to the cross-industry middle on most headline metrics, which makes it a useful baseline category against where more specialized verticals (legal, healthcare, and home services) stand out as outliers.

Metric	2026 Benchmark	Context
Search Ads Conversion Rate (cross-industry average)	8.18%	Up from 7.52% in 2025; conversion rate improved as CPC rose modestly
Search Ads CPC (cross-industry average)	$5.42	Real Estate saw the largest YoY increase (+27.27%); Arts & Entertainment remained the cheapest category
Search Ads Cost Per Lead (cross-industry average)	$66.69	First measured YoY decrease in CPL since before 2020

Sources: WordStream/LocaliQ Search Advertising Benchmarks 2026; Search Engine Journal, "What Are Good Google Ads Benchmarks In 2026?"

E-commerce

E-commerce — retail conducted entirely online — is where the on-site funnel metrics from Chapter 4 (Website Analytics) carry the most direct weight on revenue. Because every step from landing page to checkout is fully instrumented, e-commerce is the rare industry where an analyst can usually diagnose exactly where a funnel is leaking rather than inferring it indirectly.

Metric	2026 Benchmark	Context
Site-wide Conversion Rate	~1.4%	Range reflects methodology across panels; Food & Beverage runs as high as 4.5% - 6.1%, Luxury & Jewelry as low as 0.9% - 1.2%
Cart Abandonment Rate	70.22%	Baymard Institute's meta-analysis of 50 studies; roughly 40% of abandonment is attributed to unexpected costs (shipping) revealed at checkout
Add-to-Cart Rate	~7% (5% - 10% considered healthy)	Stores with ATC rates above 10% consistently converted above 3.8% site-wide in one 21-store analysis
Average Order Value	~$150 - $180 globally	AOV also varies meaningfully by device, with desktop orders typically outpacing mobile

Sources: Baymard Institute Cart Abandonment Rate Statistics; Elogic Commerce B2B Ecommerce Conversion Rate Benchmarks 2026; Triple Whale Ecommerce Benchmarks; DTC Pages Ecommerce Conversion Rate Benchmarks 2026.

B2B (Business-to-Business)

B2B marketing is defined by a long, multi-stage funnel and a buying committee rather than a single buyer, which is why a single "conversion rate" is almost meaningless without specifying which stage of that funnel it describes. The MQL-to-SQL handoff introduced in Chapter 9 is the single most consequential checkpoint in this funnel, and it has been getting harder, not easier, as buying committees grow and qualification criteria tighten. Marketers (and analysts) have to make sure that not only is conversion managed, but that there is a strategy to go from MQL-to-SQL-to-Customer.

Metric	2026 Benchmark	Context
Median B2B Cost per Lead	$213	Top-quartile programs achieve $84; bottom-quartile sits at $397 - a 4.7x spread
MQL-to-SQL Conversion Rate	~9.8%	Down from 13% in 2024; Forrester and Demand Gen Report data show a 24% compression over two years
Lead-to-Customer Conversion (all sources, blended)	~0.94%	Roughly 1 in 106 captured leads become closed-won revenue
Website Conversion Rate (median, all industries)	2.9%	Legal services lead at ~7.4%; B2B e-commerce trails at ~1.8%, a 311% spread between categories
Average Buying Committee Size (deals over $50k)	11.2 stakeholders	Up from 9.7 in 2024; larger committees lengthen mid-market cycles to ~121 days and enterprise cycles to ~218 days

Sources: Digital Applied, B2B Marketing Statistics 2026 and Lead Generation Statistics 2026; SalesHive B2B Digital Marketing Benchmarks for Lead Generation; First Page Sage B2B Conversion Rates By Industry — 2026.

Insight: The Same Acronym, But a Different Number Every Year

Chapter 9 introduced MQL-to-SQL conversion as a benchmark worth tracking. Here, you may note the change in results over the past two years, a drop from roughly 13% to 9.8% over two years, is a reminder that even well-established benchmarks shift, sometimes quickly, as buyer behavior and qualification discipline change. There are still a number of so-called "benchmarks" on the internet regarding everything from open rate to CTR. Make sure you have the latest information because using an old benchmark from two years ago is a bit risky. Treat every number in this chapter as a snapshot of a specific year and not a permanent target.

SaaS (Software as a Service)

SaaS is the industry most responsible for popularizing the retention-driven analytics philosophy running through this entire book. It is even the industry that popularized some of the frameworks you've seen thus far and will see in the last chapter. Why? In SaaS, revenue is recurring rather than a one-time accomplishment, thus, a SaaS company's health depends less on any single month's new sales and more on whether existing customers stay, expand, or churn. This is why SaaS benchmarks revolve so heavily around ratios including LTV, CAC, and retention rather than raw totals.

Metric	2026 Benchmark	Context
LTV:CAC Ratio	3:1 minimum; 4:1+ for top performers	Below 3:1 signals overspending relative to customer value; ratios should be segmented by channel and customer tier, not blended

Metric	2026 Benchmark	Context
CAC Payback Period	~12-15 months (median); under 6 months for elite	Benchmarkit and ChartMogul both flag payback over 18 months as a cash-trap warning sign for investors
Net Revenue Retention (NRR)	~82% median; 100%+ considered healthy; 110%+ enterprise	Companies above 100% NRR grow at roughly double the rate of companies below it
Monthly Churn	~3.5% to 3.7% median B2B	SMB-focused products often see 5% - 8% monthly churn without active intervention; under 3% is considered excellent

Sources: ChartMogul SaaS Retention Report 2025; Benchmarkit B2B SaaS Performance Metrics Benchmark Report; Eagle Rock CFO SaaS Benchmarks by Stage 2026; The SaaS Library, SaaS Metrics 2026.

Professional Services and Home Services

Professional services (legal, accounting, consulting) and home services (HVAC, plumbing, roofing, and similar trades) are grouped together here because both share a defining analytics trait. These relationships frequently start with the phone call, not the web form. This makes call tracking one of the single highest-leverage analytics investments either category can make, and it's a recurring theme across the sourced benchmarks on the next page.

Metric	2026 Benchmark	Context
Cost per Lead, Home Services (B2C)	$144 average	Roofing runs highest ($80 - $180 via paid search) given large average job sizes; house cleaning runs lowest ($20 - $45)
Phone Lead Conversion Rate	46% (versus 7.8% blended average across channels)	37% of phone leads convert on the very first call; response within 60 seconds improves conversion rates by up to 391%
Cost per Lead, Legal Services	$130 - $650+ dependent on practice area	Personal injury and mass tort cases justify some of the highest CPLs in any industry given high case settlement values
Cost per Lead, Financial Advisory / Wealth Management	$80 - $200	Driven by high client lifetime value; CPL for commercial insurance can run $100 - $300

Sources: WebFX, 2026 Home Services Marketing Benchmarks; Estatehub, 2026 Benchmarks for Lead Conversion Rates in Home Services; LeadsuiteNow, Cost Per Lead Benchmarks by Industry in 2026; Click-Vision, Home Services Marketing Statistics 2026.

Side Quest: Why is a Missed Call an Analytics Problem?

It's tempting to treat a missed or mishandled phone call as a customer service failure rather than a marketing analytics issue. However, the two are inseparable in professional and home services. A call that isn't tracked back to the specific ad, keyword, or campaign that generated the call makes the success of that campaign invisible to further optimization. A marketing team could be quietly funding the channel that drives the fewest closed jobs simply because its calls were never properly attributed back to the source. Dynamic number insertion (swapping a tracked phone number based on traffic source) is the technical fix, but the primary issue is the handoff from source to source. Without that handoff, you can accidentally cut off critical channels thinking that you're cutting poorly performing campaigns.

Manufacturing

Manufacturing marketing operates at the long-sales-cycle, high-consideration end of the B2B spectrum. In manufacturing, you may be selling to highly specific engineering or procurement buyers rather than a broad market. The target is small, yet findable. For that reason, marketers in this industry can expect, and should budget for, conversion rates and CPLs that would be disconcerting in any other industry.

Metric	2026 Benchmark	Context
B2B Cost per Lead	\$82 - \$1,055 (wide range by sub-sectors)	Higher-value, longer-cycle categories like aerospace components justify CPLs at the top of this range

Metric	2026 Benchmark	Context
Website Conversion Rate	~2.2% average; 3% - 5% considered a strong stretch goal	Notably lower than the cross-industry B2B median of 2.9%, reflecting longer sales cycles and smaller addressable audiences
Marketing Budget as a % of Revenue	~3 - 5.7%	Among the lowest marketing budgets of any B2B category, alongside the lowest growth in AI tooling and account-based marketing adoption relative to software and SaaS
Sales Cycle (complex / engineered products)	6 - 12 months	Semiconductor, circuit board, and similar tech-manufacturing categories commonly fall in this range given enterprise buyer involvement

Sources: WebFX, 2026 Manufacturing Marketing Benchmarks Every Industrial Firm Must Track; Digital Applied, B2B Marketing Statistics 2026; First Page Sage, B2B Conversion Rates By Industry — 2026; SalesHive, B2B Digital Marketing Benchmarks for Lead Generation.

Healthcare

Healthcare was one of the few industries I had no experience in when I joined Forum Communications. I quickly learned the industry and it's challenging for a number of reasons. Healthcare marketing carries two pressures in particular that most other industries in this chapter don't face simultaneously: high-intent, urgent search behavior (a patient searching for same-day care converts at some of the highest rates in all of paid search) and a strict regulatory environment around patient data that intersects directly with not only the privacy frameworks discussed earlier, but also additional regulation. An analyst working in healthcare has to be fluent in both healthcare and the marketing world all at once.

Metric	2026 Benchmark	Context
Search Ads Conversion Rate	~24.3% (among the highest of any tracked industry)	Reflects high-intent, often urgent search behavior (symptom and same-day-care searches)
B2B/B2C Website Conversion Rate (clinical & services)	3% – 5%	Clusters with professional services and finance in the broader B2B conversion benchmark set
Search Ads CTR / CPC	Lower CTR, higher CPC than most categories	Healthcare sits alongside legal and insurance among the lowest-CTR, highest-CPC verticals tracked, which compresses Quality Score and raises cost per click further

Sources: Foundry CRO, Google Ads CPC, CTR & Conversion Rate Benchmarks 2026; Digital Applied, Google Ads Benchmarks 2026: CPC, CTR & CVR by Industry; SalesHive, B2B Digital Marketing Benchmarks for Lead Generation.

Financial Services and Insurance

Financial services and insurance share a structural trait that pushes their benchmarks to an extreme unlike few industries. A single closed client can be worth so much over a multi-year relationship that firms in this category will tolerate cost-per-lead figures that would be unthinkable in most other consumer-centric or even B2B industries, provided the conversion math at the back end still works.

Metric	2026 Benchmark	Context
Cost per Lead, Financial Services (blended)	~$653 average	Among the highest CPL of any industry tracked, alongside legal services (~$649)
Cost per Lead, Auto Insurance	$15 – $50	Heavily aggregator-driven (EverQuote, SmartFinancial); high lead volume but intense channel competition
Cost per Lead, Mortgage	$80 – $250 depending on rate environment	Low-rate refinance booms push CPL toward the top of the range as competition for the same borrower pool intensifies
Search Ads CTR (Finance & Insurance)	>9%	One of the higher-CTR categories in search advertising despite also carrying some of the highest CPCs

Sources: Martal, Cost Per Lead by Industry: 2026 Benchmarks & Data; LeadsuiteNow, Cost Per Lead Benchmarks by Industry in 2026; LocalIQ, Search Advertising Benchmarks for Every Industry [2026 Data].

A Cross-Industry Snapshot

No single table can substitute for the sector-specific detail above, but the comparison on the following page is useful for orienting a number that's been pulled out of context. For instance, in a meeting where someone asks "is a 3% conversion rate good?" without specifying which industry they mean, here are some ranges to help guide those sorts of conversations.

Industry	Typical Conversion Rate Range	Why?
Retail / Shopping (paid search)	~8% (cross-industry average)	High purchase intent on branded and product-specific search terms
E-Commerce (site-wide)	1.4% – 3.0%	Wide variance by category, price point, and device mix
B2B (website, all industries)	~2.9% median	Long, multi-stage funnel with buying committees rather than single buyers
SaaS (free trial to paid)	8% – 20%	Varies heavily by product-led vs. sales-led motion
Professional/ Home Services (phone leads)	~46%	High-intent inbound calls convert far above blended digital averages
Manufacturing	~2.2% (website)	Small addressable audience, long engineering / procurement cycles
Healthcare (paid search)	~24.3%	Urgent, high-intent searches (same-day care, symptoms)
Financial Services / Insurance	Highly variable by product	Extremely high CLV justifies tolerance for high CPL in categories like wealth management

Being Practical: An Example

Consider a marketing agency managing accounts for two clients at once: a direct-to-consumer (DTC) apparel e-commerce brand and a regional HVAC company. The apparel brand's paid search campaign converts at 2.4% comfortably within e-commerce's typical 1.4% to 3.0% range. The HVAC company's Google Ads campaign converts at 7.8%, which sounds dramatically stronger in isolation. However, against the home services benchmark of phone leads converting at 46%, that 7.8% reveals something the apparel comparison would never have surfaced. Most of the HVAC company's leads are still arriving through web forms rather than phone calls, in a category where the phone is consistently the higher-converting, faster-closing channel.

Applying this chapter's framework, rather than comparing either client to a generic cross-industry average, changes the recommendation entirely. For the apparel brand, the next move should be focused on checking add-to-cart and checkout completion rates separately rather than considering the 2.4% conversion rate a success. For the HVAC company, the agency needs to work to drive phone calls, not form completions, and needs to consider how to manage the campaign to drive users to their phones. Call tracking should be considered and the campaign restructured around driving and capturing phone calls. Neither client was underperforming in any absolute sense. Each was being measured, until this analysis, against the wrong implicit benchmark.

In the final chapter of this book, we bring everything together under the idea of lean analytical strategies — how to apply the frameworks, metrics, and industry context covered so far without requiring an enterprise budget or a large analytics team to do it well.

References

2026 Benchmarks for Lead Conversion Rates in Home Services. (n.d.). Estatehub. https://www.estatehub.io/articles/2026-benchmarks-lead-conversion-rates-home-services

Agustin, N. (2026, April 4). *Ecommerce Conversion Rate Benchmarks 2026: Real Data from 21 Shopify Stores*. DTC Pages. https://www.dtcpages.com/blog/ecommerce-conversion-rate-benchmarks-2026

B2B Conversion Rates By Industry — 2026 (2025, December 23). First Page Sage. https://firstpagesage.com/reports/b2b-conversion-rates-by-industry-fc/

B2B Marketing Statistics 2026: 180+ Essential Data Points. (2026, April 21). Digital Applied. https://www.digitalapplied.com/blog/b2b-marketing-statistics-2026-essential-data-points

Burnett, B. (2025, March 18). *B2B Digital Marketing Benchmarks for Lead Generation (2026)*. SalesHive. https://saleshive.com/blog/b2b-lead-benchmarks-digital-marketing-gen

Cost Per Lead Benchmarks by Industry in 2026 (USA Data) (2026, May). LeadsuiteNow. https://leadsuitenow.com/blog/lead-generation-cost-per-lead-benchmarks-2026

Display Advertising Benchmarks 2026: 150+ Data Points. (2026, April 20). Digital Applied. https://www.digitalapplied.com/blog/display-advertising-benchmarks-2026-data-points

Ecommerce Conversion Rate Benchmarks by Industry [2026]. (2026, July 8). Elogic Commerce. https://elogic.co/blog/b2b-ecommerce-conversion-rate-benchmarks/

eCommerce & Shopify Average Conversion Rate Benchmarks 2026. (2026, June 16). Blend Commerce. https://blendcommerce.com/blogs/shopify/ecommerce-conversion-rate-benchmarks-2026

Email Marketing Benchmarks 2026: Region & Industry Data. (2026, May 27). Brevo. https://www.brevo.com/blog/email-marketing-benchmarks/
Google Ads Benchmarks 2026: CPC, CTR & CVR by Industry (2026, April 5). Digital Applied. https://www.digitalapplied.com/blog/google-ads-benchmarks-2026-cpc-ctr-cvr-industry

Heitman, S. (2026, June 1). *NEW 2026 Search Advertising Benchmarks (+ Tips)*. LocalIQ. https://localiq.com/blog/search-advertising-benchmarks/

Home Services Marketing Statistics. (2026, June 4). Click-Vision. https://click-vision.com/home-services-marketing-statistics

Hu, N., & Newberry, C. (2026, April 14). *Social media benchmarks: 2026 data + tips*. Hootsuite. https://blog.hootsuite.com/social-media-benchmarks/

Jones, B. (2026, April 13). *Google Ads CPC, CTR & Conversion Rate Benchmarks 2026*. Foundry CRO. https://foundrycro.com/blog/google-ads-benchmarks-by-industry-2026/

Lead Generation Statistics 2026: 140+ Marketing Data. (2026, April 21). Digital Applied. https://www.digitalapplied.com/blog/lead-generation-statistics-2026-marketing-data

Lukes, J. (n.d.). *The social media benchmarks to guide your 2026 strategy*. Emplifi. https://emplifi.io/resources/social-media-benchmarks/

Marino, S. (2026, May 19). *Google Ads Benchmarks 2026: Competitive Data & Insights for Every Industry*. WordStream. https://www.wordstream.com/blog/2026-google-ads-benchmarks

Net Promoter Score Benchmarks by Industry 2026: Average NPS Data. (n.d.). StealthAgents. https://stealthagents.com/research/net-promoter-score-benchmarks-2026

Putra, M. (2026, May 29). *Average ecommerce cart abandonment rate by vertical (2026): the 70.2% anchor and the 45-91% spread underneath it*. Eightx. https://eightx.co/blog/average-ecommerce-cart-abandonment-rate-by-vertical-2026

Rovner, A. (2026, February 23). *Best LTV to CAC Ratio Benchmarks for B2B SaaS in 2026*. SaaSHero. https://www.saashero.net/strategy/b2b-saas-ltv-cac-benchmarks/

SaaS Finance Metrics Benchmarks. (n.d.). Eagle Rock CFO. https://www.eaglerockcfo.com/blog/research/saas-finance-metrics-benchmarks

SaaS Metrics Explained: ARR, MRR, LTV & CAC With Real Benchmarks. (2026, May 10). The SaaS Library. https://thesaaslibrary.com/saas-metrics-explained/

Velasquez, A. (2025, September 16). *2026 Home Services Marketing Benchmarks: What Providers Must Know (+ Insights & Strategies)*. WebFX. https://www.webfx.com/blog/home-services/home-services-marketing-benchmarks/

Velasquez, A. (2025, September 10). *2026 Manufacturing Marketing Benchmarks Every Industrial Firm Must Track*. WebFX. https://www.webfx.com/blog/manufacturing/manufacturing-marketing-benchmarks/

What is a Good Net Promoter Score?. (2026 NPS Benchmark). (n.d.). Retently. https://www.retently.com/blog/good-net-promoter-score/

Young, K. (2026, May 29). *Cost Per Lead by Industry: 2026 Benchmarks & Actionable Strategies*. Martal. https://martal.ca/cost-per-lead-by-industry-lb/

Chapter 18
Lean Analytics Strategies

We opened this book by describing data as something organizations are drowning in. Sixteen chapters and dozens of platforms, metrics, and frameworks later, that observation should feel more true than ever, not less. Every channel we've covered produces a genuine flood of numbers. The discipline this book has tried to build is knowing which of those numbers deserves your attention right now and having the courage to ignore the rest until necessary.

This closing chapter brings that discipline together under a name: lean analytics. The term and much of the thinking behind it come from Alistair Croll and Benjamin Yoskovitz's 2013 book, *Lean Analytics: Use Data to Build a Better Startup Faster*, which took Eric Ries's Lean Startup philosophy (build something small, measure what happens, learn from it, repeat) and turned it into a working measurement discipline. Much of my own career has been built around this model when possible and learning every step of the way. So what better way to end this book than unpacking that discipline, then pair it with the agile project-management frameworks, Scrum and Kanban among them, that let a team actually operationalize lean analytics week after week.

Build, Measure, Learn

Eric Ries's *Lean Startup* methodology, which Croll and Yoskovitz extend directly, centers on a simple loop: build the smallest possible version of something, measure what real customers actually do with it, and learn from that measurement before building the next iteration. This methodology is not prescriptive, but prevents a number of major mistakes. Without it, organizations tend to build a complete strategy, launch it in full, and only then ask whether any of it worked which leads to analysis paralysis and massive failures that are too late to correct. Build-Measure-Learn conceptually forces the measurement step to happen early and often enough that learning can still change the next decision, rather than only explaining the last one.

The One Metric That Matters

Croll and Yoskovitz's signature contribution is a discipline they call the One Metric That Matters (OMTM). At any given moment in an organization's efforts, they should identify the single number that reflects its biggest current risk, rally the team around moving it, and consciously set aside every other metric until that risk is addressed. Readers of this book will recognize the underlying idea immediately. It's the same idea behind the North Star Metric framework introduced in Chapter 13, and the two concepts are close cousins. The meaningful difference is that a North Star Metric is usually meant to stay relatively fixed over a long stretch of a company's life, while the OMTM is explicitly expected to change as a company moves through different stages of growth.

Croll and Yoskovitz are equally specific about what makes a metric worth choosing in the first place, building directly on the vanity-versus-actionable distinction. A good metric, in their framing, is *comparative* (it means something next to another number, like a past period or a competitor), *understandable* (a person outside the data team can grasp it quickly), expressed as a ratio or rate rather than a raw count, and most importantly, *actionable*, it changes what the team does next.

The Five Stages of Growth

The organizing structure of Lean Analytics is a five-stage model of how a business matures. The stages of this model are Empathy, Stickiness, Virality, Revenue, and Scale with a different OMTM appropriate for each stage as well as an explicit warning against skipping ahead. Croll and Yoskovitz are blunt about what happens to companies that pour acquisition spend into Virality before they've actually solved Stickiness and their recommendation is wise. If you can't keep your customers, you simply acquire users faster than you lose them, which feels like progress right up until it doesn't and you fail.

Stage	Primary Question	OMTM
Empathy	Is this a real problem people will pay to solve?	Qualitative validation through completed customer interviews, problem-fit signal strength
Stickiness	Will people who try this keep using it?	D7/D30 retention, DAU/MAU stickiness ratio
Virality	Can existing users help bring in new customers?	Viral coefficient (K-factor), referral-driven share of new users
Revenue	Can this generate sustainable, profitable income?	Customer lifetime value, contribution margin, LTV:CAC ratio
Scale	Can this grow efficiently across channels and markets?	Channel-by-channel customer acquisition cost, marginal efficiency by segment, sustainable growth rate

Insight: Don't Pour Water Into a Leaky Bucket

The most repeated warning in *Lean Analytics*, and the one most directly relevant to a marketing is this: spending on acquisition (Virality) or monetization (Revenue) before a product or campaign has cleared its Stickiness bar is close to the most common way organizations waste a marketing budget. If the organization's engagement and retention metrics are weak, the right response is almost never "spend more to bring in more." Before you do, you must fix what's causing people to leave before doing anything else. Croll and Yoskovitz call this the "line in the sand" for each stage: a specific, numeric bar that has to be cleared before it's worth investing further.

Knowing Your Business Model Changes What "Good" Means

Lean Analytics pairs its five stages with six common digital business models as illustrations because the same stage can call for a meaningfully different metric depending on which kind of business is asking. This should feel familiar after Chapter 16: it's the same underlying lesson as benchmarking by industry, applied one level deeper, to the mechanics of the business model itself rather than the vertical it operates in. I've listed those early stage metrics below:

Business Model	Early-Stage Metric
e-Commerce	Annual and 90-day repurchase rate
Software as a Service (SaaS)	Monthly logo churn (citing under 2% as healthy)
Free Mobile Apps	D30 retention (cited benchmark of 15%+ as healthy for a consumer app)
Media Site	CPM and engaged time per visit
User-Generated Content Platform	Ratio of content creators to content consumers
Two-Sided Marketplace	Liquidity, or the probability a buyer's search finds a matching seller within a defined time window

Agile Frameworks: Operationalizing the Loop

Knowing which metric matters and actually building a team rhythm around moving it are two different problems, and this is where agile project-management frameworks earn their place. Originally built for software development, now widely adopted as agile marketing, a variety of agile principles have been modified to function in the field of marketing. Training courses and even certifications have been developed to help marketers learn to use agile techniques to effectively plan, and win, in their prospective industries. Agility comes with its own set of rules and requirements similar to any of the other frameworks or models in business. Scrum, the most structured of these frameworks, organizes work into fixed-length sprints (commonly two weeks) built around four recurring ceremonies: sprint planning (deciding what the team will tackle this sprint), the daily standup (a short check-in on progress and blockers), the sprint review (showing stakeholders what was completed), and the sprint retrospective (the team privately examining how it worked, not just what it built).

Applied to analytics specifically, this rhythm maps directly onto the Build-Measure-Learn loop and onto SOSTAC®'s Control stage. A sprint plans a specific test or campaign adjustment tied to the current OMTM (Build), runs it and tracks results throughout the sprint (Measure), and closes with a retrospective that asks not just whether the metric moved, but whether the team's own process for measuring and reacting to it actually worked (Learn). Kanban, a looser alternative, replaces fixed sprints with a continuously flowing board and work-in-progress limits, which often suits marketing and analytics teams better than rigid Scrum because so much real-world marketing work arrives unpredictably rather than on a clean schedule. Many marketing organizations also have landed on a hybrid often called Scrumban: Scrum's planning and retrospective rhythm layered over Kanban's flexible, continuous-flow board.

Side Quest: The Agile Marketing Manifesto

Software's original Agile Manifesto (2001) inspired a parallel Agile Marketing Manifesto, which reframes the same core principles for marketing teams: focusing on customer value and business outcomes over activity and outputs, delivering value early and often over waiting for perfection, learning through experiments and data over opinions and conventions, cross-functional collaboration over silos and hierarchies, and responding to change over following a static plan. Read against everything covered in this book, the manifesto is essentially a guiding light through much of this book.

Tip: Focus the Retrospective on the OMTM

A sprint review answers "what did we ship and how did it perform." A sprint retrospective, held separately, should answer a different question entirely: "did our process for choosing, tracking, and reacting to our OMTM actually work this sprint, or did we get distracted by a vanity metric, a dashboard we didn't use, or a stakeholder request that pulled focus away from the riskiest part of the business?" Most teams that adopt agile ceremonies for marketing can merge these two meetings and only ever run the campaign-focused review. The retrospective helps enforce the idea of the North Star Metric and ensures you keep your eyes on the right analytical measures.

Being Practical: An Example

Consider a mid-sized SaaS company six months after launch. Using the Lean Analytics stage model, the team correctly diagnoses that it hasn't cleared Stickiness. The company's D30 retention sits at 9%, well below the roughly 15% a healthy consumer product should expect, and nowhere near the much higher logo-retention bar a mature SaaS business eventually needs. Leadership's instinct is to increase paid acquisition spend to hit a quarterly growth target. The lean analytics framework says no: pouring more users into a leaky bucket only grows the rate at which the company loses them.

Instead, the team adopts a two-week Scrum cadence focused entirely on one OMTM: D30 retention. Sprint planning each cycle selects one specific onboarding or engagement experiment tied to that number. The team decides to develop a shorter setup flow, a more targeted first-week email sequence, and a redesigned in-app prompt. Daily standups keep the small cross-functional team of three staff members aligned without long meetings. Each sprint retrospective asks the harder question from this chapter's Tip box: did the team stay focused on D30 retention, or did a tempting vanity metric that was found (a spike in signups from an unrelated press mention) pull attention away from the actual risk? After four sprints, D30 retention crosses 15%. Only then, following Croll and Yoskovitz's own sequencing, does the team shift its OMTM to a Virality-stage metric and begin investing in acquisition in earnest confident, for the first time, that the users they bring in will actually stay.

Closing Thoughts

This book began with a simple premise: digital marketing produces an overwhelming amount of data and it should be easier to sort through. I recall the first time I was asked to pull together a report from a massive marketing research study I led as an intern. It was overwhelming. Pages and pages of information about each location related to individual experiences, in-store experiences, and global experiences with the brand. I still have the 200 page report I gave to leadership. Thinking back on it now, I literally handed them a book for the purpose of analysis paralysis! And frankly, that's what I hope this book helps you prevent.

From the beginning, every chapter since has added a channel, a platform, or a framework to that stack from website and search analytics, to social, video, email, and paid, earned media and mobile, North Stars and RACEs, and guidance on how to pull it all together. This final chapter has tried to give you a way to hold all of it without drowning in it. For everything that you do, there is one metric that matters (OMTM) and the rest should serve as the guardrails to which you make decisions. If the metrics you are tracking don't lead to decisions, then why are you tracking them? The answer is likely vanity (or for someone's vanity) and that's not how you'll ever move the organization forward.

So, if there is one closing instruction worth carrying forward past the last page of this book, it's this: pick your OMTM that matters most to you and the organization right now, build a small, repeatable loop to measure and improve upon it, and resist the pull to do anything else until you've met the goal. Everything else in this book is in service of that single discipline. So, go! Practice it. And, use the data to help your organization win.

References

Agile Marketing: Implementing Scrum and Kanban in Your Marketing Team. (2024, November 6). Academy of Continuing Education. https://www.academyofcontinuingeducation.com/blog/agile-marketing-implementing-scrum-and-kanban-in-your-marketing-team

Book Summary — Lean Analytics: Use Data to Build a Better Startup Faster. (n.d.). ReadinGraphics. https://readingraphics.com/book-summary-lean-analytics/

Brooks, A. (2026, April 6). *How to Plan a Marketing Sprint*. Venture Harbour. https://ventureharbour.com/marketing-sprints/

Chin, C. (2019, July 6). *Lean Analytics Part 1: An Introduction to Analytical Thinking*. Holistics. https://www.holistics.io/blog/lean-analytics-part-1-an-introduction-to-analytical-thinking/

Croll, A., & Yoskovitz, B. (2013). *Lean Analytics: Use Data to Build a Better Startup Faster*. O'Reilly Media.

Fryrear, A. (n.d.). *Using Scrum for Marketing: An In-Depth Introduction*. AgileSherpas. https://www.agilesherpas.com/blog/scrum-marketing-intro

Halsey, E. (n.d.). *Are You Getting the Most Out of Your Agile Ceremonies?*. AgileSherpas. https://www.agilesherpas.com/blog/agile-ceremonies

Hughes, A. (2019, August 11). *Lean Analytics — Alistair Croll, Benjamin Yoskovitz*. Alex J. Hughes. https://www.alexjhughes.com/books/2019/8/11/lean-analytics-alistair-croll-benjamin-yoskovitz

Maurya, A. (2013, March 19). *Lean Analytics — The One Metric That Matters And Other Provocations*. Medium. https://medium.com/lean-stack/lean-analytics-the-one-metric-that-matters-and-other-provocations-fd3006aab17

Radigan, D. (n.d.). *A guide to agile ceremonies and scrum meetings*. Atlassian. https://www.atlassian.com/agile/scrum/ceremonies

White, K. (2026, June 22). *Lean Analytics by Croll and Yoskovitz — Cliff Notes Summary*. Pulse RevOps. https://pulserevops.com/sales-book-summaries/bs0197

Why brands need agile marketing for faster growth in 2026. (2026, March 24). Nectar. https://www.thinknectar.com/blog/why-brands-need-agile-marketing-faster-growth-2026-en

About the Author

From financial services to national retail, small businesses to international conglomerates, Nick Kastner has spent nearly 25 years helping organizations develop and implement marketing strategies that positively impact every part of their business. He serves as director of brand and digital strategy at Forum Communications, a full-service marketing agency that helps organizations find their voice in a crowded marketplace.

After initially pursuing music, Nick earned a BA in Business Administration with a marketing concentration and an MBA in leadership from Piedmont College. He is a graduate of the American Bankers Association School of Bank Marketing and Management at Northwestern University, where he became the school's first instructor of digital marketing. He holds certifications across the Google Ads and Analytics suites and HubSpot Inbound, and is a Certified ScrumMaster and Certified Agile Marketing Specialist. He is a member of the Harvard Business Review Advisory Council and the University of North Georgia's Digital Marketing Advisory Board, serves as a juror for the AIVA Davey and Communicator Awards, and has earned more than 20 industry awards as a strategic project lead. His writing has appeared in publications ranging from ABA Bank Marketing to Inc., alongside co-authored academic work on agile project management and video in B2B marketing.

For more than 17 years, Nick has also been an adjunct instructor at the University of North Georgia, teaching undergraduate and graduate marketing courses. He was the university's first instructor of digital marketing and the original architect of its digital marketing program — the classroom counterpart to the work in this book.

Nick and his wife, Brandy, live in Gainesville with their two children, Grace and Lorelei.

For dashboard templates, benchmarks, updates, visit forumspeaks.com, or connect with him through Forum Communications.

www.ingramcontent.com/pod-product-compliance
Ingram Content Group UK Ltd.
Pitfield, Milton Keynes, MK11 3LW, UK
UKHW020838290926
15470UKWH00004B/1418

9 798997 133207